iPhone® 5

FOR

DUMMIES®

6TH EDITION

iPhone® 5

FOR

DUMMIES®

6TH EDITION

by Edward C. Baig
USA Today Personal Tech columnist

and

Bob LeVitus
Houston Chronicle "Dr. Mac" columnist

WILEY

John Wiley & Sons, Inc.

iPhone® 5 For Dummies® 6th Edition

Published by
John Wiley & Sons, Inc.
111 River Street
Hoboken, NJ 07030-5774

www.wiley.com

For general information on our other products and services, please contact our Customer Care Department within the U.S. at 877-762-2974, outside the U.S. at 317-572-3993, or fax 317-572-4002.

For technical support, please visit www.wiley.com/techsupport.

Wiley publishes in a variety of print and electronic formats and by print-on-demand. Some material included with standard print versions of this book may not be included in e-books or in print-on-demand. If this book refers to media such as a CD or DVD that is not included in the version you purchased, you may download this material at http://booksupport.wiley.com. For more information about Wiley products, visit www.wiley.com.

Library of Congress Control Number: 2012950500

ISBN 978-1-118-35201-4 (pbk); ISBN 978-1-118-46099-3 (ebk); ISBN 978-1-118-55278-0 (ebk); ISBN 978-1-118-55279-7 (ebk)

Manufactured in the United States of America

10 9 8 7 6 5 4 3 2

WILEY

About the Authors

Edward C. Baig writes the weekly Personal Technology column in *USA TODAY* and makes regular video appearances on the web and TV. He appears weekly on ABC News's *TechBytes,* shown on local ABC TV affiliate stations across the nation. Ed is also the author of *Macs For Dummies,* 10th Edition, and cowriter (with Bob LeVitus) of *iPad For Dummies.* Before joining *USA TODAY* as a columnist and reporter in 1999, Ed spent six years at *Business Week,* where he wrote and edited stories about consumer tech, personal finance, collectibles, travel, and wine tasting, among other topics. He received the Medill School of Journalism 1999 Financial Writers and Editors Award for contributions to the "*Business Week* Investor Guide to Online Investing." That followed a three-year stint at *U.S. News & World Report,* where Ed was the lead tech writer for the News You Can Use section but also dabbled in numerous other subjects.

Ed began his journalist career at *Fortune* magazine, gaining the best basic training imaginable during his early years as a fact checker and contributor to the Fortune 500. Through the dozen years he worked at the magazine, Ed covered leisure-time industries, penned features on the lucrative "dating" market and the effect of religion on corporate managers, and was heavily involved in the Most Admired Companies project. Ed also started *Fortune*'s Products to Watch column, a venue for low- and high-tech items.

Bob LeVitus, often referred to as "Dr. Mac," has written or cowritten more than 65 popular computer books, including *iPad For Dummies, Incredible iPhone Apps For Dummies, OS X Mountain Lion For Dummies,* and *Microsoft Office 2011 for Mac For Dummies* for John Wiley & Sons, Inc.; *Stupid Mac Tricks* and *Dr. Macintosh* for Addison-Wesley; and *The Little iTunes Book,* 3rd Edition, and *The Little iDVD Book,* 2nd Edition, for Peachpit Press. His books have sold millions of copies worldwide. Bob has also penned the popular "Dr. Mac" column for the *Houston Chronicle* for the past 15 years and has been published in pretty much every magazine that ever used the word *Mac* in its title. His achievements have been documented in major media around the world. (Yes, that was Bob juggling a keyboard in *USA TODAY* a few years back!)

Bob is known for his expertise, trademark humorous style, and ability to translate techie jargon into usable and fun advice for regular folks. Bob is also a prolific public speaker, presenting more than 100 Macworld Expo training sessions in the United States and abroad, keynote addresses in three countries, and Macintosh training seminars in many U.S. cities.

Dedications

I dedicate this book to my beautiful and amazingly supportive wife, Janie, for making me a better person every day I am with her. And to my incredible kids: my adorable little girl, Sydney (if my iPhone is missing, chances are she has it), my little boy, Sammy (who is all smiles from the moment he wakes up in the morning), and my canine "daughter," Sadie. It is also written in the memory of my "doggie son," Eddie, Jr. They all got their hands (or paws) on the iPhone at one time or another — and gave me a valuable perspective of the device through youthful eyes. I am madly in love with you all.

— Ed Baig

As always, this book is dedicated to my incredible wife, Lisa, who taught me almost everything I know about almost everything I know (except technology), and has put up with me for almost 30 years with no (major) complaints. And, like every book I write, I dedicate this one to my two children-who-aren't-kids-anymore, Allison and Jacob, who love their iPhones almost as much as I love them (my kids, not my iPhones).

— Bob LeVitus

Authors' Acknowledgments

Special thanks to everyone at Apple who helped us turn this book around so quickly: Katie Cotton, Natalie Kerris, Steve Dowling, Greg (Joz) Joswiak, John Richey, Keri Walker, Teresa Brewer, Trudy Muller, Jen Martin, Natalie Harrison, Monica Sarkar, Tom Neumayr, Jennifer Bowcock, Janette Barrios, Christine Monaghan, and everyone else. We couldn't have done it without you. We apologize if we missed anybody.

Big-time thanks to the gang at Wiley: Bob "You can do it" Woerner, Jodi "I'm calm now, really" Jensen, Susan "just one more thing . . ." Pink, Andy "The Boss" Cummings, and our technical editor, Dennis R. Cohen, who also has no humorous nickname but once again did a rocking job in record time. We also want to thank our invaluable proofreader, Debbye Butler, who did a tremendous job. Editorial assistant Leslie Saxman also deserves our thanks; she handled a bevy of last-minute tasks with panache. Finally, thanks to everyone at Wiley we don't know by name. If you helped with this project in any way, you have our everlasting thanks.

Bob adds: Special thanks to my super-agent, Carole "Still the Swifty Lazar of Tech Agentry" Jelen. You've been my agent for more than 21 years and you're *still* the best. Thanks also to my family and friends for putting up with me throughout my hibernation during this book's gestation. Finally, thanks to Saccone's for killer New Jersey–style thin-crust pizza, John Mueller's and Black's for BBQ beyond compare, Chuy's for burritos as big as yo' face, Torchy's Tacos for the most unusual and tasty tacos ever, Mighty Fine for good, cheap, tasty burgers, and Quad Café Americana, the breakfast of champions (and tech writers).

Ed adds: Thanks to my agent Matt Wagner for again turning me into a *For Dummies* author. It is a privilege to be working with a first-class guy and true professional. I'd also like to thank Jim Henderson, Geri Tucker, Nancy Blair, and the rest of my *USA TODAY* friends and colleagues for your enormous support and encouragement. Most of all, thanks to my loving family for understanding my nightly (and weekend) disappearances as we raced to get this project completed on time. They all keep me sane.

And finally, thanks to you, gentle reader, for buying our book.

Publisher's Acknowledgments

We're proud of this book; please send us your comments at http://dummies.custhelp.com. For other comments, please contact our Customer Care Department within the U.S. at 877-762-2974, outside the U.S. at 317-572-3993, or fax 317-572-4002.

Some of the people who helped bring this book to market include the following:

Acquisitions and Editorial

Project Editor: Susan Pink

Executive Editor: Bob Woerner

Copy Editor: Susan Pink

Technical Editor: Dennis Cohen

Editorial Manager: Jodi Jensen

Editorial Assistant: Leslie Saxman

Sr. Editorial Assistant: Cherie Case

Cover Photo: © onur kocamaz/iStockphoto.com

Cartoons: Rich Tennant (www.the5thwave.com)

Composition Services

Project Coordinator: Katherine Crocker

Layout and Graphics: Joyce Haughey, Christin Swinford

Proofreader: Dwight Ramsey

Indexer: Glassman Indexing Services

Publishing and Editorial for Technology Dummies

Richard Swadley, Vice President and Executive Group Publisher

Andy Cummings, Vice President and Publisher

Mary Bednarek, Executive Acquisitions Director

Mary C. Corder, Editorial Director

Publishing for Consumer Dummies

Kathleen Nebenhaus, Vice President and Executive Publisher

Composition Services

Debbie Stailey, Director of Composition Services

Contents at a Glance

Table of Contents

Introduction

*P*recious few products ever come close to generating the kind of buzz seen with the iPhone. Its messianic arrival received front-page treatment in newspapers and top billing on network and cable TV shows. People lined up days in advance just to ensure landing one of the first units. Years from now, people will insist, "I was one of them."

But we trust you didn't pick up this book to read yet another account about how the iPhone launch was an epochal event. We trust you *did* buy the book to find out how to get the very most out of your remarkable device. Our goal is to deliver that information in a light and breezy fashion. We expect you to have fun using your iPhone. We equally hope you have fun spending time with us.

About This Book

Let's get one thing out of the way right from the get-go. We think you're pretty darn smart for buying a *For Dummies* book. That says to us that you have the confidence and intelligence to know what you don't know. The *For Dummies* franchise is built around the core notion that all of us feel insecure about certain topics when tackling them for the first time, especially when those topics have to do with technology.

As with most Apple products, every iPhone to date is beautifully designed and intuitive to use. And though our editors may not want us to reveal this dirty little secret (especially on the first page, for goodness' sake), the truth is you'll get pretty far just by exploring the iPhone's many functions and features on your own, without the help of this (or any other) book.

Okay, now that we spilled the beans, let's tell you why you shouldn't run back to the bookstore and request a refund. This book is chock-full of useful tips, advice, and other nuggets that should make your iPhone experience all the more pleasurable. So keep this book nearby and consult it often.

Conventions Used in This Book

First, we want to tell you how we go about our business. *iPhone For Dummies*, 6th Edition, makes generous use of numbered steps, bullet lists, and pictures. Web addresses look like this: www.boblevitus.com. For those reading the e-book version, links are live so you can click them.

We also include a few sidebars with information that is not required reading (not that any of this book is) but that we hope will provide a richer understanding of certain subjects. Overall, we aim to keep technical jargon to a minimum, under the guiding principle that with rare exceptions you need not know what any of it really means.

How This Book Is Organized

Here's something we imagine you've never heard before: Most books have a beginning, a middle, and an end, and you do well to adhere to that linear structure — unless you're one of those knuckleheads out to ruin it for the rest of us by revealing that the butler did it.

Fortunately, there's no ending to spoil in a *For Dummies* book. Although you may want to digest this book from start to finish — and we hope you do — we won't penalize you for skipping ahead or jumping around. Having said that, we organized *iPhone 5 For Dummies,* 6th Edition, in an order that we think makes the most sense, as follows.

Part I: Getting to Know Your iPhone

In the introductory chapters of Part I, you tour the iPhone inside and out, find out how to activate the phone, and get hands-on (or, more precisely, fingers-on) experience with the iPhone's superb virtual multitouch display. Finally, because the iPhone does have *phone* in its name, you'll discover all the ways you can make and receive calls on the device — even video calls, where two (or more) people can see each other.

Part II: The PDA iPhone

PDA is a quaint old acronym that stands for Personal Digital Assistant, yet another thing at which your iPhone excels. In this part, you see how to exchange text and iMessages, how to set up appointments with Calendar, and the various faces of the Clock app. You also calculate with Calculator, and talk to yourself with Voice Memo. Last, but certainly not least, you find out about Siri, the intelligent assistant (in the iPhone 4S and 5) that understands what you say and (usually) what you mean, and then does what you said.

Part III: The Multimedia iPhone

Part III is where the fun truly begins. This is the iPhone as an iPod, a camera, and yes, even a camcorder, meaning that music, videos, movies, pictures, and other diversions come to life.

Part IV: The Internet iPhone

Part IV covers the mobile Internet. You master the Safari browser, e-mail, maps, and more. And speaking of maps, your iPhone has the capability to locate your whereabouts through GPS and other location-tracking methods.

Part V: The Undiscovered iPhone

In Part V, you find out how to apply your preferences through the iPhone's internal settings, how to find and obtain new apps at the iTunes App Store, and discover where to go for troubleshooting assistance if your iPhone should misbehave.

Part VI: The Part of Tens

The Part of Tens: Otherwise known as the *For Dummies* answer to David Letterman. The lists presented in Part VI steer you to some of our favorite iPhone apps as well as some very handy tips and shortcuts.

Icons Used in This Book

Little round pictures (icons) appear in the left margin throughout this book. Consider these icons miniature road signs, telling you something extra about the topic at hand or hammering a point home.

Here's what the five icons used in this book look like and mean.

This text contains the juicy morsels, shortcuts, and recommendations that might make the task at hand faster or easier.

This icon emphasizes the stuff we think you ought to retain. You may even jot down a note to yourself in the iPhone's Reminders app.

Put on your propeller beanie hat and pocket protector; this text includes truly geeky stuff. You can safely ignore this material, but we wouldn't have bothered to write it if it weren't interesting or informative.

You wouldn't intentionally run a stop sign, would you? In the same fashion, ignoring warnings may be hazardous to your iPhone and (by extension) your wallet. There, you now know how these warning icons work, for you have just received your very first warning!

Denotes a feature that's either new in iOS 6, new in iTunes, or new in the latest and greatest iPhone, the iPhone 5. What do we mean by *new*? Mostly that it wasn't available last year and wasn't covered in previous editions of this book.

Where to Go from Here

Where to turn to next? Why straight to Chapter 1, of course (without passing Go).

In all seriousness, we wrote this book for you, so please let us know what you think. If we screwed up, confused you, left something out, or — heaven forbid — made you angry, drop us a note. And if we hit you with one pun too many, it helps to know that as well.

Because writers are people too (believe it or not), we also encourage positive feedback if you think it's warranted. So kindly send e-mail to Ed at baig dummies@gmail.com and to Bob at iPhoneLeVitus@boblevitus.com. We'll do our best to respond to reasonably polite e-mail in a timely fashion.

Most of all, we want to thank you for buying our book. Please enjoy it along with your new iPhone.

Note: At the time we wrote this book, all the information it contained was accurate for the iPhone 4, 4S, and 5, as well as the latest versions of iTunes and iOS 6, the iPhone operating system. Apple will probably introduce a new iPhone model or versions of the operating system and iTunes between book editions. If you've bought a new iPhone or your version of iTunes looks a little different, be sure to check out what Apple has to say at www.apple. com/iphone. You'll no doubt find updates on the company's latest releases.

Occasionally, John Wiley & Sons, Inc., has updates to its technology books. If this book does have technical updates, they will be posted at www.dummies. com/go/iphonefdupdates.

Part I
Getting to Know Your iPhone

The 5th Wave — By Rich Tennant

"Other than this little glitch with the landscape view, I really love my iPhone."

*Y*ou have to crawl before you walk, so consider this part basic training for crawling. The four chapters that make up Part I serve as a gentle introduction to your iPhone.

We start out nice and easy in Chapter 1, with a big-picture overview, even letting you know what's in the box (if you haven't already peeked). Then we examine just some of the cool things your iPhone can do. We finish things off with a quick-and-dirty tour of the hardware and the software, so that you'll know where things are when you need them.

Next, after you're somewhat familiar with where things are and what they do, we move right along to a bunch of useful iPhone skills, such as turning the darn thing on and off (which is very important) and locking and unlocking your phone (which is also very important). Chapter 2 ends with useful tips and tricks to help you master iPhone's unique multitouch interface so that you can use it effectively and efficiently.

Then, in Chapter 3, we explore the process of synchronization and how to get data — contacts, appointments, movies, songs, podcasts, and such — between your computer, your iPhone, iCloud, and other iDevices, quickly and painlessly.

In Chapter 4, we explore how to use typical mobile phone features, starting with all the neat ways to make an outgoing phone call. You also find out how to answer or ignore the calls that come in and discover iPhone's clever visual voicemail feature, which lets you take in messages on your terms, rather than in the order in which the messages arrived on the phone. You also figure out how to juggle calls, merge calls, and select a ringtone.

Unveiling the iPhone

Congratulations. You've selected one of the most incredible handheld devices we've ever seen. Of course, the iPhone is one heck of a wireless telephone, but it's actually *four* handheld devices in one. At least it's four devices right out of the box. Add some iPhone apps, and your iPhone becomes a PDA, an e-book reader, a handheld gaming device, a memory jogger, an exercise assistant, and ever so much more. We discuss optional apps — how to obtain, install, and delete them — throughout the book and particularly in Chapters 15, 17, and 18.

For now, we focus on the four awesome handheld devices your iPhone is the day you take it out of the box. In addition to being a killer cell phone, the iPhone is a gorgeous widescreen video iPod, a decent 5-megapixel (iPhone 4) or 8-megapixel (iPhone 4S and 5) camera/ camcorder, as well as the smallest, most powerful Internet communications device yet.

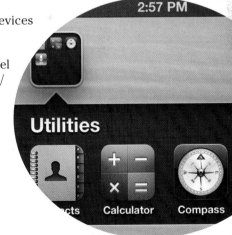

In this chapter, we offer a gentle introduction to all four devices that make up your iPhone, plus overviews of its revolutionary hardware and software features.

The Big Picture

The iPhone has many best-of-class features, but perhaps its most unusual feature is the lack of a physical keyboard or stylus. Instead, it has a super-high-resolution touchscreen (326 pixels per inch for iPhone 4, 4S, and 5; 160 pixels per inch for other models) that you operate using a pointing device you're already intimately familiar with: your finger.

What's in the box?

Somehow we think you've already opened the elegant box that the iPhone came in. But if you didn't, here's what you can expect to find inside:

- **Stereo headset or EarPods (iPhone 5 only):** Use it for music, videos, and, yes, phone calls. The headset contains a built-in microphone for making yourself heard during phone calls.

- **Dock connector or Lightning (iPhone 5 only)–to–USB cable:** Use this handy cable to sync or charge your iPhone. You can plug the USB connector into your PC or Macintosh to sync or into the included USB power adapter. By the way, if you prefer to have your iPhone standing up on your desk while you charge or sync it, as we do, check out one of the optional charging/syncing docks available from Apple and others.

- **USB power adapter:** Use this adapter to recharge your iPhone from a standard AC power outlet.

- **Some Apple logo decals:** Of course.

- **A quick start guide:** You'll find handy tips from Apple on using the new object of your affection.

- ***Important Product Information Guide* pamphlet:** Well, it must be important because it says so right on the cover. You'll find basic safety warnings, a bunch of legalese, warranty information, and info on how to dispose of or recycle the iPhone. *What! We're getting rid of it already?* A few other pieces of advice: Don't drop the iPhone if you can help it, keep the thing dry, and — as with all cell phones — give full attention to the road while driving.

- **SIM eject tool:** Alas, iPhone users have no SIM eject tool; they'll have to use a straightened paper clip or something. All previous iPhone models included this handy tool used to eject your SIM card when necessary. (See Chapter 16 for more on the SIM eject tool and bent paper clips.)

- **iPhone:** You were starting to worry. Yes, the iPhone itself is also in the box.

And what a display it is. We venture that you've never seen a more beautiful screen on a handheld device in your life.

Another feature that still knocks our socks off is the iPhone's built-in sensors. An accelerometer detects when you rotate the device from portrait to landscape mode and adjusts what's on the display accordingly. A proximity sensor detects when the iPhone gets near your face, so it can turn off the display to save power and prevent accidental touches by your cheek. A light sensor adjusts the display's brightness in response to the current ambient lighting situation. (Let's see your BlackBerry do *that!*) The iPhone even has a gyroscope for advanced motion sensing and includes GPS sensors so your phone can determine where in the world you are.

In this section, we take a brief look at some of the iPhone's features, broken down by product category.

The iPhone as a phone and digital camera/camcorder

On the phone side, the iPhone synchronizes with the contacts and calendars on your Mac or PC, as well as contacts and events on iCloud, Google, Yahoo!, and Facebook. It includes a full-featured QWERTY soft, or virtual, keyboard, which makes typing text easier than ever before — for some folks. Granted, the virtual keyboard takes a bit of time to get used to. But we think that many of you eventually will be whizzing along at a much faster pace than you thought possible on a mobile keyboard of this type.

The 5-megapixel (iPhone 4) or 8-megapixel (iPhone 4S and 5) digital camera is accompanied by a decent photo management app, so taking and managing digital photos and videos on it is a pleasure rather than the nightmare it can be on other phones. Plus, you can automatically synchronize iPhone photos and videos with the digital photo library on your Mac or PC. Okay, we still wish the iPhone camera took better photos and shot better video. But models prior to iPhone 4 are still better than some other phone cameras we've used, and the iPhone 5 camera is almost certainly the best phone camera we've seen to date.

Another of our favorite phone accoutrements is visual voicemail. (Try saying that three times fast.) This feature lets you see a list of voicemail messages and choose which ones to listen to or delete without being forced to deal with every message in your voice mailbox in sequential order. Now, *that's* handy!

Finally, the iPhone 4S and 5 come with Siri, an intelligent voice-controlled assistant that not only understands what you tell her (usually), but also figures out what you mean (again, usually) and determines which (if any) iPhone app to use to find the right answer. And, like a real personal assistant, she replies in a natural sounding human voice. Last but certainly not least, she takes dictation!

If you've tried voice control before, forget everything you've learned and give Siri a try. We think you'll be as impressed as we are.

We've mentioned just the highlights of the iPhone's superb set of features. But because we still have the entire book ahead of us, we'll put the extended coverage on hold for now (pun intended).

The iPhone as an iPod

We agree with the late Steve Jobs on this one: The iPhone is a better iPod than any iPod Apple has ever made. (Okay, we can quibble about the iPod touch and the iPad, as well as wanting more storage, but you know what we mean.) You can enjoy all your existing iPod content — music, audiobooks, audio and video podcasts, iTunes U courses, music videos, television shows, and movies — on the iPhone's gorgeous high-resolution color display, which is bigger, brighter, and richer than any iPod display that came before it.

Bottom line: If you can get the content — be it video, audio, or whatever — into iTunes on your Mac or PC, you can synchronize it and watch or listen to it on your iPhone.

The iPhone as an Internet communications device

But wait — there's more! Not only is the iPhone a great phone and a stellar iPod, but it's also a full-featured Internet communications device with — we're about to drop a bit of industry jargon on you — a rich HTML e-mail client that's compatible with most POP and IMAP mail services, with support for Microsoft Exchange ActiveSync. (For more on this topic, see Chapter 12.) Also on board is a world-class web browser (Safari) that, unlike on most other phones, makes web surfing fun and easy.

Another cool Internet feature is Maps, which is all-new in iOS 6. By using GPS, Maps can determine your location, let you view maps and satellite imagery, and obtain driving directions and traffic information regardless of where in the United States you happen to be. You can also find businesses such as gas stations, pizza restaurants, hospitals, and Apple Stores with just a few taps. And the Compass app not only displays your current GPS coordinates but also orients Maps to show the direction you're facing.

You might also enjoy using Stocks, an included app that delivers near real-time stock quotes and charts any time and any place, or Weather, another included app that obtains and displays the weather forecast for as many cities as you like.

The Internet experience on an iPhone is far superior to the Internet experience on any other handheld device we've seen, except the iPad. (Technically, we'd call the iPad a "two-hands-held device" because it's difficult to hold in one hand for more than a few minutes. But we digress.)

Technical specifications

One last thing before we proceed. Here's a list of everything you need before you can actually *use* your iPhone:

- An iPhone
- In the United States, a wireless contract with AT&T, Verizon, Sprint, or one or of the smaller carriers, such as C Spire or Cricket.
- An Apple ID
- Internet access (required) — broadband wireless Internet access recommended

In previous editions of this book, we said you *needed* one of the following. But now that you can activate, set up, update, back up, and restore your iPhone wirelessly and without a computer (a welcome feature added in iOS 5), we've amended our advice. Although you don't technically *need* a computer to use your iPhone, we think you'll find many tasks are faster and easier if you perform them on a computer with iTunes instead of on your iPhone's much smaller screen. And some tasks, such as reordering Home screens, can *only* be accomplished in iTunes.

If you decide to introduce your iPhone to your computer (and we think you should), here's what's required:

- **For Macs:** A Mac with a USB 2.0 or 3.0 port, Mac OS X version 10.5.8 or later, and iTunes 10.7 or later

- **For Windows:** A PC with a USB 2.0 or 3.0 port; Windows 7 or 8, Windows Vista, or Windows XP Home or Professional Edition with Service Pack 3 or later; and iTunes 10.7 or later (free download at www.itunes.com/download)

One last thing: Although the preceding specifications are correct, if you want to use iCloud (and you probably will), the system requirements are somewhat more stringent. You need a more current version of Mac OS X (Lion 10.7.2 or higher) or Windows (Windows 7 or Vista Service Pack 2 or later). Finally, although not officially supported (and still in beta at press time), iCloud appears to work fine with Windows 8 previews.

A Quick Tour Outside

The iPhone is a harmonious combination of hardware and software. In this section, we take a brief look at what's on the outside. In the next section, we peek at the software.

On the top and side

On the top of your iPhone, you'll find the headset jack (unless you have an iPhone 5, which has its headset jack on the bottom), a microphone, and the sleep/wake button, as shown in Figure 1-1. The SIM card tray is on one side and the ring/silent switch and volume buttons are on the other side. We describe these elements more fully in the following list:

- **Headset jack:** The headset jack lets you plug in the included iPhone headset (iPhone 4 and 4S), which looks a lot like white iPod earbuds, or EarPods (iPhone 5), which are also white but have a unique elliptical shape. Unlike iPod earbuds, however, both types of iPhone headsets have a microphone so that you can talk as well as listen.

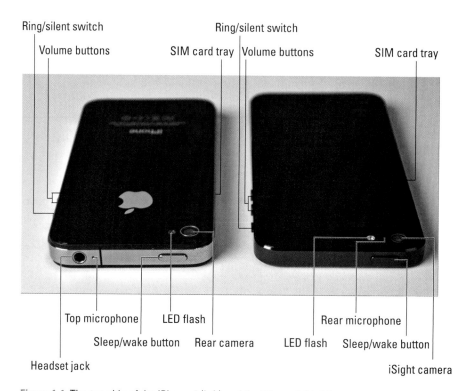

Figure 1-1: The top side of the iPhone 4 (left) and the iPhone 5 (right).

- ✔ **Microphone:** Used for FaceTime calls and noise suppression during phone calls.

- ✔ **SIM card tray:** The SIM card tray is where you remove or replace the SIM card inside your iPhone.

  A SIM (Subscriber Identity Module) card is a removable smart card used to identify mobile phones. It allows users to change phones by moving the SIM card from one phone to another. Kind of — the iPhone 4 and 4S use a micro-SIM, while the iPhone 5 uses a smaller version called a nano-SIM. And, of course, they're not compatible.

- ✔ **Sleep/wake button:** This button is used to lock or unlock your iPhone and to turn your iPhone on or off. When your iPhone is locked, you can still receive calls and text messages, but nothing happens if you touch its screen. When your iPhone is turned off, all incoming calls go directly to voicemail.

✔ **Ring/silent switch:** This switch, which is on the left side of your iPhone, lets you quickly switch between ring mode and silent mode. When the switch is set to ring mode — the up position, with no orange dot — your iPhone plays all sounds through the speaker on the bottom. When the switch is set to silent mode — the down position, with an orange dot visible on the switch — your iPhone doesn't make a sound when you receive a call or when an alert pops up on the screen.

Silent mode is overridden, however, by alarms you set in the built-in Clock app, iPod audio, and selecting sounds such as ringtones and alert sounds in the Settings app.

If your phone is set to ring mode and you want to silence it quickly, press the sleep/wake button on the top of the iPhone or press one of the volume buttons.

✔ **Volume buttons:** Two volume buttons are just below the ring/silent switch. The upper button increases the volume; the lower one decreases it. You use the volume buttons to raise or lower the loudness of the ringer, alerts, sound effects, songs, and movies. And during phone calls, the buttons adjust the voice loudness of the person you're speaking with, regardless of whether you're listening through the receiver, the speakerphone, or a headset.

Finally, when you open the Camera from the Lock screen (see Chapter 9), the volume up button acts as the shutter release button and shoots a picture when you press it.

On the bottom

On the bottom of your iPhone, you'll find the microphone, the dock connector or Lightning connector, the speaker, and the headset jack (on the iPhone 5), as shown in Figure 1-2:

✔ **Microphone:** The microphone lets callers hear your voice when you're not using a headset.

The iPhone 4 and 4S have two microphones (top and bottom); the iPhone 5 has three (top front, top back, and bottom). The top ones are used for FaceTime calls and also work with the main mic (located on the bottom) to suppress unwanted and distracting background sounds on phone calls using dual-mic noise suppression or beam-forming technology.

✔ **Dock or Lightning connector:** The dock connector (Lightning connector on the iPhone 5) has three purposes. One, you can use it to recharge your iPhone's battery. Simply connect one end of the included dock connector or Lightning–to–USB cable to the dock connector or Lightning port and the other end to the USB power adapter. Two, you can use the dock connector or Lightning port to synchronize. Connect one end of the cable to the dock connector or Lightning port and the other end to a USB port on your Mac or PC. And three, you can use the dock connector or Lightning port to connect your iPhone to other devices such as a camera or television using an adapter such as the Camera Connection Kit or one of Apple's A/V adapter cables (not supported by Lightning at press time).

✔ **Speaker:** The speaker is used by the iPhone's built-in speakerphone and plays audio — music or video soundtracks — if no headset is plugged in. It also plays the ringtone you hear when you receive a call.

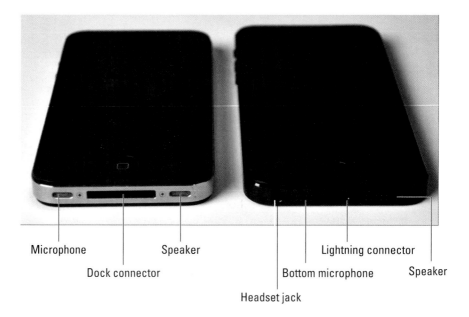

Microphone   Speaker   Lightning connector

Dock connector   Bottom microphone   Speaker

Headset jack

Figure 1-2: The bottom side of the iPhone 4 (left) and the iPhone 5 (right).

On the front

On the front of your iPhone, you'll find the following (labeled in Figure 1-3):

✔ **Camera:** The camera on the front of the iPhone is tuned for FaceTime, so it has just the right field of view and focal length to focus on your face at arm's length, which presents you in the best possible light.

✔ **Receiver:** The receiver is the speaker that the iPhone uses for telephone calls. It naturally sits close to your ear whenever you hold your iPhone in the "talking on the phone" position.

You should be the only one who hears sound coming from the receiver. If you have the volume set above about 50 percent and you're in a location with little or no background noise, someone standing nearby may be able to hear the sound, too. So be careful.

If you require privacy during phone calls, use the included Apple headset (or any compatible third-party wired or wireless headset — as discussed in Chapter 14).

✔ **Status bar:** The status bar displays important information, as you'll discover in a page or two.

✔ **Touchscreen:** You find out how to use the iPhone's gorgeous high-resolution color touchscreen in Chapter 2. All we have to say at this time is . . . try not to drool all over it.

✔ **Home button:** No matter what you're doing, you can press the Home button at any time to display the Home screen, which is the screen shown in Figure 1-3.

✔ **App buttons:** Each button on the Home screen launches an included iPhone app or one you've acquired from the App Store, with two exceptions. The Utilities button is a folder containing four app buttons: Contacts, Calculator, Compass, and Voice Memos. The Utilities button appears only on iPhones that came with iOS 4 or 5 preinstalled. If you upgraded an older iPhone to iOS 4 or 5, or are restoring from a backup, those four apps are still wherever they were before the upgrade, so yours won't be in a Utilities folder unless you created a Utilities folder and put them there as described in Chapter 2. The Newsstand button is also a folder (as explained in Chapter 16).

Status bar

Receiver

Front camera

Home button

App icon   Touchscreen

Figure 1-3: The front of the iPhone 5 is a study in elegant simplicity.

On the back

On the back of your iPhone is a camera lens. It's the little circle in the top-left corner. The iPhone also has a little LED next to the camera lens that's used as a flash for still photos and as a floodlight for videos. For more on using the camera and shooting videos, see Chapters 9 and 10, respectively. Finally, the iPhone 5 has its third microphone on the back, as shown in Figure 1-1.

Status bar

The status bar, which is at the top of every Home screen and displayed by many (if not most) apps, displays tiny icons that provide a variety of information about the current state of your iPhone:

- ✓ **Cell signal:** The strength of the cellular signal. The cell signal icon tells you whether you're within range of your wireless telephone carrier's cellular network and therefore can make and receive calls. The more bars you see (five is the highest), the stronger the cellular signal. If you're out of range, the bars are replaced with the words *No service.* And if your iPhone is looking for a cellular signal, the bars are replaced with *Searching.*

  If you have only one or two bars, try moving around a little bit. Even walking just a few feet can sometimes mean the difference between no service and three or four bars.

- ✓ **Airplane mode:** Turns off all wireless features of your iPhone. — the cellular, 3G, GPRS (General Packet Radio Service), and EDGE networks, Wi-Fi, and Bluetooth. You're allowed to use your iPod on a plane after the captain gives the word. But you can't use your cell phone except when the plane is in the gate area before takeoff or after landing. Fortunately, your iPhone offers an airplane mode, which turns off all wireless features of your iPhone and makes it possible to enjoy music or video during your flight.

  Some flights now offer on-board Wi-Fi. If you're on such a flight, you can turn on Wi-Fi even when airplane mode is enabled. Just don't turn it on until the captain says it's okay.

- ✓ **LTE (iPhone 5 only):** LTE, your wireless carrier's highest-speed data network, is available and that you can connect to the Internet via LTE.

- ✓ **3G:** Your wireless carrier's high-speed 3G data network is available and your iPhone can connect to the Internet via 3G.

- ✓ **GPRS:** Your wireless carrier's GPRS data network is available and your iPhone can use it to connect to the Internet.

- ✓ **EDGE:** Your wireless carrier's EDGE (Enhanced Datarate for GSM Evolution) network is available and you can use it to connect to the Internet.

✔ **Wi-Fi:** Your iPhone is connected to the Internet over a Wi-Fi network. The more semicircular lines you see (up to three), the stronger the Wi-Fi signal. If you have only one or two semicircles of Wi-Fi strength, try moving around a bit. If you don't see the Wi-Fi icon in the status bar, Internet access is not currently available.

Wireless (that is, cellular) carriers may offer one of four data networks. The fastest is the LTE (4G) data network, which is available only on the iPhone 5; the next fastest is 3G; the slowest are EDGE and GPRS. The device looks for the fastest available network and then, if it can't find one, looks for a slower network.

Wi-Fi networks, however, are even faster than any cellular data network. So all iPhones will connect to a Wi-Fi network if one is available, even if a 3G, GPRS, or EDGE network is also available.

Last but not least, if you *don't* see one of these icons — LTE, 3G, GPRS, EDGE, or Wi-Fi — you don't currently have Internet access.

 ✔ **Do Not Disturb:** The Do Not Disturb feature (see Chapter 4) is enabled.

 ✔ **Personal Hotspot:** The iPhone is providing a personal hotspot connection to another iPhone or other device.

 ✔ **Network activity:** Some network activity is occurring, such as over-the-air synchronization, sending or receiving e-mail, or loading a web page. Some third-party apps also use this icon to indicate network or other activity.

 ✔ **Syncing:** Your iPhone is syncing with iTunes.

 ✔ **Call forwarding:** Call forwarding is enabled on your iPhone.

 ✔ **VPN:** Your iPhone is currently connected to a virtual private network (VPN).

 ✔ **Lock:** Your iPhone is locked. See Chapter 2 for information on locking and unlocking your iPhone.

 ✔ **Play:** Audio is currently playing. You find out more about playing songs in Chapter 8.

 Portrait orientation: The iPhone is in portrait orientation mode, but not locked in that mode. (See next entry.)

 ✔ **Portrait orientation lock:** The iPhone screen is locked in portrait orientation. To lock your screen in portrait orientation, double-press the Home button, flick the dock (at the bottom of the screen) from left to right, and then tap the portrait orientation button.

 ✔ **Alarm:** You've set one or more alarms in the Clock app.

 ✔ **Location Services:** An application is using Location Services, a topic we describe in Chapter 13.

- **Bluetooth:** The current state of your iPhone's Bluetooth connection. If the icon is blue, Bluetooth is on and a device (such as a wireless headset or car kit) is connected. If the icon is gray, Bluetooth is turned on but no device is connected. If you don't see a Bluetooth icon at all, Bluetooth is turned off. Chapter 14 goes into more detail about Bluetooth.

- **Battery:** The level of your battery's charge. The icon is completely filled with green when your battery is fully charged, and then empties as your battery becomes depleted. You'll see a lightning bolt inside the icon when your iPhone is recharging.

- **TTY:** Your iPhone is set up to work with a teletype (TTY) machine, which is used by those who are hearing- or speech-impaired. You need an optional Apple iPhone TTY Adapter (suggested retail price $19) to connect your iPhone to a TTY machine.

Home Sweet Home Screen

The first page of your Home screen offers a bevy of icons, each representing a different bundled app or function. Because the rest of the book covers each and every one of these babies in full and loving detail, we merely provide brief descriptions here.

To get to the first Home screen, press the Home button. If your iPhone is asleep when you press, the Unlock screen appears. Once unlocked, you'll see whichever page of icons was on the screen when it went to sleep. If that screen happens to have been the first Home screen, you're golden. If it wasn't, merely press the Home button again to summon your iPhone's first (main) Home screen.

Three steps let you rearrange icons on your iPhone:

1. **Press and hold any icon until all of the icons begin to jiggle.**

2. **Drag the icons around until you're happy with their positions.**

3. **Press the Home button to save your arrangement and stop the jiggling.**

If you haven't rearranged your icons, you'll see the following apps on your Home screen, starting at the top left:

- **Messages:** The Messages app lets you exchange text messages (SMS) and multimedia messages (MMS) with almost any other cell phone user, as described in Chapter 5.

The Messages app also lets you exchange iMessages with anyone using an Apple device with iOS 5 or higher or a Mac running Mountain Lion (OS X 10.8) or higher, which is to say other iPhone users as well as iPad, iPod touch, and Mac owners. We've used a lot of mobile phones in our day, and this app is as good as it gets.

- **Calendar:** No matter what calendar program you prefer on your Mac or PC (as long as it's Calendar. iCal; Microsoft Entourage, Outlook, or Exchange, or the online calendars from Google or Yahoo!), you can synchronize events and alerts between your computer and your iPhone. Create an event on one and it's automatically synchronized with the other the next time they're synced. Neat stuff.

- **Photos:** This app is the iPhone's terrific photo manager. You can view pictures that you took with the iPhone's built-in cameras, transferred from your computer, received through e-mail, saved from Safari, or acquired as part of your photo stream. You can zoom in or out, create slideshows, e-mail photos to friends, and much more. Other phones may let you take pictures; the iPhone lets you enjoy them in many ways.

- **Camera:** Use this app when you want to shoot a picture or video with the iPhone's built-in cameras.

- **Videos:** This handy app is the repository for your movies, TV shows, music videos, video podcasts, and some iTunes U courseware. You add videos via iTunes on your Mac or PC, or by purchasing them from the iTunes Store using the iTunes app on your iPhone. Check out Chapter 9 to find out more.

The Videos and Music apps were new in iOS 5; in earlier releases, both audio and video content appeared in a single app called iPod.

- **Maps:** This app is among our favorites. View street maps or satellite imagery of locations around the globe, or ask for driving, walking, or public transportation directions, traffic conditions, or even the location of a nearby pizza joint.

- **Weather:** This app monitors the six-day weather forecast for as many cities as you like.

- **Passbook:** This app stores gift cards, coupons, tickets, boarding passes, and other passes in a single location.

- **Notes:** This program lets you type notes while you're out and about. You can send the notes to yourself or anyone else through e-mail or just save them on your iPhone until you need them.

- **Reminders:** This app was new in iOS 5 and may be the only to-do list you ever need. It integrates with iCal/Calendar, Outlook, and iCloud, so to-do items and reminders sync automatically with your other devices, both mobile and desktop. You'll read much more about this great app and its shiny location-based reminders, but you'll have to wait until Chapter 6.

- **Clock:** This program lets you see the current time in as many cities as you like, set one or more alarms for yourself, and use your iPhone as a stopwatch or a countdown timer.

- **Stocks:** This app lets you monitor your favorite stocks, which are updated in near-real time.

↙ **Newsstand:** This app is where you find publication-specific apps for magazines and newspapers. Shop for subscriptions at the App Store; you read more about Newsstand in Chapter 15.

↙ **iTunes:** Tap here to access the iTunes Store, where you can browse, preview, and purchase songs, albums, movies, and more.

↙ **App Store:** This icon enables you to connect to and search the iTunes App Store for iPhone apps you can purchase or download for free over a Wi-Fi or cellular data network connection.

↙ **Game Center:** This is Apple's social-networking app for game enthusiasts. Compare achievements, boast of your conquests and high scores, or challenge your friends to battle. You hear more about Game Center in Chapter 15.

↙ **Settings:** Use this app to adjust your iPhone's settings. If you're a Mac user, think System Preferences; if you're a Windows person, think Control Panel.

You won't find the Utilities folder, which we're about to describe, on your Home screen — it's on the *second* Home screen of apps (which you find out about in Chapter 2). If you just can't wait to see them, swipe your finger across the screen from right to left and they'll appear like magic.

↙ **Utilities:** The Utilities icon is a folder that contains four utility apps:

  • **Contacts:** This app stores information about your contacts, which can be synced with iCloud, Mac OS X Address Book or Contacts, Yahoo! Address Book, Google Contacts, Microsoft Outlook 2003, Microsoft Outlook 2007, Microsoft Outlook 2010 (Windows XP, Windows Vista, or Windows 7), Windows Address Book (Windows XP), Windows Contacts (Windows Vista or Windows 7), Microsoft Entourage 2004, Microsoft Entourage 2008, or Microsoft Outlook 2011 for Mac.

  • **Calculator:** The Calculator app lets you perform addition, subtraction, multiplication, and division. Period.

  • **Compass:** The Compass app is kind of like having a magnetic needle compass inside your iPhone, but better.

  • **Voice Memos:** This handy little app turns your iPhone into a convenient handheld recording device.

Again, note that the Utilities folder appears only on iPhones that had iOS 4 or 5 preinstalled. iPhones that have been upgraded to iOS 4 or 5 from previous versions or iPhones restored from a previous backup won't have a Utilities folder if the backup didn't have a Utilities folder.

Finally, four icons at the bottom of the Home screen are in a special area known as the *dock*. When you switch Home screens (see Chapter 2), all the icons above the dock change; the four items in the dock remain available on all Home screens.

If the four apps in the dock aren't the ones that you use most, you can move different apps to the dock, as described in Chapter 2.

✔ **Phone:** Tap this app icon to use the iPhone as a phone. What a concept!

✔ **Mail:** This app lets you send and receive e-mail with most POP3 and IMAP e-mail systems and, if you work for a company that grants permission, Microsoft Exchange accounts, too.

✔ **Safari:** Safari is your web browser. If you're a Mac user, you know that already. If you're a Windows user who hasn't discovered the wonderful Safari for Windows, think Internet Explorer on steroids.

✔ **Music:** This icon unleashes all the power of an iPod right on your phone.

Okay, then. Now that you and your iPhone have been properly introduced, it's time to turn it on and actually use it. Onward!

iPhone Basic Training

In This Chapter

▶ Activating your iPhone

▶ Turning the device on and off

▶ Locking your iPhone

▶ Mastering multitouch

▶ Multitasking with your iPhone

▷ Organizing folders

▶ Spotlighting search

▶ Keeping alert through notifications

*I*f you were caught up in the initial iPhone frenzy of 2007, you may have plotted for months about how to land one. After all, the iPhone quickly emerged as the ultimate fashion phone. And the chic device hosted a bevy of cool features.

Owning the hippest and most-hyped handset on the planet came at a premium cost compared with rival devices. To snag the very first version, you may have saved your pennies or said, "The budget be damned."

Sign In with an Apple ID

Create a Free Apple ID

Several years later, the iPhone is no less hip or cool, though you now get more bang for your buck. Apple has lowered the price of the iPhone 4 to — drumroll, please — zero dollars. Yes, you read right, zero. And the iPhone 4S, as of this writing, fetches just $99, while the new iPhone 5 costs $199 (for 16GB), $299 (32GB), or $399 (64GB). The original iPhone from AT&T commanded $599. All these are subsidized prices that in the United States require a mandatory two-year contract. For existing iPhone customers, the upgrade price for a new model depends on how far you're into your previous contract, how prompt you are at paying your bill, and other factors.

Activating the iPhone

Purchasers of the iPhone 4 and beyond experience a new and better activation experience than those 2007 buyers who were part of the bleeding edge. Back then, no salesperson was going to guide you through the process, whether you picked up your newly prized possession in an Apple retail store, an AT&T retail store, or on the web. Instead, you handled activation solo, in the comfort of your home.

Unless you were among those people who encountered activation hiccups in the days soon after the phone was released in June 2007, the process of getting up to speed with the iPhone was (for the most part) dirt simple and fun — as it is with most products with an Apple pedigree. Still, there were some well-publicized issues in those days, so Apple eventually changed the protocol.

You're now supposed to activate the iPhone where you bought the thing, just as you do with other cell phones. However, if you buy your iPhone from Apple's online store, they'll ship it to you and you activate it through iTunes, just like the old days, or through iCloud. If you're already a customer upgrading from an earlier iPhone or a different phone, you can convert your plan during the ordering process. You also choose your desired monthly bucket of voice minutes and SMS (Short Message Service) or text messages as well as your allotment of wireless data minutes right in the store.

Verizon Wireless and Sprint have started selling versions of the iPhone. As of this writing, AT&T, Sprint, and Verizon each had a plan that started around $80 a month. But Sprint was the only carrier to offer unlimited data plans starting at that price combined with a bucket of 450 voice minutes. Verizon and AT&T used to offer unlimited data plans but now charge based on usage, though those of you who signed up for such a plan previously have been grandfathered in.

AT&T has a $20-a-month plan with 300MB of data, but that's not much. You're looking at roughly enough data to send or receive about 900 e-mails without attachments, or send or receive about 100 messages with photo attachments, or view about 300 web pages, or post about 200 photos on social media sites, or watch about ten minutes of streaming video. These numbers are estimates. As the well-worn cliché goes, your actual mileage will vary.

If you exceed your allotment, AT&T is all too happy to sell you an additional bucket of data — an extra 300MB of usage costs $20 within the cycle.

A step-up AT&T plan costs $30 per month and gives you 3GB of data, enough to send or receive approximately 5,000 e-mails without attachments, or send or receive 800 e-mails with photo attachments, or view 4,000 web pages, or post 700 photos to social media sites, or watch 140 minutes of streaming video. If you exceed 3GB, you can get another 1GB for $10.

AT&T has claimed that 98 percent of smartphone customers use less than 2GB. So think long and hard about your anticipated usage before choosing a plan. It's also worth noting that these charges apply only to accessing cellular networks and don't count when you connect via Wi-Fi in your home, office, or elsewhere.

If you plan on tapping into the faster 4G LTE (Long Term Evolution) networks that the iPhone 5 is capable of making nice with, you may end up consuming more data, and ultimately paying more.

AT&T also has a $50 5GB plan that includes *tethering,* or the capability to use your iPhone as a broadband modem for other devices you might carry, such as laptops and netbooks, but alas not Apple's own iPad tablet or iPod touch.

Verizon has a number of different voice and data plans. For around $100 monthly, you can get unlimited voice and 2GB of data.

Verizon also lets you use your iPhone 4, iPhone 4S, and iPhone 5 as a mobile hotspot (Wi-Fi connection) for up to five devices.

It's not surprising why Apple, AT&T, Verizon, and Sprint want you in their stores: After they get you in the door, they have the opportunity to sell you other stuff. And they can help crack down on techies who want to unlock, or "jailbreak," the iPhone to defect to a rival carrier.

Two small regional carriers, C Spire and Cricket, were gearing up to sell the iPhone 5 as this book went to press. Without the same kind of large subsidies offered by AT&T, Sprint, and Verizon, you can count on paying more upfront with these companies.

The two prerequisites for enjoying the iPhone that have been in place since the original release remain — at least for most U.S. customers. First, unless you're already in the fold, there's the aforementioned business of becoming an AT&T, Verizon, or Sprint subscriber: You'll have to ink that new two-year term. If you're in the middle of a contract with a rival carrier, read the sidebar titled "The Great Escape: Bailing out of your wireless contract."

Second, make sure you download the latest version of iTunes software for syncing with your PC or Mac. Apple doesn't supply the software in the box, so head to `www.apple.com/itunes` if you need to fetch a copy, or launch your current version of iTunes and then choose iTunes⇨Check for Updates (Mac) or Help⇨Check for Updates (Windows).

The Great Escape: Bailing out of your wireless contract

In most instances, a wireless provider will sell you a deeply discounted phone or even issue you a free model, as is now the case with the iPhone 4. But this deal has one expensive catch: You're subject to hefty termination fees if you bail out of your (typical) two-year contract early.

In the U.S., the iPhone is available only through AT&T, Verizon, Sprint, and small regional carriers such as C Spire and Cricket, so you'll have to wave sayonara to other carriers if you want this device. But breaking a cell phone contract is not easy, and some options for doing so may not be quite the out you had in mind: You can enlist in the military, move overseas, or die.

Fortunately, other strategies are available, although none are assured of working:

- **Complain loudly and often:** If you've been having problems with your existing carrier, contact the phone company and tell them about your lousy coverage. Document your complaints in writing and be as specific as possible about spots where your calls drop out.

- **Keep an eye out for price hikes:** If the carrier ups rates dramatically on text messaging, say, you may have a legal out in your contract. The Consumerist website (www.consumerist.com) advises you to read any notices of changes to your Terms of Service that come your way. These changes may void the original agreement, and you'll have about a month to cancel your contract.

- **Use online matchmaking:** Sites such as www.celltradeusa.com and www.cellswapper.com are in the business of matching users who want to get out of their contracts with folks who are seeking a bargain. The person trying to ditch a contract pays a modest fee to these sites. So what's the motivation for the person who takes the contract off your hands? Those who get their phone service this way need not pay an activation fee to the carrier, and they incur no long-term commitment of their own.

- **Roam, roam on the range:** If you keep using your phone outside your carrier's network, it may become uneconomical for *them* to want to keep you because your phone company picks up expensive roaming charges.

For the uninitiated, iTunes is the nifty Apple jukebox software that iPod owners and many other people use to manage music, videos, and more. iTunes is at the core of the iPhone as well because an iPod is built into the iPhone. You'll employ iTunes to synchronize a bunch of stuff on your computer and iPhone, including apps, photos, podcasts, videos, ringtones, and (of course) music — that is, unless you eschew your computer directly and manage all this stuff through iCloud.

We get into all that syncing business in Chapter 3.

Turning the iPhone On and Off

Apple has taken the time to nearly fully charge your iPhone, so you'll get some measure of instant gratification. After taking the phone out of the box, press and hold the sleep/wake button on the top-right edge. (Refer to Chapter 1 for the location of all buttons.) If the phone has been activated — and at least in Apple Stores, a salesperson will happily handle this for you — the famous Apple logo appears on your screen, followed a few seconds later with the word *iPhone* overlaid on top of a gray background. If the phone is shipped to you from the Apple Store, you get a Connect to iTunes screen so that the device can connect to your provider's servers and perform the activation. Or you can go computer-free through iCloud.

Over the next several screens that appear, you'll set up your phone. You get to choose your language (English by default) and country or region. You then choose a Wi-Fi network, if available, or proceed using your cellular connection.

Next, you decide whether to enable Location Services. Agreeing to this step means the iPhone knows where you are, which is useful for Maps and other apps that rely on your whereabouts.

The interrogation continues. Do you want to set up the device as a new iPhone, restore the phone from an iCloud backup (see the next chapter), or restore it from an iTunes backup?

After that business is decided, you're asked to agree to the Terms and Conditions. And just what took the lawyers so long to get involved?

Next, you sign in with an Apple ID (if you already have one) or create a new one. Apple ID is the credential used to set up your iCloud, App Store, and iTunes Store accounts. You can use iCloud to store photos, apps, contacts, calendars, and more and have them wirelessly pushed to your devices. You can also have the iPhone back up data to iCloud daily over Wi-Fi or back up instead to your computer.

As part of the setup, you're asked whether you want to take advantage of the Find My iPhone feature. Seems like a no-brainer to us: Why wouldn't you want to turn on a tool that can possibly help you retrieve a lost or stolen phone? (For more on Find My iPhone, check out Chapter 14.)

You also get to choose or verify the phone number and e-mail addresses that folks might use to get in touch with you, via FaceTime video calling (see Chapter 4) or via iMessage (see Chapter 5).

Then, only for owners of the iPhone 4S or iPhone 5 (as of this writing), you determine whether you will use the Siri voice assistant.

Training your digits

Rice Krispies has Snap! Crackle! Pop! Apple's response for the iPhone is Tap! Flick! Pinch! Oh yeah, add Drag!

Fortunately, tapping, flicking, pinching, and dragging are not challenging gestures, so you'll be mastering many of the iPhone's features in no time:

✔ **Tap:** Tapping serves multiple purposes, as will become evident throughout this book. You can tap an icon to open an app from the Home screen. Tap to start playing a song or to choose the photo album you want to look through. Sometimes you'll double-tap (tapping twice in rapid succession), which has the effect of zooming in (or out) of web pages, maps, and e-mails.

✔ **Flick:** A flick of the finger on the screen itself lets you quickly scroll through lists of songs, e-mails, and picture thumbnails. Tap the screen to stop scrolling, or merely wait for the list to stop scrolling.

✔ **Pinch/spread:** On a web page or picture, pinch your fingers together to shrink the image, or spread your fingers apart to enlarge the image. Pinching and spreading (or what we call *unpinching*) are cool gestures that are easy to master and sure to wow an audience.

✔ **Drag:** Slowly press your finger against the touchscreen and then, without lifting your finger, move it. You might drag to move around a map that's too large for the iPhone's display area.

Apple makes one more request at this stage. They'd love for you to have your iPhone automatically send them daily diagnostic and usage data, including your location. Armed with such information, Apple says they can better improve the company's products and services. We think the request is harmless. If you find the prospect unappealing, just say no — or to be more precise, choose Don't Send.

From then on, you're pretty much good to go.

To turn the device completely off, press and hold the sleep/wake button again until a red arrow appears at the top of the screen. Then drag the arrow to the right with your finger. Tap Cancel if you change your mind.

Locking the iPhone

Carrying a naked cell phone in your pocket is asking for trouble. Unless the phone has some locking mechanism, you may inadvertently dial a phone number. Try explaining to your boss why he or she got a call from you at 4 a.m. Fortunately, Apple makes it a cinch to lock the iPhone so this scenario won't happen to you.

In fact, you don't need to do anything to lock the iPhone; it happens automatically, as long as you don't touch the screen for one minute. (You can change this duration in iPhone Settings, a topic in Chapter 14.)

Can't wait? To lock the iPhone immediately, press the sleep/wake button. To unlock it, press the sleep/wake button again. Or press the Home button on the front of the screen. Either way, the on-screen slider appears. To unlock the device, drag the slider to the right with your finger and then, in some cases, also enter a passcode, another topic reserved for Chapter 14.

By now, you're picking up on the idea that your fingers play an instrumental role in controlling your iPhone. We talk more about the responsibility your digits have later in this chapter.

The iOS 5 software upgrade introduced a Notification Center that clues you in on, well, notifications. These include, but are not limited to, missed calls, texts, e-mails, and the weather. What's more, Apple is kind enough to serve up notifications right on the iPhone's Lock screen.

You can act upon notifications by swiping your finger. More on notifications later in this chapter — and more on the Lock screen in Chapter 9, where we clue you in on how to launch the Camera app from the Lock screen.

Mastering the Multitouch Interface

Until the iPhone came along, virtually every cell phone had a physical (typically plastic) dialing keypad, if not also a more complete QWERTY-style keyboard, to bang out e-mails and text messages. The iPhone dispenses with both. Apple is once again living up to an old company advertising slogan to "Think Different."

Indeed, the iPhone removes the usual physical buttons in favor of a *multitouch display.* This display is the heart of many things you do on the iPhone, and the controls change depending on the task at hand.

Unlike other phones with touchscreens, don't bother looking for a stylus. You are meant, instead — at the risk of lifting another ancient ad slogan — to "let your fingers do the walking."

It's important to note that you have at your disposal several keyboard layouts in English, all variations on the alphabetical keyboard, the numeric and punctuation keyboard, and the more punctuation and symbols keyboard. Six keyboards are shown in Figure 2-1. The layout you see depends on the app you are working in. For instance, the keyboards in Safari differ from the keyboards in Notes.

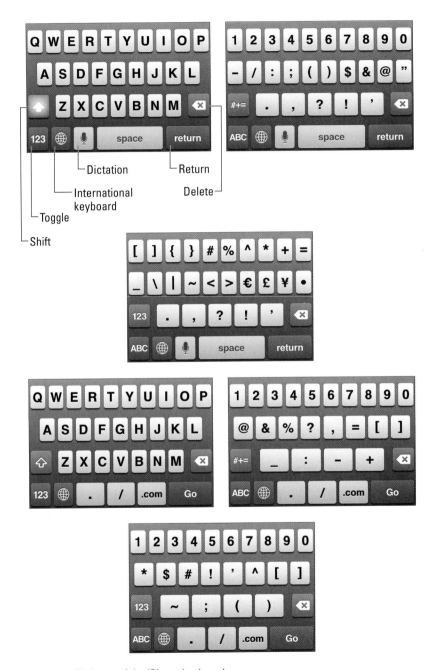

Figure 2-1: Six faces of the iPhone keyboard.

What's more, if you rotate the iPhone to its side, you'll get wider variations of the respective keyboards. A single example of a wide keyboard in the Notes app is shown in Figure 2-2.

Figure 2-2: Going wide on the keyboard.

Discovering the special-use keys

The iPhone keyboard contains five keys that don't actually type a character (refer to Figure 2-1). These special-use keys follow:

- **Shift key:** Switches between uppercase and lowercase letters if you're using the alphabetical keyboard. If you're using keyboards that show only numbers and symbols, the traditional shift key is replaced by a key labeled #+= or 123. Pressing that key toggles between keyboards that have just symbols and numbers.

  To turn on caps lock mode and type in all caps, you first need to enable caps lock. You do that by tapping the Settings icon, then tapping General, and then tapping Keyboard. Tap the Enable Caps Lock item to turn it on. After the caps lock setting is enabled (it's disabled by default), you double-tap the shift key to turn on caps lock. (The shift key turns blue when caps lock is on.) Tap the shift key again to turn off caps lock. To disable caps lock completely, just reverse the process by turning off the Enable Caps Lock setting (tap Settings, General, Keyboard).

- **Toggle key:** Switches between the different keyboard layouts.

- **International keyboard key:** Shows up only if you've turned on an international keyboard, as explained in the sidebar titled "A keyboard for all borders," later in this chapter.

- ✒ **Delete key:** Erases the character immediately to the left of the cursor.

  If you hold down the delete key for a few seconds, it begins erasing entire words rather than individual characters.

- ✒ **Return key:** Moves the cursor to the beginning of the next line.

- ✒ **Microphone/Siri key (iPhone 4S and iPhone 5 only):** Tapping this key, which appears in apps such as Notes and Messages, lets you use Siri to dictate your words. More on Siri in Chapter 7.

Google's Chrome web browser app, available free in the App Store, adds a row of keys above the QWERTY row. You see a semicolon (:), a period (.), a hyphen (-), a slash (/), and .com.

The incredible, intelligent, and virtual iPhone keyboard

Before you consider how to actually *use* the keyboard, we'd like to share a bit of the philosophy behind its so-called intelligence. Knowing what makes this keyboard smart will help you make it even smarter when you use it. The iPhone keyboard

- ✒ Uses a bundled English dictionary that even includes words from today's popular culture.

- ✒ Adds your contacts to its dictionary automatically.

- ✒ Uses complex analysis algorithms to predict the word you're trying to type.

- ✒ Suggests corrections as you type, and then offers you the suggested word just below the word you typed. When you decline a suggestion and the word you typed is *not* in the iPhone dictionary, the iPhone adds that word to its dictionary and offers it as a suggestion if you mistype a similar word in the future.

  Remember to decline suggestions (by tapping the characters you typed as opposed to the suggested words that appear below what you've typed), because doing so helps your intelligent keyboard become even smarter.

- ✒ Reduces the number of mistakes you make as you type by intelligently and dynamically resizing the touch zones for certain keys. You can't see it, but the iPhone increases the zones for keys it predicts might come next and decreases the zones for keys that are unlikely to come next.

Navigating beyond the Home screen

The Home screen, which we discuss in Chapter 1, isn't the only screenful of icons on your phone. After you start adding apps from the iTunes App Store (see Chapter 15), you'll likely have multiple screens.

A keyboard for all borders

Apple continues to expand the iPhone's global reach by supplying international keyboard layouts for more than 50 languages. To access a keyboard that isn't customized for Americanized English, tap Settings, General, Keyboard, Keyboards, Add New Keyboard. (Alternatively, tap Settings, General, International, Keyboards, Add New Keyboard.) Up pops the list shown in the first figure, with custom keyboards for Russian, Slovak, Swedish, and other languages. Apple even supplies two versions of Portuguese to accommodate customers in Brazil and Portugal, and three versions of French (including keyboards geared to Canadian and Swiss users). Heck, there's even a U.K. version of English and one for Australian English, and keyboards for "right-to-left" languages such as Arabic and Hebrew.

Have a multilingual household? You can select, in turn, as many international keyboards as you want. When you're working in an app that summons a keyboard, tap the international keyboard button, between the toggle and space keys (refer to Figure 2-1), until you see the keyboard you want. Note that the space key momentarily displays the name of the keyboard language and then translates the word *space* itself to the language of the keyboard in use. Tap again to select the next keyboard in the list of international keyboards that you turned on in Settings. If you keep cycling, you eventually come back to your original English layout. Here's an alternative method for summoning a keyboard you've enabled: Press your finger against the international keyboard key until a pop-up window displays all the keyboards that are ready for action. Slide your finger along the list until it lands on the keyboard you want to use, and then release it to select that keyboard.

You can use handwriting character recognition for simplified and traditional Chinese, as shown here. Just drag your finger in the box provided. We apologize in advance for not knowing what the displayed characters here mean. We certainly don't want to offend.

Initially, you see three tiny dots above the Phone, Mail, Safari, and Music icons. Each dot denotes an additional screen, containing up to 16 additional icons (up to 20 on the iPhone 5) for apps or folders of apps. The leftmost dot, which is dimmed (and, on close inspection, is shaped like a tiny magnifying glass), denotes the Search screen, which you access by flicking from left to right across the middle of the screen or by tapping directly on the dot. The second dot, which is all white, represents the Home screen, or the screen you're currently viewing. The next dot to the right is the first additional screen in which you can park icons. You get to it by flicking right to left (assuming you're on the first screen) or tapping the dot. Including the Search screen, you can have 12 screens in all; as you add screens, you add dots.

You must be precise when tapping a dot. Otherwise, you'll open one of the app or folder icons instead of switching screens.

The four icons in the bottom row — Phone, Mail, Safari, and Music — are in a part of the screen known as the *dock*. When you switch from screen to screen as just described, these icons remain on the screen.

You can easily move icons within a screen or from screen to screen. Simply press and hold any icon until all the icons on the screen begin to jiggle. Then drag the icon you want to park elsewhere to its new location. The other icons on the screen kindly step aside to make room. To move an icon to an entirely new screen, drag it to the right or left edge of the screen. When you're satisfied with the new layout, press the Home button to stop the jiggling.

Want to jump back to the first screenful of icons or the Home screen? Simply press the Home button. Pressing a second time brings you to a handy Spotlight search feature, which we address at the end of this chapter, in the "Searching" section.

If you press two times in rapid succession, you won't jump to the first Home screen or Spotlight Search screen. Instead, the multitasking tray (described in the "Multitasking" section, later in this chapter) appears. So remember to pause briefly between presses if you want to jump to the Home or Spotlight Search screens, and press twice in rapid succession to invoke multitasking.

Press and hold the Home key for more than a second or so to summon Siri on the iPhone 4S and iPhone 5, or Voice Control on all older iPhones except the original model (unless you turn the feature off in Settings).

Finger-typing on the virtual keyboards

Apple's multitouch interface just might be considered a stroke of genius. And it just might as equally drive you nuts, at least initially.

Fingers or thumbs?

Should you use your fingers or thumbs to type? The answer is: both. It seems somewhat easier to hold the iPhone in your nondominant hand (that is, your left hand if you're right-handed or vice versa) and type with the index finger of your dominant hand, especially when you're starting out with the iPhone. And that's what we suggest you try first.

When you get the hang of typing with one index finger, try to speed things up by using both hands. You can type two-handed in two ways:

✔ Set the iPhone on a sturdy surface (such as a desk or table) and tap with both index fingers. You can't easily use this technique when you're standing up with no stable surface at the proper height.

✔ Cup the iPhone with both hands and type with both thumbs. This technique has the advantage of being possible in almost any situation, with or without a sturdy surface. The downside is that your thumbs are bigger than your other fingers, so typing accurately with them takes more practice — and if you have larger-than-average thumbs, well, you're flirting with trouble.

Which technique is better? Don't ask us — try both ways and use the method that feels the most comfortable or lets you type with the best accuracy. Better still, master both techniques and use whichever is more appropriate at the time.

If you're patient and trusting, you'll get the hang of finger-typing in a week or so. You have to use the virtual keyboard that appears when you tap a text field to enter notes, compose text messages, type the names of new contacts, and so forth.

Apple's own recommendation — with which we concur — is to start typing with just your index finger before graduating to two thumbs.

As we've noted, Apple has built a lot of intelligence into its virtual keyboard, so it can correct typing mistakes on the fly and take a stab at predicting what you're about to type next. The keyboard isn't exactly Nostradamus, but it does a pretty good job in coming up with the words you have in mind.

As you press your finger against a letter or number on the screen, the individual key you press gets bigger and practically jumps off the screen, as shown in Figure 2-3. That way, you know that you struck the correct letter or number.

Sending a message to an overseas pal? Keep your finger pressed against a letter, and a row of keys showing variations on the character for foreign alphabets pops up, as shown in Figure 2-4. Then you can add the appropriate accent mark. Just slide your finger until you reach the key with the relevant accent mark, and press.

Figure 2-3: The ABCs of virtual typing.

Figure 2-4: Accenting your letters.

Meanwhile, if you press and hold the .com key on a Safari keyboard, it offers you the choice of .com, .net, .edu, .us, or .org. Pretty slick stuff.

If you enabled any international keyboards, you'll see more choices when you hold down the .com key. For example, if you enabled a French keyboard, pressing and holding .com will also give you options for .eu and .fr.

Alas, typing mistakes are common at first. Say that you meant to type a sentence in the Notes app that reads, "I am typing a bunch of notes." But because of the way your fingers struck the virtual keys, you actually entered "I am typing a bunch of *npyrs.*" Fortunately, Apple knows that the *o* you meant to press is next to the *p* that showed up on the keyboard, just as *t* and *y* and the *e* and the *r* are side-by-side. So the software determines that *notes* was indeed the word you had in mind and places it in red under the suspect word, as shown in Figure 2-5. To accept the suggested word, merely tap the space key. And if for some reason you actually did mean to type *npyrs* instead, tap the suggested word (*notes* in this example) to decline it.

Because Apple knows what you're up to, the virtual keyboard is customized for the task at hand. If you're entering a web address, the keyboard inside the Safari web browser (Chapter 11) includes dedicated period, forward slash, and (the aforementioned) .com keys but no space key.

If you're using the Notes app (Chapter 5), the keyboard does have a space key. And if you're composing an e-mail message, a dedicated @ key pops up on the keyboard.

When you're typing notes or sending e-mail and want to type a number, symbol, or punctuation mark, tap the 123 key to bring up an alternative virtual keyboard. Tap the ABC key to return to the first keyboard. This extra step is not hard to get used to, but some may find it irritating.

See Chapter 19 for a slick trick (the slide) that avoids the extra step involved in moving between the 123 and ABC keys.

As mentioned, you can rotate the iPhone so that its keyboard changes to a wider landscape mode in certain apps, including Mail, Messages, and Notes. The feature was already present in Safari. The keys are slightly larger in landscape mode, a boon to those who do a lot of typing or have largish fingers.

Editing mistakes

It's a good idea to type with abandon and not get hung up over mistyped characters. The self-correcting keyboard will fix many errors. That said, plenty of typos will likely turn up, especially in the beginning, and you'll have to make corrections manually.

A neat trick when manually correcting text is to hold your finger against the screen to bring up the magnifying glass shown in Figure 2-6. Use it to position the pointer to the spot where you need to make the correction.

Cutting, copying, pasting, and suggesting

Being able to copy and paste text (or images) from one place on a computer to another has seemingly been a divine right since Moses, but getting to this Promised Land on the iPhone took awhile. Apple eventually added Copy and Paste (and Cut) — and, in its own inimitable way, brought pizzazz to this long-requested feature. Apple also has provided another helpful remedy for correcting errors: a Suggest pop-up option that appears when you double-tap a word. (A Define option is here too.)

Figure 2-5: When the keyboard bails you out.

Figure 2-6: Magnifying errors.

Here's how to exploit the copy-and-paste feature. Say you're in the Notes app, jotting down ideas that you want to copy into an e-mail message. Double-tap a word to select it, and then drag the blue grab points or handles to select a larger block of text, as shown in Figure 2-7. (You can use the handles to contract selected text too.) After you've selected the text, tap Copy. (If you want to delete the text block, tap Cut instead.

Now open the Mail program (Chapter 12) and start composing a message. When you decide where to insert the text you just copied, tap the cursor. Up pop commands to Select, Select All, and Paste, as shown in Figure 2-8. Tap Paste to paste the text into the message.

Here's the pizzazz part. If you make a mistake while you're cutting, pasting, suggesting, or typing, shake the iPhone. It undoes the last edit.

Figure 2-7: Drag the grab points to select text.

Figure 2-8: Tap Paste to make text appear from nowhere.

Or suppose that you notice a typo in what you've entered. In Figure 2-9, for example, we inadvertently typed *their* instead of *there*. By tapping Suggest, we can easily make a fix. Upon doing so, the iPhone serves up a few suggested replacement words. If the word you have in mind as a substitute is, um, there, tap it and the iPhone automatically makes the switch. Another example: Say you inadvertently typed *Freek*. When you tap Suggest, the iPhone presents alternatives such as Greek, Freak, and Freed.

Meanwhile, if you want to know exactly what a word means, you can double-tap a word and choose the Define option instead. The first time you tap Define, you'll be presented with the option to download the dictionary.

Figure 2-9: Tap Suggest and then tap a substitute word to make a switch.

Multitasking

Back when Apple introduced the iOS 4 software upgrade (which, of course, predated iOS 5 and iOS 6), the company added a bevy of important features, with the long-overdue multitasking feature arguably the most significant. *Multitasking* simply lets you run numerous apps in the background simultaneously or easily switch from one app to another. For example, music from a third-party app such as Slacker can play in the background while you surf the web, peek at pictures, or check e-mail. Before multitasking hit the iPhone, Slacker would shut itself down the moment you started performing tasks in another app. (Previously, Apple did let you multitask by, for example, playing audio in the background with its iTunes app. But multitasking was limited to Apple's own apps, not those produced by outside developers.)

But that's not all. If you use an Internet voice-calling app such as Skype, you'll be able to receive notification of an incoming call even if you haven't launched the Skype app. The multitasking feature also lets a navigation app employing GPS update your position while you're listening to an Internet radio app such as Pandora. From time to time, the navigation app or Apple's own Maps app, which arrived with iOS 6, will pipe in with turn-by-turn directions, lowering the volume of the music so you can hear the instructions.

And if you're uploading images to a photo website and the process is taking longer than you'd like, you can switch to another app, confident that the images will continue to upload behind the scenes. We've also been able to leave voice notes in the Evernote app while checking out a web page.

Multitasking couldn't be easier. Double-press the Home button, and a tray appears at the bottom of the screen, as shown in Figure 2-10, left. The tray holds icons for the most recently used apps. Scroll to the right to see more apps (see Figure 2-10, right). Tap the app you want to switch to: The app remembers where you left off. (Scroll all the way to the left and you'll also see volume controls, AirPlay controls, and an orientation lock.)

Figure 2-10: Scroll the tray to see the apps you've recently used.

Apple insists (and our experience generally leads us to believe) that multitasking will not drain the iPhone battery or exhaust system resources. The iPhone conserves power and resources by putting apps in a state of suspended animation. But as we just mentioned, you can wake them up instantly and return to what you were doing.

 To remove an app from the tray holding icons of the most recently used apps — and thus remove the app from those in the multitasking rotation — press and hold your finger against any app until all the apps start to wiggle. Then tap the red circle with the white line that appears inside the app you want to remove. Poof, it's gone.

Multitasking works only on iPhones dating back to the 3GS model. Older iPhones don't have the resources to handle the feature.

Note that multitasking on the iPhone doesn't work quite the same way as multitasking on a PC or a Mac. You can't display more than one window on the screen at a time — given the size of the iPhone screen, you'd have trouble viewing multiple windows anyway.

Moreover, there's some philosophical debate whether this feature is multitasking, or fast task-switching, or some combination. Rather than getting bogged down in the semantics, we're just glad that multitasking, or whatever it is, is available.

Organizing Icons into Folders

Finding the single app you want to use among apps spread out over 11 screens is a daunting task. But Apple felt your pain, and with iOS 4, the company introduced a handy organizational tool called Folders. The Folders feature enables you to create folder icons, each holding up to a dozen apps. You might want to create folders for social apps, photography, travel, and any number of other categories.

To create a folder, press your finger against an icon until all the icons on the screen jiggle, as shown in Figure 2-11. Decide which apps you want to move to a folder, and drag the icon for the first app on top of the second app. The two apps now share living quarters inside a newly created folder, as shown in Figure 2-12. Apple names the folder according to the category of apps inside the folder, but you can easily change the folder name by tapping the X in the bar where the folder name appears and substituting a new name.

To launch an app that's inside a folder, tap that folder's icon and then tap the icon for the app that you want to open.

You can drag apps into and out of any folder as long as there's room for them — remember that you can have no more than 12 apps in a folder. If you drag all the apps outside the folder, it automatically disappears.

Folders are a great organizational tool. But if you have numerous apps on the phone, it's a lot easier to create and arrange folders not from the phone but when syncing your phone in iTunes.

Figure 2-11: Keeping apps in their place using folders.

Figure 2-12: Dragging one app on top of another to create a folder.

Searching

Using the Safari browser (see Chapter 11), you can search the web using Google, Yahoo!, or Microsoft Bing. But you can also search for people and programs across your iPhone or within specific apps. We show you how to search within apps in the various chapters dedicated to Mail, Contacts, Calendar, Notes, and Music.

Searching across the iPhone, meanwhile, is based on the Spotlight feature familiar to Mac owners. To access Spotlight, flick to the left of the main Home screen (or press the Home button from the Home screen, as mentioned earlier in this chapter).

In the bar at the top of the screen that slides into view, enter your search query using the virtual keyboard. The iPhone starts spitting out results the moment you type a single character, and the list narrows as you type additional characters.

The results are pretty darn thorough. Say you entered *Bell* as your search term, as shown in Figure 2-13. Contacts whose names have Bell in them will show up, along with folks who work for companies named Bell. If your iTunes library has the song "One Last Bell to Answer" or music performed by violinist Joshua Bell, those will show up, too. Same goes for a third-party iPhone app called The Bell. Tap any listing to jump to the contact, ditty, or app for which you're searching.

TIP

If you don't find what you're looking for, you can take your search into cyberspace. At the very bottom of the search results that popped up are two additional options, Search Web and Search Wikipedia. Tap the latter to fire up Safari and visit the vast online Wikipedia encyclopedia. The search term you entered *(Bell)* is already selected. If you tap Search Web instead, Safari brings you to a Google, Yahoo!, or Bing search page, prepopulated with the search term you selected.

Figure 2-13: Putting the spotlight on search.

You have some control over the type of search that Spotlight conducts. From the Home page, tap Settings⇨General⇨Spotlight Search. Make sure there's a check mark next to each bundled app on the iPhone that you'd like searched automatically. By default, all the options — Contacts, Applications, Music, Podcasts, Videos, Audiobooks, Notes, Events, Mail, Voice Memos, Reminders, and Messages — are selected. Tap to remove the check mark from any app that you don't want automatically included in your search.

Notifications

When you stop to think about it, a smartphone is smart because of all the things it can communicate, from stock prices to social-networking friend requests.

Notification Center gives you an at-a-glance, timely view of everything you want to keep on top of: new e-mails, texts, the current temperature, appointments and reminders, Tweets, and more.

If you provide your Facebook user credentials in Settings, you can post directly to the world's most popular social network right from Notification Center. Similarly, if you provide your Twitter information, you can Tweet from Notification Center.

Although it's useful to keep tabs on all this stuff, you don't want to be hit over the head with the information, thus distracting you from whatever else you're doing on the iPhone. So Apple delivers notifications unobtrusively by displaying banners at the top of the screen that then disappear until you actively choose to view them. And when you want to do just that, you can summon Notification Center, shown in Figure 2-14, just by swiping down from the top of the screen.

You can also choose which notifications you will see. Tap Settings⟶ Notifications and then tap the notifications you want to see. What's more, you can customize the way the notifications you do want to see appear.

By way of example, in Settings, tap Reminders under the list of apps and widgets that you can include in Notification Center. Figure 2-15 displays your options.

Figure 2-14: Staying in the loop with Notification Center.

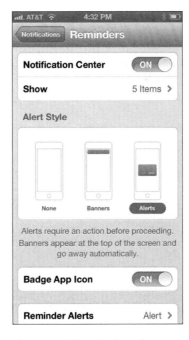

Figure 2-15: Choosing how alerts should appear.

You can decide whether reminders should appear in Notification Center and indicate whether you want to see just a single reminder item, up to five reminders, or up to ten of these items. Next, choose an alerts style: whether such reminder notifications appear as a banner at the top of the screen that disappears automatically or as an alert that requires your response before you can do anything else.

You also get to decide whether to receive reminder notifications when your phone is locked.

If you don't want to be bothered with notifications at all, turn on the Do Not Disturb option, new in iOS 6. When enabled, alerts that would otherwise grab your attention will be silenced. You can even schedule the time that the Do Not Disturb feature is turned on. As you see in Chapter 4, you can also turn on Do Not Disturb to silence incoming phone calls.

And with that, you are hereby notified that you've survived basic training. The real fun is about to begin.

3

Synchronicity: Getting Stuff to and from Your iPhone

In This Chapter

▷ Starting your first sync

▷ Understanding iCloud

▷ Syncing iPhone with iTunes

▷ Synchronizing contacts, calendars, e-mail accounts, and bookmarks

▷ Synchronizing ringtones, music, podcasts, video, photos, and applications

*A*fter you pass basic training (in Chapter 2), the next thing you're likely to want to do is get some or all of the following into your iPhone: contacts, appointments, events, mail settings, bookmarks, ringtones, music, movies, TV shows, podcasts, books, courseware, photos, documents, and applications.

We have good news and . . . more good news. The good news is that you can easily copy any or all of those items from your computer to your iPhone. And the more good news is that after you do that, you can synchronize your contacts, appointments, and events so they're kept up-to-date automatically everywhere you might need them — on your computer, iPhone, iPad, and iPod touch. So when you add or change an appointment, an event, or a contact on your iPhone, that information automatically appears on your computer and other devices.

This communication between your iPhone and computer is called *syncing* (short for synchronizing). Don't worry: Syncing is easy and you find out how it works in this very chapter.

Podcasts

☑ Automatically include 3 most recent unpl

Podcasts

The Mac Observer's Apple Conte
● 3 new episodes

The Mac Observer's Mac Geek G
● 1 new episode (3 total)

Power Users

Here's even more good news: iOS 5 and 6 let you use your iPhone PC-free, which means it doesn't *require* you to connect to a computer running iTunes. You'll discover how to sync both with and without connecting your iPhone to a computer in this chapter. But bear in mind that certain tasks — such as rearranging icons on your Home screens and managing media — are quite a bit easier on a computer than on the iPhone's smaller screen. And some tasks, such as rearranging the order of Home screens, are only possible using iTunes on a computer.

The information in this chapter is based on iTunes version 10.7 and iOS 6.0, which were the latest and greatest when these words were written. If your screens don't look exactly like ours, you probably need to upgrade to iTunes 10.7 or higher (choose iTunes➪Check for Updates) or to iOS 6 or higher (click the Check for Update button on the Summary tab shown in the upcoming Figure 3-2 and follow the instructions for updating your iPhone), or both. By the way, both upgrades are free, and both offer useful new features and have significant advantages over their predecessors.

You start this chapter with a description of how to set up a new iPhone both with and without a computer. Next, you take a quick look at iCloud, Apple's free wireless storage and synchronization solution, and find out how it can make using your iPhone better. Finally, you get started syncing.

Setting Up a New iPhone

In this section, you discover how to set up a brand new iPhone.

Unless your iPhone is brand spanking new and fresh out of the box, chances are you've already performed the steps that follow. If so, please skip ahead to the next section.

That said, here's how to set up a brand new iPhone:

1. **Turn on the iPhone or wake it if it's sleeping.**

    An arrow appears near the bottom of the screen, flashing messages in many languages. We're pretty sure they all say, *Slide to Set Up,* because that's what the English rendition says.

2. **Swipe the Slide to Set Up arrow to the right.**

    The first thing you see on your shiny new (or freshly restored) iPhone is the Language Selection screen.

3. **Tap the language you want this iPhone to use, and then tap the blue arrow near the top-right of the screen.**

   The Country or Region screen appears.

4. **Tap your country or region, and then tap the blue Next button.**

   The Choose a Wi-Fi Network screen appears.

5. **Tap to choose a Wi-Fi network, type a password if necessary, tap the blue Join button, and then tap the blue Next button.**

   Tapping Next initiates the activation process, which requires either a Wi-Fi network or your wireless carrier's cellular network and may take up to five minutes.

   If neither network is available, you'll see an alert that says you need to connect your iPhone to your computer and use iTunes to complete the activation and setup process, as described in the first four steps in "The Kitchen Sync" section, later in this chapter.

   After your iPhone has been activated, the Location Services screen appears.

6. **Tap to enable or disable Location Services, and then tap the blue Next button.**

   Location Services is your iPhone's way of knowing your precise geographical location. The Maps app, for example, relies on Location Services to determine where in the world you are. (See Chapter 13 for more on Maps.)

   You can turn Location Services on or off globally or for individual apps in Settings, as you discover in Chapter 14.

   The Set Up iPhone screen appears.

7. **Do one of the following:**

   • **If you're replacing an old iPhone with this one:** Choose either Restore from iCloud Backup or Restore from iTunes Backup to have the new iPhone restored with the settings and data from your previous one. You'll see either the iCloud Sign In screen or the Connect to iTunes screen. Follow the on-screen instructions and choose the backup you want to restore from. In a few minutes (or more if your old iPhone contained a lot of data), your new iPhone will contain all the apps, media files, and settings from your old iPhone. You're finished and can skip ahead to the next section, "A Brief iCloud Primer."

- **If this is your first iPhone:** You won't have any backups of your iPhone yet, so unless you want to restore it with the data from an iPod touch or iPad, you should choose Set Up as New iPhone and tap the blue Next button. The Apple ID screen appears.

8. **Tap Sign In with Your Apple ID or tap Create a Free Apple ID. Then (you know) tap the blue Next button.**

   You can tap Skip This Step and proceed without supplying an Apple ID, but we advise against that choice. You'll need a free Apple ID to take advantage of the myriad excellent and free features — including iCloud — described in this and other chapters.

   The Terms and Conditions screen appears.

9. **To agree to the terms and conditions, tap the blue Agree button in the lower-right corner.**

   A Terms and Conditions alert appears.

10. **Tap the Agree button and then tap the blue Next button.**

    What happens if you disagree? You don't want to know. And, of course, you won't be able to use your iPhone.

    The Set Up iCloud screen appears.

11. **Do one of the following:**

    - **If you want to use iCloud:** Good choice! Tap Use iCloud and then tap the blue Next button. Follow the instructions on the Back Up to iCloud screen, and tap the blue Next button again.

      If you're committed to using your iPhone PC-free, we urge you to use iCloud to back up your iPhone.

    - **If you don't want to use iCloud:** Tap Don't Use iCloud, and then tap the blue Next button.

    The iCloud Backup screen appears.

12. **Tap Back Up to iCloud to back up your iPhone to iCloud daily over Wi-Fi; tap Back Up to My Computer to back up to your computer's hard drive; then tap the blue Next button.**

    The Find My iPhone screen appears next.

13. **Tap Use Find My iPhone or tap Don't Use Find My iPhone, and then tap the blue Next button.**

    Find My iPhone is a seriously cool feature that lets you locate and secure your iPhone if it ever gets lost or stolen, as you'll discover in Chapter 14.

14. Tap the phone numbers and e-mail addresses you want to use for iMessages and FaceTime calls, and then tap the blue Next button.

People can use an e-mail address or your phone number to send you iMessages and place FaceTime calls to your iPhone. Tap all the ones you want to enable. Don't sweat your decisions; you can always add and remove addresses in Settings⇨Messages.

If you have an iPhone 4, you don't have Siri, so you can skip the next step.

15. If you have an iPhone 4S or 5, tap Use Siri or tap Don't Use Siri, and then tap the blue Next button.

Siri is an intelligent voice-controlled assistant available only on the iPhone 4S and 5. It's so wickedly cool we devote all of Chapter 7 to its use.

We can't think of a good reason not to enable Siri, but if that's your choice, you'll still be able to use voice commands for dialing the phone and controlling the Music app.

If you just can't wait to hear what Siri can do for you, tap the What Is Siri link at the bottom of the screen for a brief description. When you're finished, tap the blue Done button.

The Diagnostics screen appears.

16. Tap either Automatically Send or Don't Send, and then tap the blue Next button.

If you tap Automatically Send, anonymous diagnostic and usage data will be sent to Apple.

The Thank You screen appears.

17. Tap Start Using iPhone to, well, start using your iPhone.

Your iPhone's Home screen appears in all its glory.

One last thing: Apple's free iCloud wireless storage and synchronization service (described in the following section) is strictly optional, but it's especially useful if you're planning to use your iPhone PC-free or only plan to sync it with a computer occasionally.

A Brief iCloud Primer

Apple's iCloud service is more than just a wireless hard drive in the sky. iCloud is a complete wireless storage and data synchronization solution. In a nutshell, iCloud is designed to store and manage your digital stuff — your music, photos, contacts, events, and more — keeping everything updated on all your computers and iDevices automatically with no physical (wired) connection or action on your part. Like so many things Apple makes, iCloud just works.

iCloud pushes information such as e-mail, calendars, contacts, and bookmarks to and from your computer and to and from your iPhone and other iDevices, and then keeps those items updated on all devices wirelessly and without human intervention. iCloud also includes nonsynchronizing options, such as Photo Stream (see Chapter 9) and e-mail (see Chapter 12).

Your free iCloud account includes 5GB of free storage, which is all many (if not most) users will need. If you find yourself needing more storage, 10-, 20-, and 50-gigabyte upgrades are available for $20, $40, and $100 a year, respectively.

A nice touch is that music, apps, books, periodicals, movies, and TV shows purchased from the iTunes Store, as well as your photo stream and iTunes Match content (see Chapter 8), don't count against your 5GB of free storage. You'll find that the things that do count — such as mail, documents, photos taken with your iPhone camera, account information, settings, and other app data — don't use much space, so that 5GB should last you a long time.

If you plan to go PC-free, but want to have your e-mail, calendars, contacts, and bookmarks synchronized automatically and wirelessly (and believe us, you do), here's how to enable iCloud syncing on your iPhone:

1. **Tap Settings on your Home screen.**
2. **Tap iCloud in the list of settings on the left.**
3. **Tap Account and provide your Apple ID and password.**
4. **Tap Done.**

Now tap any of the individual On/Off switches to enable or disable iCloud sync for any of the following options:

- Mail
- Contacts
- Calendars
- Reminders
- Bookmarks
- Notes
- Photo Stream
- Documents & Data
- Find My iPhone

You find out much more about iCloud in the rest of this chapter and several other chapters, so let's move on to syncing your iPhone.

The Kitchen Sync

If you're using your iPhone PC-free because you don't own or have access to a computer, you can skip the rest of the chapter. Why? If you don't have a computer, you don't have any data or media to sync with your iPhone and can skip ahead to Chapter 4 now.

First things first: About iPhone backups

Whether you know it or not, your iPhone backs up your settings, app data, and other information on your iPhone whenever you connect to a computer and use iTunes to:

- Sync with your iPhone
- Update your iPhone
- Restore your iPhone

Every time you sync your iPhone and computer, most (but not all) of your iPhone content — photos in the camera roll, text messages, notes, contact favorites, sound settings, and more — is backed up to either your computer's hard drive or iCloud before the sync begins. Most of your media, including songs, TV shows, and movies, *isn't* backed up in this process. This shouldn't be a problem because these files are usually restored when you sync with iTunes again.

Backups are saved automatically and stored on your computer by default. You can instead choose to back up to iCloud by clicking the appropriate button in the iTunes Summary pane.

To switch to backing up to iCloud using iTunes on your computer (or vice versa), follow these steps:

1. **Connect the iPhone to the computer.**

   If iTunes doesn't launch automatically when you connect the iPhone, launch it now.

2. **In the sidebar on the left side of iTunes, select your iPhone.**

3. **Click the Summary tab.**

4. **Click Back Up to iCloud or Back Up to This Computer.**

   If you choose to back up to your computer, you can encrypt your backups with a password by selecting the Encrypt iPhone Backup check box.

If anything goes wonky or you get a new iPhone, you can restore most (if not all) of your settings and files that aren't synced with iCloud or iTunes on your computer. Or, if you've backed up an iPhone, iPod touch, or another iPhone, you can restore the new iPhone from the older device's backup.

If you're using an iPhone computer-free, here's how to enable backing up to iCloud from your iPhone, which we strongly suggest you do without further delay:

1. **Tap Settings⇨iCloud⇨Storage & Backup.**

2. **Tap iCloud Backup to switch it on.**

Choosing this option means your iPhone no longer backs up automatically if you connect it to a computer.

If you're a computer-free iPhone user, you don't care because you never connect your iPhone to a computer. But if you sync your iPhone with your computer, as many folks do, give some thought to which option suits your needs. Restoring from a computer backup requires physical or Wi-Fi access to that computer, but you don't need Internet access. Restoring from iCloud requires Internet access and can happen anywhere on Earth that has that access.

One last thing to look at in the Backup section: If you want to password-protect your iPhone backups (your iPhone creates a backup of its contents automatically every time you sync), be sure to also select the Encrypt iPhone Backup check box from the Backup area.

Backups are good; choose one or the other and move on.

Sync prep 101

For those who want to sync using iTunes on the computer, either with the included dock or Lightning connector–to–USB cable or wirelessly over Wi-Fi, follow the instructions in the rest of this chapter.

In other words, unless you don't have a computer at all, just follow these steps and you'll be ready to sync via cable or wirelessly in just a few minutes:

1. **Start by connecting your iPhone to your computer with the Lightning or dock connector–to–USB cable included with your iPhone.**

   When you connect your iPhone to your computer, iTunes should launch automatically. If it doesn't, chances are you plugged the cable into a USB port on your keyboard, monitor, or hub. Try plugging it into one of the USB ports on your computer instead. Why? Because USB ports on your computer supply more power to a connected device than other USB ports or most hubs.

   If iTunes still doesn't launch automatically, try launching it manually.

   If you don't see an iPhone in the source list and you're sure your iPhone is connected to a USB port on your computer (not on the keyboard, monitor, or hub), try restarting your computer.

2. **If your photo management software launches, either import the photos you've taken with the iPhone or don't.**

   If you've taken any photos with your iPhone since the last time you synced it, your photo management software (iPhoto, Image Capture, or Aperture on the Mac; Adobe Photoshop Elements on the PC) opens and ask whether you want to import the photos from your phone. (You find out all about this in the "Photos" section, later in this chapter.)

3. **Select your iPhone in the iTunes source list.**

   If you're setting up this iPhone for the first time, you'll see the Set Up Your iPhone pane shown in Figure 3-1. If you've already named your iPhone, skip to Step 5.

Source list

iPhone selected in Source list

Figure 3-1: This is the first thing you see in iTunes.

4. **Name your iPhone.**

   We've named this one *Bob's iPhone 4S.*

5. **Choose what, if anything, you want iTunes to automatically synchronize, and then click Done.**

   You can sync only your iPhone, or you can sync only your contacts, calendars, bookmarks, notes, e-mail accounts, and applications, or you can sync everything.

However, we suggest that you leave both boxes unchecked and set everything up manually, as described in the remainder of this section. That way, you'll see additional options for syncing contacts, calendars, bookmarks, notes, e-mail accounts, and apps, as well as how to sync media including movies, TV shows, and podcasts.

6. **Click the Summary tab near the top of the window, as shown in Figure 3-2.**

If you don't see a Summary tab, make sure your iPhone is still selected in the source list.

Summary tab

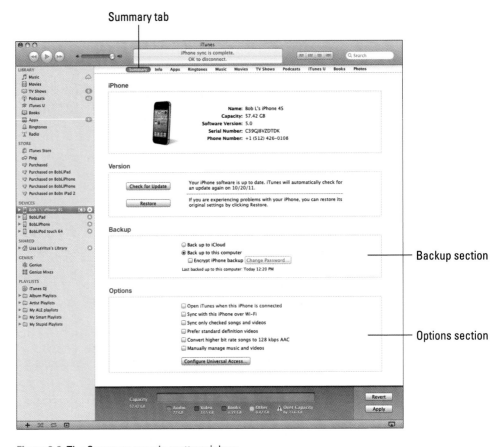

Figure 3-2: The Summary pane is pretty painless.

7. **In the Backup section of the Summary pane, click either Back Up to iCloud or Back Up to This Computer.**

   Your iPhone creates a backup of its contents automatically every time you sync, regardless of whether you sync using a USB cable or wirelessly.

   If you choose to store your backups locally, on your computer, you can encrypt and password-protect them by selecting the Encrypt iPhone Backup check box section.

   That's all there is to the Backup section. The remaining steps deal with the check boxes in the Options section (refer to Figure 3-2).

8. **If you want iTunes to launch automatically and sync your iPhone whenever you connect it to your computer, click to put a check mark in the Open iTunes When This iPhone Is Connected check box (in the Options section).**

   If the Prevent iPods, iPhones, and iPads from Syncing Automatically option in the Devices pane of iTunes Preferences (iTunes⇨Preferences on a Mac; Edit⇨Preferences on a PC) is selected (checked), the Open iTunes When This iPhone Is Connected option in the Summary tab is deselected.

   Your choice in this step is not set in stone. If you select the Open iTunes When This iPhone Is Connected check box, you can still prevent your iPhone from syncing automatically in two ways:

   • **Way #1:** After you connect the iPhone to your computer, click the Summary tab in iTunes and deselect the Open iTunes When This iPhone Is Connected check box. Removing the check mark prevents iTunes from opening automatically when you connect the iPhone. If you use this method, you can still start a sync manually by clicking the Sync button.

   • **Way #2:** Launch iTunes *before* you connect your iPhone to your computer. Then press and hold down ⌘+Option (Mac) or Shift+Ctrl (PC) and connect your iPhone. Keep pressing the keys until you see your iPhone appear in the iTunes source list. This method prevents your iPhone from syncing automatically without changing any settings.

9. **If you want to sync automatically over your Wi-Fi connection, select the Sync with This iPhone over Wi-Fi check box.**

10. **If you want to sync only items that have check marks to the left of their names in your iTunes library, select the Sync Only Checked Songs and Videos check box.**

11. **If you want high-definition videos you import to be automatically converted into smaller standard-definition video files when you transfer them to your iPhone, select the Prefer Standard Definition Videos check box.**

    Standard-definition video files are significantly smaller than high-definition video files. You'll hardly notice the difference when you watch the video on your iPhone, but you can have more video files on your iPhone because they take up less space.

    That said, if you choose to watch video from your iPhone on an HDTV either with one of the A/V adapters for iPhone 4 or 4S (no such adapters were announced for the iPhone 5 at press time) mentioned next or wirelessly via AirPlay (as discussed in Chapter 8), you'll definitely notice a big difference.

    Finally, if you have a wireless network at home, you don't need to sync video you intend to watch at home with your iPhone. Instead, you can stream it from your computer to your iPhone or your iPhone to your HDTV (with an Apple TV), as described in Chapter 8.

    The conversion from HD to standard definition takes a *long* time, so be prepared for very long sync times when you sync new HD video and have this option enabled.

12. **If you want iTunes to automatically create smaller audio files (so you can fit more music on your iPhone), select the Convert Higher Bit Rate Songs to 128Kbps AAC check box.**

    A *higher* bit rate means that the song will have better sound quality but use more storage space. Songs that you buy at the iTunes Store or on Amazon, for example, have bit rates of around 256 Kbps. So, a 4-minute song with a 256 Kbps bit rate is around 8MB; convert it to 128 Kbps AAC and it's roughly half that size (that is, around 4MB), while sounding almost as good.

    Most people don't notice much (if any) difference in audio quality when listening to music on most consumer audio gear. So unless you expect to hook your iPhone up to a great amplifier and superb speakers or headphones, you probably won't hear much difference, but your iPhone will hold roughly twice as many tunes with this option enabled. Put another way, we're very picky about our audio, and we both enable this option to allow us to carry more music around with us on our iPhones. And neither of us has noticed much impact on sound quality with the headphones or speakers we use with our iPhones.

13. **If you want to turn off automatic syncing in just the Music and Video panes, select the Manually Manage Music and Videos check box.**

And, of course, if you decide not to select the Open iTunes When This iPhone Is Connected check box, you can synchronize manually by clicking the Sync button in the bottom-right corner of the window. Note, however, that if you've changed any sync settings since the last time you synchronized, the Sync button will say Apply instead of Sync.

Syncing Your Data

Did you choose to set up data synchronization manually (by not selecting the Automatically Sync Contacts, Calendars, Bookmarks, Notes, and Email Accounts check box or the Automatically Sync Applications check box in the Set Up Your iPhone pane shown in Figure 3-1)? If you did, your next order of business is to tell iTunes what data you want to synchronize between your iPhone and your computer. You do this by clicking the Info tab, which is to the right of the Summary tab.

The Info pane has five sections: Sync Contacts, Sync Calendars, Sync Mail Accounts, Other, and Advanced. The following sections look at them one by one.

If you are using iCloud to sync contacts, calendars, bookmarks, or notes, DO NOT enable those items in iTunes, as we're about to describe. There's a warning in fine print at the bottom of each section that says so, but some folks don't read the fine print, so here's our warning in big type: IF YOU ENABLE SYNCING WITH iCLOUD AND ALSO ENABLE IT IN iTUNES, YOU MAY END UP WITH DUPLICATED DATA ON YOUR iPHONE. We guarantee you won't like that, so enable syncing one way or the other — via iCloud or in the iTunes Info pane.

Syncing address book contacts

The Sync Address Book Contacts section of the Info pane determines how synchronization is handled for your contacts. One method is to synchronize all your contacts, as shown in Figure 3-3. Or you can synchronize any or all groups of contacts you've created in your computer's address book program; just select the appropriate check boxes in the Selected Groups list, and only those groups will be synchronized.

The iPhone syncs with the following address book programs:

- **Mac:** Address Book and other address books that sync with Address Book, such as Microsoft Outlook 2011 or the discontinued Microsoft Entourage

- **PC:** Windows Contacts (Vista and Windows 7), Windows Addressbook (XP), Microsoft Outlook, and Microsoft Outlook Express

- **Mac and PC:** Yahoo! Address Book and Google Contacts

Figure 3-3: Want to synchronize your contacts? This is where you set things up.

Now, here's what each option in the Sync Contacts section does:

- **All Contacts:** One method is to synchronize all your contacts, as shown in Figure 3-3. This will synchronize every contact in your Mac or PC address book with your iPhone's Contacts app.

- **Selected Groups:** You can synchronize any or all groups of contacts you've created in your computer's address book program. Just select the appropriate check boxes in the Selected Groups list, and only those groups will be synchronized.

- **Yahoo! or Google Contacts:** If you use Yahoo! Address Book, select the Sync Yahoo! Address Book Contacts check box and then click the Configure button to enter your Yahoo! ID and password. If you use Google Contacts, select the Sync Google Contacts check box and then click the Configure button to enter your Google ID and password.

  If you use Yahoo!, note that syncing doesn't delete a contact from your Yahoo! Address Book if the contact has a Yahoo! Messenger ID, even if you delete that contact on the iPhone or on your computer. To delete a contact that has a Yahoo! Messenger ID, log on to your Yahoo! account with a web browser and delete the contact in your Yahoo! Address Book.

If you sync with your employer's Microsoft Exchange calendar and contacts, any personal contacts or calendars already on your iPhone will be wiped out.

Syncing calendars

The Calendars section of the Info pane determines how synchronization is handled for your appointments and events. You can synchronize all your calendars, as shown in Figure 3-4. Or you can synchronize any or all individual calendars you've created in your computer's calendar program. Just select the appropriate check boxes.

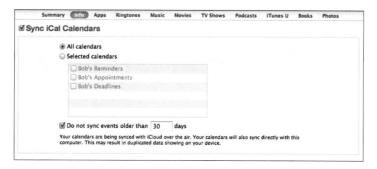

Figure 3-4: Set up sync for your calendar events here.

The Calendars section is named Sync iCal Calendars because Figure 3-4 was captured in iTunes for the Mac. If you use a PC, this section is named Sync Calendars with Outlook. As before, don't worry — regardless of its name, it works the same on either platform.

The iPhone syncs with the following calendar programs:

✔ **Mac:** iCal and Calendar

✔ **PC:** Microsoft Exchange and Outlook 2003, 2007, and 2010

✔ **Mac and PC:** Google and Yahoo! Calendars

Syncing e-mail accounts

You can sync account settings for your e-mail accounts in the Sync Mail Accounts section of the Info pane. You can synchronize all your e-mail accounts (if you have more than one) or individual accounts, as shown in Figure 3-5. Just select the appropriate check boxes.

Figure 3-5: Transfer e-mail account settings to your iPhone here.

The iPhone syncs with the following mail programs:

- **Mac:** Mail
- **PC:** Microsoft Outlook 2003, 2007, or 2010
- **Mac and PC:** Gmail, Yahoo! Mail, iCloud, AOL, Hotmail, other POP and IMAP accounts

E-mail account settings are synchronized only one way: from your computer to your iPhone. If you make changes to any e-mail account settings on your iPhone, the changes will *not* be synchronized back to the e-mail account on your computer. Trust us, this is a very good feature and we're glad Apple did it this way.

By the way, the password for your e-mail account may or may not be saved on your computer. If you sync an e-mail account and the iPhone asks for a password when you send or receive mail, do this: On the Home screen, tap Settings, and then tap Mail, Contacts, Calendars. Tap your e-mail account's name, and then type your password in the appropriate field.

Syncing bookmarks and notes

The Other section of the Info pane has only two options. Select the Sync Safari Bookmarks check box if you want to sync the bookmarks on your computer with bookmarks on your iPhone. The iPhone can sync bookmarks with the following web browsers:

- **Mac:** Safari
- **PC:** Microsoft Internet Explorer and Safari

Select the second option, the Sync Notes check box, to sync notes in the Notes app on your iPhone with Notes in Apple Mail on a Mac or Microsoft Outlook on a PC. To sync notes on a Mac, you must have Mac OS X 10.5.7 or later installed.

Advanced syncing

Every so often, the contacts, calendars, mail accounts, or bookmarks on your iPhone get so screwed up that the easiest way to fix things is to erase that information on your iPhone and replace it with information from your computer.

If that's the case, just click to select the appropriate check boxes in the Advanced section of the Info pane, as shown in Figure 3-6. Then the next time you sync, that information on your iPhone will be replaced with information from your computer.

Figure 3-6: Replace the information on your iPhone with the information on your computer.

Because the Advanced section is at the bottom of the Info pane and you have to scroll down to see it, it's easy to forget that it's there. Although you probably won't need to use this feature very often (if ever), you'll be happy you remembered that it's there if you do need it.

One last thing: Check boxes in the Advanced section are disabled for items not selected, as described in the previous sections (Contacts, Calendars, and Mail Accounts in Figure 3-6). If you're using iCloud and you want to replace any of these items on your iPhone, you must first enable that item as discussed in the previous sections of this chapter. In other words, if we wanted to replace Contacts, Calendars, or Mail Accounts in Figure 3-6, we'd first have to select Sync Contacts, Sync Calendars, and Sync Mail Accounts, as we've just described.

Synchronizing Your Media

If you chose to let iTunes manage synchronizing your data automatically, welcome back. This section looks at how you get your media — your ringtones, music, movies, TV shows, podcasts, video, iTunes U courses, books, and photos — from your computer to your iPhone.

Sharp-eyed readers may notice that we aren't covering syncing iPhone apps in this chapter. Apps are so darn cool that we've given them an entire chapter, namely Chapter 15. In that chapter, you discover how to find, sync, rearrange, review, and delete apps, and much, much more.

Podcasts and videos (but not photos) from your computer are synced only one way: from your computer to your iPhone. If you delete a podcast or a video that got onto your iPhone via syncing, the podcast or video will not be deleted from your computer when you sync.

That said, if you buy or download any of the following items on your iPhone, the item *will* be copied back to your computer automatically when you sync:

- ✔ Songs
- ✔ Podcasts
- ✔ Videos
- ✔ iBooks, e-books, and audiobooks
- ✔ Apps
- ✔ Playlists that you create on your iPhone

And if you save pictures from e-mail messages, from the iPhone camera, from web pages (by pressing and holding down on an image and then tapping the Save Image button), or from screen shots (by pressing the Home and Sleep/Wake buttons simultaneously), these too can be synced.

Taking a screen shot creates a photo of what's on your screen. It's a handy tool, and it's what we used to generate almost every figure in this book.

You use the Apps, Tones, Music, Podcasts, Movies, TV Shows, iTunes U, Books, and Photos panes to specify the media that you want to copy from your computer to your iPhone. The following sections explain the options you find in each pane.

To view any of these panes, make sure that your iPhone is still selected in the sidebar and then click the appropriate button near the top of the window.

The following sections focus only on syncing. Need help acquiring apps, music, movies, podcasts, or anything else for your iPhone? This book contains chapters dedicated to each of these topics. Just flip to the most applicable chapter for help.

Ringtones, music, movies, and TV shows

You use the Tones, Music, Movies, TV Shows, Podcasts, and iTunes U panes to specify the media that you want to copy from your computer to your iPhone. To view any of these panes, make sure that your iPhone is still selected in the source list, and then click the appropriate tab near the top of the window.

Ringtones

If you have custom ringtones in your iTunes library, select the Sync Ringtones check box in the Tones pane. Then you can choose either all ringtones or individual ringtones by selecting their check boxes. Ringtones can be used also as text tones and alarms.

Music, music videos, and voice memos

To transfer music to your iPhone, select the Sync Music check box in the Music pane. You can then select the option for Entire Music Library or Selected Playlists, Artists, and Genres. If you choose the latter, click the check boxes next to particular playlists, artists, and genres you want to transfer. You also can choose to include music videos or voice memos or both by selecting the appropriate check boxes at the top of the pane (see Figure 3-7).

Figure 3-7: Use the Music pane to copy music, music videos, and voice memos from your computer to your iPhone.

If none of the options just mentioned sounds just right (pun intended), you can drag individual songs onto the Manually Added Songs section near the bottom of the Music pane, as you see at the bottom of Figure 3-7.

How much space did I use?

If you're interested in knowing how much free space is available on your iPhone, look near the bottom of the iTunes window while your iPhone is selected in the source list. You'll see a chart that shows the contents of your iPhone, color-coded for your convenience. As you can see in the figure (which shows three different charts), this 64GB iPhone 5 has 25.8GB of free space.

If you click once on the chart, it will display the number of items in each category, as shown in the middle chart in the figure. And if you click

it again, it will display how long it will take to listen to all your audio or watch all your video, as shown in the bottom chart. Click again and the display returns to gigabytes and megabytes, as shown in the top chart.

You can find similar information about space used and space remaining on your iPhone by tapping Settings➪General➪Usage. The iPhone's display isn't as pretty as the one pictured here, but it is useful when you need that info and you're not near your computer.

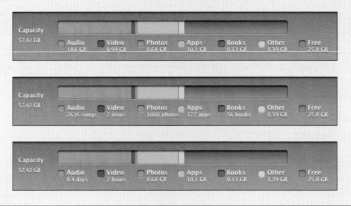

If you choose Entire Music Library and have more songs in your iTunes library than storage space on your iPhone, you'll see one or both of the error messages shown in Figure 3-8 when you try to sync. You'll also see a yellow alert on the right side of the Capacity chart at the bottom of the screen, along with how much over your iPhone's capacity adding the entire music library would make you. To avoid such errors, select playlists, artists, and genres that total less than the free space on your iPhone, which is also displayed in the Capacity chart at the bottom of the iTunes screen.

Music, podcasts, and video are notorious for using massive amounts of storage space on your iPhone. If you try to sync too much media, you'll see lots of error messages like the ones in Figure 3-8. Forewarned is forearmed.

Finally, if you select the Automatically Fill Free Space with Songs check box, iTunes fills any free space on your iPhone with music.

Movies

To transfer movies to your iPhone, select the Sync Movies

Figure 3-8: If you have more music than your iPhone has room for, this is what you'll see when you sync.

check box and then choose an option for movies you want to include automatically from the pop-up menu, as shown in Figure 3-9. If you choose an option other than All, you can optionally select individual movies and playlists by checking the boxes in appropriate sections.

Figure 3-9: Your choices in the Movies pane determine which movies are copied to your iPhone.

TV shows

The procedure for syncing TV shows is slightly different from the procedure for syncing movies. First, select the Sync TV Shows check box to enable TV show syncing. Then choose how many episodes to include and whether you want all shows or only selected shows from the two pop-up menus, as shown in Figure 3-10. If you want to also include individual episodes or episodes on playlists, select the appropriate check boxes in the Shows, Episodes, and Include Episodes from Playlists sections of the TV Shows pane.

Figure 3-10: The TV Shows pane determines how TV shows are synced with your iPhone

Podcasts, iTunes U, and books

You can also sync podcasts, educational content from iTunes U, two types of books — e-books for reading and audiobooks for listening — and photos.

TIP

If you like to watch or listen to podcasts, iTunes U courses, or e-books, visit the App Store (see Chapter 15) and grab copies of Apple's free Podcasts, iBooks, and iTunes U apps. Audiobooks, on the other hand, don't require a special app; you can listen to them using the Music app (see Chapter 8).

Podcasts

To transfer podcasts to your iPhone, select the Sync Podcasts check box in the Podcasts pane. Then you can automatically include however many podcasts you want by making selections from the two pop-up menus, as shown in Figure 3-11. If you have podcast episodes on playlists, you can include them by selecting the appropriate check box in the Include Episodes from Playlists section.

iTunes U

To sync educational content from iTunes U, first select the Sync iTunes U check box to enable iTunes U syncing. Then choose how many episodes to include and whether you want all collections or only selected collections from the two pop-up menus. If you want to also include individual items or items on playlists, select the appropriate check boxes in the Items section and Include Items from Playlists section of the iTunes U pane.

Figure 3-11: The Podcasts pane determines which podcasts are copied to your iPhone.

Books

By now we're sure you know the drill: You can sync all your e-books or audiobooks or just sync selected titles by choosing the appropriate buttons and check boxes in the Books pane.

To sync e-books, you need the free iBooks app from the App Store. For more information on apps and the App Store, read Chapter 15.

Photos

Syncing photos is a little different from syncing other media because your iPhone has a built-in camera — two cameras, actually — and you may want to copy pictures or videos you take with the iPhone to your computer, as well as copy pictures stored on your computer to your iPhone.

The iPhone syncs photos and videos, too, with the following programs:

- **Mac:** Aperture version 3.2 or later or iPhoto version 9.2 or later
- **PC:** Adobe Photoshop Elements or Adobe Photoshop Album

You can also sync photos with any folder on your computer that contains images.

In the Photos pane, select the Sync Photos From check box, and then choose an application or folder from the pop-up menu (which says Aperture in Figure 3-12).

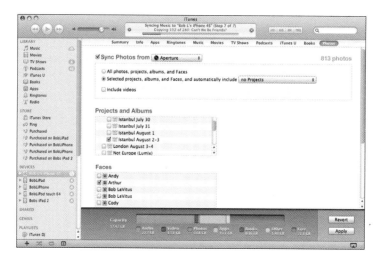

Figure 3-12: The Photos pane determines which photos will be synchronized with your iPhone.

If you choose an application that supports photo albums (such as Photoshop Elements, Aperture, or iPhoto), projects (Aperture), events (iPhoto), facial recognition and Places (Aperture or iPhoto), or any combination thereof, you can automatically include recent projects (Aperture), events (iPhoto), or faces (Aperture and iPhoto) by making a selection from the same pop-up menu (refer to Figure 3-12).

If you're using iPhoto, you can also type a word or phrase in the search field (an oval with a magnifying glass) to search for a specific event or events. We're using Aperture in Figure 3-12, which is why you don't see the search field.

If you choose a folder full of images, you can create subfolders inside it that will appear as albums on your iPhone. But if you choose an application that doesn't support albums or events, or a single folder full of images with no subfolders, you have to transfer all or nothing.

Because we selected Aperture in the Sync Photos From menu, and Aperture 3 (the version installed on our Mac) supports projects and faces in addition to albums and photos, we have the option of syncing any combination of photos, projects, albums, and faces.

If you've taken any photos with your iPhone or saved images from a web page, an e-mail, an MMS message, or an iMessage since the last time you synced, the appropriate program launches (or the appropriate folder is selected), and you have the option of uploading the pictures to your computer.

Understanding the Phone-damentals

*Y*ou may well have bought an iPhone for its spectacular photo viewer, its marvelous widescreen display, its multimedia capabilities, and the best darn pocket-sized Internet browser you've ever come across. Not to mention its overall coolness.

For most of us, though, cool goes only so far. The iPhone's most critical mission is the one from which its name is derived — it is first and foremost a cell phone. And no matter how capable it is at all those other things, when push comes to shove, you had best be able to make and receive phone calls.

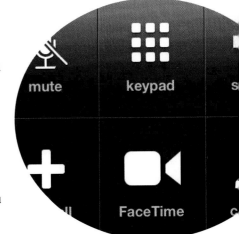

That requirement puts a lot of responsibility in the hands of AT&T, Sprint, and Verizon, the iPhone's main wireless carriers in the United States. As with any cell phone, the strength of the wireless signal depends a great deal on your location and the robustness of the carrier's network.

As noted in Chapter 1, the cell signal status icon at the upper-left corner of the screen can clue you in on what your phone-calling experience may be like. Simply put, more bars supposedly equate to a better experience. What you hope to avoid are those two dreaded words: *No Service.* Cell coverage aside, this chapter is devoted to all the nifty ways you can handle wireless calls on an iPhone.

And when we say *nifty,* we mean nifty. If you and the person you're gabbing with have an iPhone 4, 4S, or 5 plus a good Wi-Fi or cellular connection, you can *see* each other. That's right: We're talking about video calling, through a remarkable feature called FaceTime. (FaceTime also lets you make a video call to a friend with an iPad 2 or later tablet, a fourth-generation or later iPod touch, or a Mac computer.)

The promise of video calling has been around since LBJ occupied the White House. But despite various efforts to bring video calling or video chat to computers and certain other mobile handsets, video calling has never really gone Main Street.

We're betting that with FaceTime, Apple is going to do as much as any outfit this side of Microsoft-owned Skype to change that. Don't take our word for it; give FaceTime a try. Sorry, but we're going to leave you hanging until the end of the chapter to figure out how to do that. (Trust us, giving FaceTime a whirl isn't hard.)

In the meantime, we present more conventional but no less important ways to make and receive calls on your iPhone. Somewhere, Alexander Graham Bell is beaming.

Making a Call

Start by tapping the Phone icon on the Home screen. You can then make calls by tapping any of the icons that show up at the bottom of the screen: Favorites, Recents, Contacts, Keypad, or Voicemail, in that order. In this section, we describe these options one by one.

The iPhone 3GS and iPhone 4 have another way of calling, by using the aptly named Voice Control feature to dial a name or phone number by voice. As of the iOS 5 upgrade, the Siri feature on the iPhone 4S and iPhone 5 can also take on voice-dialing responsibilities. We discuss both these options in Chapter 7.

Contacts

If you read the chapter on syncing (Chapter 3), you know how to get the snail-mail addresses, e-mail addresses, and (most relevant for this chapter) phone numbers that reside on your PC or Mac into the iPhone. Assuming that you went through that drill already, all those addresses and phone numbers are hanging out in one place. Their not-so-secret hiding place is revealed when you tap the Contacts icon in the Phone app. Okay, so Contacts hangs out in the Utilities folder.

As of iOS 6, if you enter your Facebook credentials in Settings, your Facebook friends — and their phone numbers, if they were made publicly available in Facebook — will automatically populate your list of contacts.

Here's how to make those contacts work to your benefit:

1. **In the Phone app, tap Contacts.**

2. **Flick your finger so the list of contacts on the screen scrolls rapidly up or down, loosely reminiscent of the spinning Lucky 7s on a Las Vegas slot machine.**

Think of the payout on a One-Armed Bandit with that kind of power.

Don't feel like flicking? You can find a contact by

- Moving your fingers along the alphabet on the right edge of the Contacts list or tapping one of the letters to jump to names that begin with that letter, easier said than done given the tiny size of those letters.

- Starting to type in the search field near the top of the list. Try the name of the contact or the place where your contact works. You may have to flick to get the search field into view.

- Using Spotlight (refer to Chapter 2).

3. **When you're at or near the appropriate contact name, stop the scrolling by tapping the screen.**

Note that when you tap to stop the scrolling, that tap doesn't select an item in the list. This behavior may seem counterintuitive the first few times you try it, but we got used to it and now we really like it this way.

Tap the status bar to automatically scroll to the top of the list and bring the search field into view. Doing so is useful if you're really popular (or influential) and have a whole bunch of names among your contacts.

4. Tap the name of the person you want to call.

As shown in Figure 4-1, you can see a bunch of fields with the individual's phone numbers, physical and e-mail addresses, and possibly even a mug shot. You may have to scroll down to see more contact info.

If the person has more than one phone number, the hardest decision you must make is choosing which number to call.

5. Tap the phone number, and the iPhone initiates the call.

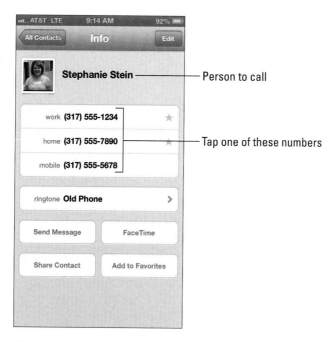

Figure 4-1: Contact me.

Your iPhone contacts reflect any groups you belong to, such as different departments in your company, friends from work, and friends from school. When you're looking at the Contacts entry for an individual person, an All Contacts button appears in the upper-left corner. Tap All Contacts to bring up the roster of all your contacts, and the button at the upper-left corner changes to Groups. Tap that button to access contacts for a given group.

Among the Groups listings you see is one for all your iCloud contacts and one for all your friends on Facebook. In some cases, your contacts will be linked — that is, information supplied by Facebook, Microsoft Exchange, or some other source will be combined into a single entry. An obvious benefit of this linking is that you can cut down on duplicate contact listings. If the iPhone doesn't automatically link appropriate contact entries, you can manually do the job from the given contact. Tap Edit, scroll to the bottom, tap Linked Contacts, and choose the appropriate entry to link with from among your entire list of contacts.

Your own iPhone phone number, lest you forget it, appears at the top of the Contacts list, provided you arrived in Contacts through the Phone app.

You can also initiate text messages and e-mails from within Contacts. Those topics are discussed in greater depth in Chapters 5 and 12, respectively.

Favorites

Favorites is where you can keep a list of the people and numbers you dial most often. Consider Favorites the iPhone equivalent of speed-dialing. Merely tap the person's name in Favorites, and your iPhone calls the person.

You can set up as many favorites as you need for a person. So, for example, you may create separate favorite listings for your spouse's office phone number, cell number, and FaceTime entry.

Setting up Favorites is a breeze. When looking at one of your contacts, you may have noticed the Add to Favorites button. When you tap this button, all the phone numbers you have for that person pop up. Tap the number you want to make into a favorite and it turns up on the list.

If any of your chosen folks happen to fall out of favor, you can easily kick them off the Favorites roster. Here's how:

1. **Tap the Edit button in the upper-left corner of the screen.**

   Note that a red circle with a horizontal white line appears to the left of each name in the list.

2. **Tap the circle next to the A-lister getting the heave-ho.**

   The horizontal white line is now vertical and a red Delete button appears to the right of the name, as shown in Figure 4-2.

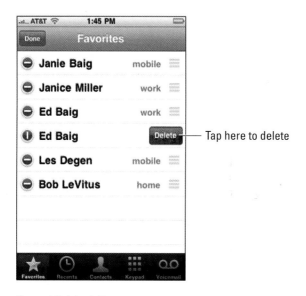

Tap here to delete

Figure 4-2: I don't like you anymore.

3. **Tap Delete.**

The person (or one of his or her given phone numbers) is no longer afforded the privilege of being in your iPhone inner circle.

Booting someone off the Favorites list does not remove that person from the main Contacts list.

You can rearrange the order in which your favorites are displayed. Tap Edit, and then, to the right of the person you want to move, press your finger against the symbol that looks like three short horizontal lines stacked on top of one another. Drag that symbol to the place on the list where you want your favorite contact to appear. Tap Done when the listings are as you like them.

You can designate new favorites by tapping the + symbol at the upper-right corner of the screen. Doing so brings you back to Contacts. From there, select the appropriate person and number. A star appears next to any contact's number chosen as a favorite.

Recents

Tapping the Recents icon displays the iPhone call log. The Recents feature houses logs of all the, well, *recent* calls made or received, as well as calls you missed. Tap All to show all the recent calls and Missed to show just those you missed. Under the All list, completed calls and missed calls that have been returned by tapping the red entry are shown in black, and missed calls that haven't been returned in this fashion are in red, along with a descriptor of the phone you were calling or received a call from (home, mobile, and so on).

By tapping the small blue circle with the right-pointing arrow next to an item in the list, you can find out the time calls were made or missed, as well as any known info about the caller from your Contacts information. Also shown is the length of the time you spoke to the person, assuming a conversation indeed took place.

To return a call, just tap anywhere on the name.

If one of the calls you missed came from someone who isn't already in your Contacts, you can add that person. Tap the right-pointing arrow, and then tap the Create New Contact button. If the person is among your Contacts but has a new number, tap the Add to Existing Contact button.

Tap Share Contact to share a contact with a friend, family member, or colleague. You have the option to send that person an e-mail or a message (MMS, text, or iMessage message). The contact info is already embedded in the message that you send.

You can clear an individual entry from the Recents list by swiping in either direction on a name and tapping the red Delete button that appears.

Keypad

From time to time, of course, you have to dial the number of a person or company who hasn't earned a spot in your Contacts. Or you need to access a keypad to navigate a voicemail system. That's when you'll want to tap the Keypad icon to bring up the large keys of the virtual touchtone keypad you see in Figure 4-3. Just tap the appropriate keys and tap Call to dial.

To add this number to your Contacts, tap the + silhouette key (that's a plus sign and the silhouette of a person) on the keypad and tap either Create New Contact or Add to Existing Contact.

You can use the iPhone's keypad also to remotely check your voicemail at work or home.

Come to think of it, what a perfect segue into the next section. It's on one of our favorite iPhone features, visual voicemail.

Visual voicemail

How often have you had to listen to four or five (or more) voicemail messages before getting to the message you really want, or need, to hear? As shown in Figure 4-4, the iPhone's clever visual voicemail presents a list of your voicemail messages in the order in which calls were received. But you need not listen to those messages in order.

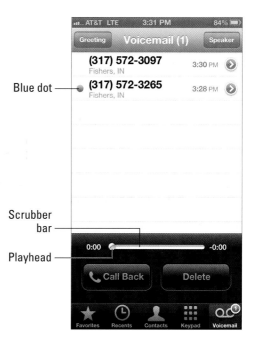

Figure 4-3: A virtually familiar way to dial.

Figure 4-4: Visual voicemail in action.

You can tell if you even have voicemail in a few ways:

✔ A red circular badge showing the number of pending messages awaiting your attention appears above the Phone icon on the Home screen or above the Voicemail icon in the Phone app.

✔ You may also see a message alert on the iPhone display that says something like *New voicemail from Ed (or Bob)* or a notification in Notification Center.

Whatever draws you in, tap that Voicemail icon to display the list of voicemails. You see the caller's phone number, assuming this info is known through Caller ID, and in some cases, his or her name. Or you see the words *Unknown* or *Private Caller.*

The beauty of all this is that you can ignore (or at least put off listening to) certain messages. We are not in the advice-giving business on what calls you can safely avoid; disregard messages from the IRS or your parole officer at your own risk, okay?

A blue dot next to a name or number signifies that you haven't heard the message yet.

To play back a voicemail, tap the name or number in question. Then tap the tiny play/pause button that shows up to the left. Tap once more to pause the message; tap again to resume. Tap the Speaker button if you want to hear the message through the iPhone's speakerphone.

Tap the blue arrow next to a caller's name or number to bring up any contact info on the person or to add the caller to your contacts.

The tiny playhead along the scrubber bar (labeled in Figure 4-4) shows you the length of the message and how much of the message you've heard. If you hate when callers ramble on forever, you can drag the playhead to rapidly advance through a message. Perhaps more importantly, if you miss something, you can replay that segment.

Returning a call is as simple as tapping the green Call Back button. If the caller's number is unknown, the Call Back button appears dimmed. And you can delete a voicemail by pressing Delete.

If you have no phone service, you'll see a message that says *Visual Voicemail is currently unavailable.*

The globetrotting iPhone

Different countries employ different radios and frequencies, and Apple has managed to cram a bunch of radios into the latest iPhones. It has GSM/EDGE radios (850, 900, 1,800, and 1,900 MHz), UMTS/HSDPA/HSUPA radios (850, 900, 1,900, and 2,100 MHz), plus CDMA EV-DO Rev. A and Rev B radios (800, 1,900, and 2,100 MHz). Oh, and radios for Bluetooth, Wi-Fi, and GPS.

When the iPhone 5 hit in September 2012, the biggest — and arguably the most welcome — news was that this latest iPhone can exploit speedy LTE (Long Term Evolution) phone networks. At the time this was written, LTE, a 4G (fourth-generation) communications standard, handles data rather than voice calls, and Verizon Wireless is by far the LTE leader (followed in order by AT&T and Sprint).

When you're cruising along at LTE speeds, you'll see the little LTE indicator on the upper-left corner of the status bar. But just to confuse you, AT&T displays a tiny 4G indicator instead of LTE when you're cruising a fast but slightly slower cellular network called HSDPA.

While we're on the topic of wireless communications, here's a bit of trivia: You may recall that in the iPhone 4, Apple built antennas into the stainless steel band on the edge of the device. Those antennas were anything but trivial in the days following the iPhone 4's launch. Some people who gripped the lower-left corner of the device in such a way as to make contact with the notch in that location actually lost reception. This controversy became known as AntennaGate.

On the iPhone 4S, Apple engineered an antenna design that intelligently switches between two antennas as needed to improve reception, even in the middle of a call. That said, we are obliged to point out that sometimes your carrier lets you down, with dropped or less than pristine quality calls. More often than not, however, we've been happy with the quality of voice calls on the iPhone.

Before the iPhone 5, the iPhone used the 3G (third-generation) networks to make calls (and do more) when you traveled abroad or stateside. Although 4G networks are being deployed on the iPhone 5, carriers still argue all the time about what 4G truly means, a debate not worth dwelling on here. Just know that LTE is plenty fast.

When you're abroad, your carrier must turn on something called *international roaming* (unless, of course, you live in a foreign land and have a local carrier). Consult your carrier for the latest international rates. If you're calling the United States while overseas, you can take advantage of Dial Assist. This feature automatically adds the proper prefix to U.S. numbers dialed from abroad. Tap Settings⇨Phone⇨Dial Assist. Make sure you see the blue On button instead of the white Off button.

You can listen to your iPhone voicemail from another phone. Just dial your iPhone number and, while the greeting plays, enter your voicemail password. You can set up such a password from the Home screen by tapping Settings⊏⊐ Phone⊏⊐Change Voicemail Password. You'll be asked to enter your current voicemail password, if you have one. If one doesn't exist yet, tap Done. If you have a password, enter it and then tap Done. You'll then be asked to type the new password and tap Done twice.

Recording a greeting

You have two choices when it comes to the voicemail greeting your callers will hear. You can accept a generic greeting with your phone number by default. Or you can create a custom greeting in your own voice as follows:

1. **In Voicemail, tap the Greeting button.**

2. **Tap Custom.**

3. **Tap Record and dictate a clever, deserving-of-being-on-the-iPhone voicemail greeting.**

4. **When you've finished recording, tap Stop.**

5. **Review the greeting by pressing Play.**

6. **If the greeting is worthy, tap Save. If not, tap Cancel and start over at Step 1.**

Voice dialing

You can make a call hands-free, just by opening your mouth. To read the details on voice control and Siri, the personal assistant who takes voice stuff to another level, see Chapter 7.

Receiving a Call

It's wonderful to have numerous options for making a call. But what are your choices when somebody calls you? The answer depends on whether you are willing to take the call or not.

Accepting the call

To accept a call, you have three options:

- ✔ Tap Answer.
- ✔ If the phone is locked, drag the slider to the right.
- ✔ If you're donning stereo earbuds or the newer EarPods, which come with the iPhone 5, tap the microphone button. Microphone adapters for standard headsets may also work.

- ✔ If you wear a wireless Bluetooth headset or use a car speakerphone, push the Answer button on your headset or speakerphone (refer to the manual if the process isn't intuitive). For more on Bluetooth, read Chapter 14.

If you're listening to music in your iPhone's iPod when a call comes in, the song stops playing and you have to decide whether to take the call. If you do take the call, the music resumes from where you left off after the conversation ends.

Rejecting the call

We're going to assume that you're not a cold-hearted person out to break a caller's heart. Rather, we assume that you're a busy person who will call back at a more convenient time.

Keeping that positive spin in mind, here are three ways to reject a call on the spot and send the call to voicemail. (A new fourth way that arrived with iOS 6 is discussed in the next section.)

- ✔ Tap Decline. Couldn't be easier than that.
- ✔ Press the sleep/wake button twice in rapid succession. (The button is on the top of the device.)
- ✔ Using the supplied headset, press and hold the microphone button for a couple of seconds, and then let go. Two beeps let you know that the call was indeed rejected.

Replying with a text message

Sometimes you can't take a call because, well, you can't take a call — you're under the gun at work or the kids demand your attention. But you want to be polite or give callers a sense that you do care about them too. Enter the handy new iOS 6 reply with a text message feature.

Simply drag up the Phone icon that appears when you see the Slide to Answer option and select Reply with Message, as shown in Figure 4-5. You can select from three canned messages (I'll Call You Later, I'm on My Way, and What's Up?) or create a custom reply.

When you tap any of these options, the caller will get your outgoing voicemail message and receive whichever of the text options you chose to send.

If you tap Remind Me Later instead of Reply with Message, you can arrange to receive a reminder notification in One Hour, When I Leave (the current location), or When I get home. Meanwhile, the caller again hears your voicemail message.

Sometimes you're perfectly willing to take a call but need to silence the ringer, lest the people sitting near you in the movie theater or corporate boardroom cast an evil eye your way. To do so, press the sleep/wake button a single time or press one of the volume buttons. You'll still have the opportunity to answer. You can use this technique also to turn off vibration mode.

Avoiding disturbances

In the middle of the night — or the middle of the day when you're playing hooky — the last thing you want is to be bothered by a phone call. Apple had such potential disturbances in mind when it devised the Do Not Disturb feature, new to iOS 6. When you turn on the feature in Settings, your incoming calls and alerts will be silenced. A moon icon, um, rises to the top of the status bar to remind you when Do Not Disturb is enabled.

Of course, you may be reluctant to turn on the feature, fretting perhaps about missing emergency calls or calls from family members or important associates. You need exceptions, right?

Right. Here's how to address those situations when Do Not Disturb is enabled. From the Home screen, tap Settings⇨Notifications⇨Do Not Disturb. Tap the Allow Calls From option (see Figure 4-6) and choose whether to allow calls from your Favorites, Everyone (kind of defeats the purpose of Do Not Disturb, eh?), No One, All Contacts, or a particular Group Name from Contacts.

You can also take advantage of the Repeated Calls option. When Repeated Calls is turned on, a second call from the same person within three minutes will not be silenced. The rationale is if somebody is trying to reach you that badly, it must be important.

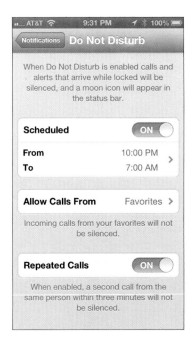

Figure 4-5: I can't take your call right now.

Figure 4-6: Now calls from my favorites can get through.

Finally, you can also schedule when Do Not Disturb is on. Tap Settings⇨ Scheduled; then tap the From To time field and choose a quiet time.

Choosing ringtones

Apple includes 25 ringtones in the iPhone, ranging from the sound of crickets to an old car horn. Read the "iTunes and ringtones" sidebar to figure out how to create your own custom ringtones.

To choose a ringtone, follow these steps:

1. **From the Home screen, tap Settings.**

2. **Tap Sounds.**

3. **Tap Ringtone to access the list of available ringtones.**

4. **Flick your finger to move up or down the list.**

5. **Tap any of the ringtones to hear what it will sound like.**

   A check mark appears next to the ringtone you've just listened to, as shown in Figure 4-7. If need be, adjust the volume slider in Sounds.

iTunes and ringtones

Apple lets you turn some of the songs you've purchased into custom ringtones. You must fork over 99¢ for songs that are already in your iTunes library on your computer or pay $1.29 for a new song from the iTunes Store online (which lets you also get full use of the track on your PC or Mac).

The ringtone-ready music in your own iTunes collection (on the computer) is designated by a little bell symbol. Clicking that symbol displays a ringtone editor that resembles Apple's GarageBand music-editing software. Drag the editor over the portion of the song you want to use as your ringtone — up to 30 seconds' worth. You can choose to have the ringtone fade in or out by selecting the appropriate boxes in the editor. Click Preview to make sure you're happy with the result, and click Buy when you're satisfied.

Connect the iPhone to your computer to synchronize the ringtone.

You can also create custom ringtones on a Mac in GarageBand and through third-party utilities such as iToner. Head to Chapter 19 for more details on GarageBand ringtoning. (We love coining new verbs.)

You can purchase and download ringtones wirelessly from your phone via the iTunes Store. From the Home screen, tap iTunes and then tap Ringtones. You can find ringtones by genre, by top ten (in a given musical category), and by poring through selections featured in the store. Note that ringtones can also be used as text tones.

6. If you're not pleased, try another.

If you're satisfied, you need do nothing more. Unbeknownst to you, you have just selected that ringtone.

You can easily assign specific ringtones to individual callers. From Contacts, choose the person to whom you want to designate a particular ringtone. Then tap Edit⇨Assign Ringtone to display the aforementioned list of ringtones. Select the one that seems most appropriate (a barking dog, say, for your father-in-law).

To change or delete the ringtone for a specific person, go back into Contacts, and then tap Edit. Either tap the right arrow to choose a new ringtone for that person or tap the red circle and Delete to remove the custom ringtone altogether.

Figure 4-7: Ring my chimes: The iPhone's ringtones.

While on a Call

You can do lots of things while talking on an iPhone, such as consulting your calendar, taking notes, or checking the weather. Press the Home button to get to the apps that let you perform these tasks.

If you're using Wi-Fi, 3G, or 4G and are on an AT&T iPhone, you can also surf the web (through Safari) while talking on the phone. But you can't surf while you talk if your only outlet to cyberspace is the AT&T EDGE network or a CDMA network such as the ones that Sprint and Verizon rely on.

Here are other things you can do while on a call:

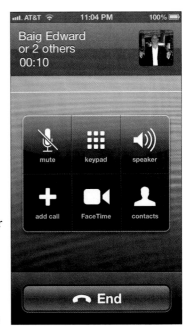

Figure 4-8: Managing calls.

✔ **Mute a call:** From the main call screen (shown in Figure 4-8), tap Mute. Now you need not mutter under your breath when the caller ticks you off. Tap Mute again to unmute the sound.

✔ **Tap Contacts to display the Contacts list:** This option is useful if you want to look up a friend's number while you're talking to another pal or you want to add someone to a conference call.

✔ **Place a call on hold:** Touch and hold the aforementioned Mute button. Tap Mute again to take the person off hold. You might put a caller on hold to answer another incoming call or to make a second call yourself. The next section shows you how to deal with more than one call at a time.

✔ **Tap Keypad to bring back the keypad:** This feature is useful if you have to type touchtones to access another voicemail system or respond to an automated menu system. Heaven forbid you actually get a live person when calling an insurance company or airline. But we digress. . . .

✔ **Use the speakerphone:** Tap Speaker to listen to a call through the iPhone's internal speakers without having to hold the device up to your mouth. If you've paired the iPhone with a Bluetooth device, the control is labeled Audio Source instead, as shown in Figure 4-9. Tap Audio Source and then tap Speaker (if you want the speakerphone), iPhone (if you want to hold up the phone to your ear), or the name of the Bluetooth device. A tiny speaker icon will appear next to your selection, as shown in Figure 4-10.

✔ **Make a conference call:** Read on.

Figure 4-9: Tap Audio Source to change how you are taking the call.

Figure 4-10: The speakerphone is active.

Juggling calls

You can field a new call when you're already talking to somebody. Or ignore the call (by tapping Ignore).

To take the new call while keeping the first caller on hold, tap the Hold Call + Answer button that appears, as shown in Figure 4-11. You can then toggle between calls (placing one or the other on hold) by tapping either the Swap button or the first call at the top of the screen.

If these phone gymnastics are too much for you and that second caller is really important, tap End Call + Answer to ditch caller number one.

Making conference calls

Now suppose caller number one and caller number two know each other. Or you'd like to play matchmaker so they get to know each other. Tap Merge Calls so all three of you can chitchat. At first, the phone number of each caller will scroll at the top of your screen like a rolling ticker. A few seconds later, the ticker is replaced by the word *Conference* with a circled right-pointing arrow to its immediate right.

Figure 4-11: Swapping calls.

Now let's assume you have to talk to your entire sales team at once. It may be time to initiate a full-blown conference call, which effectively takes this merge call idea to its extreme. You can merge up to five calls at a time. In fact, creating such a conference call on the iPhone may be simpler than getting the same five people in a physical room at the same time.

Here's how you do it. Start by making a call and then placing the caller on hold as noted in the preceding section, "Juggling calls." Tap Add Call to make another call, and then tap Merge Calls to bring everyone together. Repeat this exercise to add the other calls.

Other conference call tidbits:

- iPhone is actually a two-line phone, and one of the available lines can be involved in a conference call.
- If you want to drop a call from a conference, tap Conference, and then tap the red-circled phone icon next to the call. Tap End Call to make that caller go bye-bye.

✔ You can speak privately with one of the callers in a conference. Tap Conference, and then tap Private next to the caller you want to go hush-hush with. Tap Merge Calls to bring the caller back into the conference so everyone can hear him or her.

✔ You can add a new incoming caller to an existing conference call by tapping Hold Call + Answer followed by Merge Calls.

Seeing Is Believing with FaceTime

FaceTime video reminds us of a favorite line from The Who's rock opera *Tommy:* "See me, feel me, touch me." The "see me" (and for that matter, "see you") part arrives with FaceTime. Think of all the people who will want to see you, such as an old college roommate living halfway around the world, grandparents living miles away (okay, they really want to see your newborn), or an old flame in a distant location.

Fortunately, using FaceTime is as easy as making a regular call on the iPhone. Plus, FaceTime comes with at least two major benefits *besides* the video:

✔ FaceTime calls don't count against your regular minutes, though they will count against your data plan allotment if you make these calls over a cellular connection (a new feature in iOS 6).

✔ The audio quality on FaceTime calls, those over Wi-Fi anyway, is superior to a regular cell phone connection.

But FaceTime also has a couple of major caveats:

✔ Both you and the party you're talking to must have an iPhone 4, 4S, or 5, an iPad 2 or later model, a Mac computer, or a recent iPod touch. (Okay, so maybe that's not much of a caveat after all — the list of compatible devices keeps growing.) Apple is pushing to make FaceTime a video standard that the entire tech industry can embrace, allowing you to someday (and maybe even by the time you read this) make FaceTime calls from iPhones and other Apple devices to other handsets and computers that don't carry an Apple logo. We'll see. Skype, among others, also lets you make video calls on the iPhone over a much broader range of devices.

✔ Both you and the caller at the other end have to access Wi-Fi or a robust cellular connection. The capability to use FaceTime over cellular was another iOS 6 addition. The quality of the experience depends on a solid connection.

If you meet the requirements, here's how to make FaceTime happen:

1. **The first time you make a FaceTime call to another iPhone, dial the person's regular iPhone number as usual, using any of the methods we describe in this chapter.**

   Use an e-mail address instead if you're using FaceTime to call an iPod touch, an iPad, or a Mac.

2. **After a regular call is established and you've broached the subject of going video, you can tap the FaceTime button, as shown in Figure 4-12.**

   A few seconds later, the other person gets the option to Decline or Accept the FaceTime invitation by tapping the red button or the green button, respectively, as shown in Figure 4-13. If the answer is Accept, you'll need to wait a few seconds before you can see the other person.

You can also use the Siri voice assistant (discussed in detail in Chapter 7) to make a FaceTime call. Just ask Siri to "FaceTime with Dad" or whomever else you'd want to engage in a video call, and she'll make the proper arrangements.

When someone requests FaceTime with you, you'll appreciate being able to politely decline a FaceTime call. Cool as it can be to see and be seen, ask yourself if you really want to be seen, say, when you just got out of bed.

Figure 4-12: Tap FaceTime to literally watch what happens.

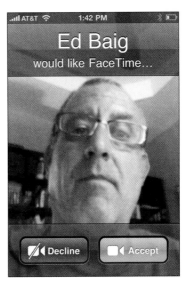

Figure 4-13: Say "yes" to see me.

Search for any FaceTime calls you previously made by tapping an entry for that call in Recents. The iPhone knows to take the call straight to video, though of course the person you're talking to has to accept the invitation each time.

You can do FaceTime also by tapping a pal's listings in Contacts.

So what is a FaceTime call like? In our experience, first-time reactions were gleeful. Not only are you seeing the other person, but the quality of the video is also typically good. You also see your own mug in a small picture-in-picture (PiP) window (as shown in Figure 4-14), which you can drag to a corner of the screen. The PiP image represents what the other person sees, so it's a good way of knowing, short of the other person telling you, if your face has dropped out of the frame.

Recipient sees this PiP

Mute audio   End call   Switch cameras

Figure 4-14: Bob can see Ed and Ed can see Bob.

You can use FaceTime in portrait or landscape mode. You might find it easier to bring another person into a scene in landscape mode.

Apple says the front camera has been fine-tuned for FaceTime usage, which in photography-speak means the camera has the proper field of view and focal length. But at times, you'll want to employ the iPhone's main camera on the rear to best show off your surroundings and give the caller an idea of where you are.

To toggle between the front and main cameras, tap the icon at the bottom-right corner of the screen (refer to Figure 4-14).

If you want to mute a FaceTime video call, tap the microphone icon with the slash running through it. The caller can continue to see you but not hear you.

Although many FaceTime calls commence with a regular AT&T, Sprint, or Verizon call, you can't go from FaceTime to an audio-only call without hanging up and redialing. Similarly, if you drop a FaceTime call because of a Wi-Fi hiccup or some other problem, you'll have to redial via FaceTime or your provider, depending on whether you want the call to be video or only audio.

To block all FaceTime calls, tap Settings from the Home screen, tap Phone, and make sure FaceTime is off. If you can't find the FaceTime button or wonder why you're not getting FaceTime calls, go back to Settings and make sure this option is turned on. While you're in FaceTime Settings, note that you can list one or more e-mail addresses by which a caller can reach you for a video call, along with your iPhone's phone number.

If you want to momentarily check out another iPhone app while on a FaceTime call, press the Home button and then tap the icon for the app you have in mind. At this point, you can still talk over FaceTime, but you'll no longer see the person. Tap the green bar at the top of the screen to bring the person back in front of you.

And there you have it. That's FaceTime, one of the coolest features in the iPhone.

You can do even more things with iPhone the phone, as you find out when we delve deeper into Settings in Chapter 14. Meanwhile, we recommend that you read the next chapter to figure out how to become a whiz at text messaging.

Part II
The PDA iPhone

The 5th Wave   By Rich Tennant

iPhone

"This model comes with a particularly useful function — a simulated static button for breaking out of long-winded conversations."

*N*ow that you've mastered all the calling and listening stuff, you're ready to become a whiz at keeping in touch and staying organized. We start with the sending and retrieving of SMS, MMS, and iMessage messages. As journalists, we especially appreciate what comes next: finding out how to become a champion note taker.

Next, you explore all those C-word programs — namely, Calendar, Calculator, and Clock — plus Voice Memos and the new Passbook app. These handy applications enable you to stay on top of your appointments, solve arithmetic problems on-the-fly (with one or two nifty calculators), show up for appointments on time — thanks to the Calendar app's alerts and Clock app's alarm clock — record memos (or lectures, or anything you can hear, really), and use tickets, boarding passes, and other credentials without having to print them first.

We close this part with a delightful little ditty about voice control and Siri, the intelligent assistant inside the iPhone 4S and 5. Marvel at how she understands what you say and then does it — most of the time and discover how easy it is to make phone calls with Voice Control.

Texting 1, 2, 3: Messages and Notes

In This Chapter

▷ Sending and receiving SMS (text) messages

▷ Sending and receiving MMS (multimedia) messages

▷ Using the Notes app

*I*f you've never used an intelligent virtual keyboard, it will probably feel awkward in the beginning. Within a few days, however, many iPhone users report that they have become not only comfortable using the virtual keyboard but also proficient virtual typists as well.

You discover how to use the virtual keyboard in Chapter 2. In this chapter, we focus on two iPhone apps that use text — namely, Messages and Notes. By the time you finish this chapter, we think you'll feel comfortable and proficient, too.

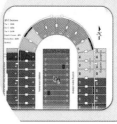

5 million Ac
Apple.

Sep 24, 2012, 9:20 AM

…Message

Getting the iMessage

The Messages app lets you exchange short text messages with any cell phone that supports the SMS protocol. You can also send and receive MMS messages, which means you can exchange pictures, contacts, videos, ringtones, other audio recordings, and locations with any cell phone that supports the MMS protocol.

SMS is the acronym for the Short Message Service protocol; MMS is the acronym for the Multimedia Messaging Service protocol. Most phones sold today support one or both protocols. MMS support has been built into iOS since version 3 and is available on the iPhone 3G and later.

In addition to the traditional SMS and MMS protocols offered by the wireless carriers (currently AT&T, Verizon, and Sprint in the United States), iOS 5 introduced a new service from Apple called iMessage, which lets you send and receive unlimited messages with text, pictures, contacts, videos, and locations. The good news is that although the wireless operators all charge something for SMS or MMS services, iMessages are free. The bad news is that you can share iMessages only with other iPhone, iPad, and iPod touch users whose devices are running iOS 5 or higher or Mac users running OS X 10.8 Mountain Lion. And, if no Wi-Fi connection is available, the message is sent as a standard MMS or SMS (Multimedia or Short Message) via your wireless carrier (and subject to the usual text message charges).

Typing text on a dumb cell phone with a 12-key numeric keypad is an unnatural act, which is why many people have never sent a single SMS or MMS message. The iPhone changes that. Its intelligent virtual keyboard makes it easy to compose short text messages, and its big, bright, high-resolution screen makes it a pleasure to read them.

But before we get to the part where you send or receive messages, let's go over some messaging basics:

- **Both sender and receiver need either an SMS- or an MMS-enabled mobile phone or an Apple device with iOS 5 or higher (and, of course, an Internet connection).** Your iPhone qualifies, as do almost any mobile phones made in the past few years and iPads and iPod touches with iOS 5 or higher. Keep in mind that if you send messages to folks using a phone that doesn't support SMS or MMS or to those who don't have an appropriate Apple device, they may never get your message or even know you sent it.

- **Some phones (not the iPhone, of course) limit SMS messages to 160 characters.** If you try to send a longer message to one of these phones, your message may be truncated or split into multiple shorter messages. The point is that it's a good idea to keep SMS messages brief.

The Messages app can count characters for you. To enable the option, you may need to tap the Settings icon on your Home screen, then tap the Messages icon and enable Character Count. When this feature is enabled, after you've typed a line or more of text, you'll see the number of characters you've typed so far, a slash, and then the number 160 (the character limit on some mobile phones, as just described) directly above the Send button.

The character count feature is disabled for iMessages sent to other iDevices, which makes sense because iMessages have no limit on their length.

- **Regardless of which carrier you choose, you'll encounter a bewildering array of pricing options.** In the United States, for example, some data plans do not include any SMS or MMS messages. Other plans offer packages of 200 or 250 messages starting at around $5 per month; and still other plans offer unlimited messages starting at around $20 per month. If you don't subscribe to a messaging plan from your wireless operator, you'll pay 20¢ or 30¢ per message sent or received. Ouch!

Each individual message in a conversation counts against this total, even if it's only a one-word reply such as "OK," or "CUL8R" (which is teenager-speak for "see you later").

If you haven't decided on a wireless carrier yet, compare prices from all three. For example, Sprint is currently offering a bundle that includes unlimited voice, text, and data for $99 a month, which is significantly less expensive than plans from AT&T and Verizon. If you use a lot of data, Sprint is almost certain to be the best deal, because neither AT&T nor Verizon currently offers unlimited data in any of their plans.

Both AT&T and Verizon used to offer unlimited data plans. If you signed up for one (as we did), you are "grandfathered" for your unlimited data plan, even if you get a new iPhone (as we did). Although a limited plan may seem cheaper, remember that if you switch, you can't go back to the unlimited plan. If you currently have an unlimited data plan, we suggest you think long and hard before you decide to switch.

- **SMS and MMS messages require access to your wireless operator's cellular network.** iMessages can be sent and received over a cellular or Wi-Fi network.

Okay, now that we have those details out of the way, let's move on to how to send a message.

You send me: Sending text messages

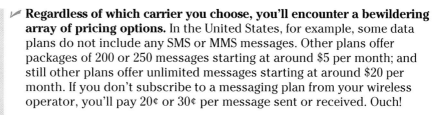

Tap the Messages icon on the Home screen to launch the Messages app, and then tap the little pencil-and-paper icon (shown in the margin) in the top-right corner of the screen to start a new text message.

At this point, the To field is active and awaiting your input. You can do three things at this point:

- If the recipient isn't in your Contacts list, type his or her cell phone number or the person's e-mail address (iMessage users only).

- If the recipient *is* in your Contacts list, type the first few letters of the name. A list of matching contacts appears. Scroll through it if necessary and tap the name of the contact.

The more letters you type, the shorter the list becomes. And, after you've tapped the name of a contact, you can begin typing another name so you can send the message to multiple recipients at once.

  ✔ Tap the blue + icon on the right side of the To field to select a name from your Contacts list.

A fourth option is available if you want to compose the message first and address it later. Tap inside the text-entry field (the oval-shaped area just above the keyboard and to the left of the Send button) to activate it, and then type your message. When you've finished typing, tap the To field and use one of the preceding techniques to address your message.

When you've finished addressing and composing, tap the Send button to send your message on its merry way.

And that's all there is to it.

Alert: You've got messages

First things first. Your iPhone can alert you to new messages with an audio alert, an on-screen alert, neither, or both.

If you want to hear a sound when a message arrives, go to the Home screen and tap Settings⇨Sounds⇨Text Tone, and then tap one of the available sounds. You can audition any sound in the list by tapping it.

You hear the sounds when you audition them in the Settings app, even if you have the ring/silent switch set to Silent. After you exit the Settings app, however, you *won't* hear a sound when a message arrives if the ring/silent switch is set to Silent.

If you *don't* want to hear an alert when a message arrives, instead of tapping one of the listed sounds, tap the first item in the list: None.

You can assign a custom alert sound to anyone in your Contacts list. Follow the instructions for assigning a custom ringtone (see Chapter 4), but instead of tapping Ringtone, tap the item directly below it, Text Tone. And because the same sounds are used for both ringtones and text tones, you can assign the same sound to a contact for both phone calls and messages, which we think is a nice touch.

In addition to playing a sound when a new message arrives, your iPhone can also display several types of on-screen alerts. To enable or disable these visual alerts, tap Settings⇨Notifications⇨Messages. You see the screen shown in Figure 5-1.

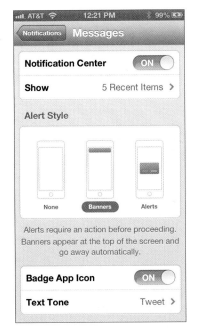

Figure 5-1: You have a myriad of options for new message notifications.

What happens when you receive a new message depends on how you've set your notification options, so let's take a look at them as they appear on the screen, starting at the top:

- **Notification Center:** This option is the master on/off switch for Messages notifications in Notification Center. Turn it on if you want to see 'em there; turn it off if you don't.

  Swipe downward from the top of any screen, except the Lock screen, to see Notification Center. Note, too, that on-screen alerts are not affected by turning this setting on or off. Rather, the Notification Center on/off switch determines whether or not notifications from the Messages app appear in Notification Center. The upshot is that if you choose banners or alerts as the Alert Style, you'll still see a banner or an alert on the screen when a new message arrives, but you won't see them in Notification Center.

- **Show:** Tap to select the number of notifications displayed in Notification Center. The options are 1, 5, or 10 Recent Items.

✏ **Alert Style:** Tap to select the appearance of on-screen notifications. With the Banners option, a banner appears at the top of the screen, as shown in Figure 5-2, and then disappears (with a slick little animation) after a few seconds. The Alerts option requires you to tap a button to proceed, as shown in Figure 5-3. And, of course, the None option means neither a banner nor an alert appears when a new message arrives.

✏ **Badge App Icon:** This on/off setting determines whether you see a badge with the number of unread new messages on the Messages icon. (The badge shows 2 in Figure 5-3.)

✏ **Text Tone:** Tap to change the sound you hear when a new message arrives (or set it to None).

✏ **Show Preview:** This setting determines whether or not you see the first line of the message in banners or alerts.

✏ **Repeat Alert:** Tap to select the number of times an alert is repeated. Your choices are Never, Once, Twice, 3 Times, 5 Times, 10 Times, or at two-minute intervals.

Figure 5-2: Banners appear at the top of the screen and then disappear after a few seconds.

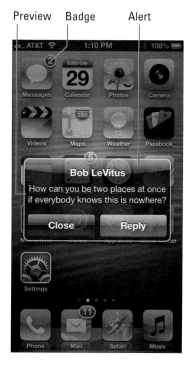

Figure 5-3: Alerts appear midscreen and remain there until you tap Close or Reply.

- ✔ **Show iMessage Alerts From:** Tap to select either Everyone or My Contacts Only.

- ✔ **View in Lock Screen:** Enable this option to see new message alerts when your iPhone is locked, as shown in Figure 5-4.

Slide to reply

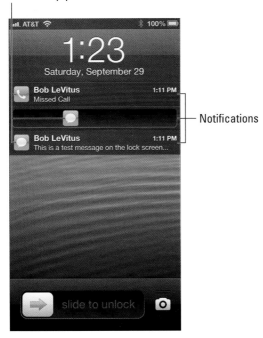

Notifications

Figure 5-4: When your iPhone is locked, notifications look like this; swipe a notification from left to right to act on it.

Notifications on the Lock screen look like the three that appear in Figure 5-4 regardless of whether you've selected banners or alerts. They will remain on the Lock screen until you swipe the Slide to Unlock slider at the bottom of the screen or slide one of the notification icons to reply.

Note that if only one notification is on the Lock screen, the slider at the bottom of the screen says Slide to Reply; if more than one notification is displayed on the Lock screen, you can swipe the icon of a specific notification (as we're doing with the middle notification in Figure 5-4) to reply to that particular message.

Being a golden receiver: Reading and replying to text messages

Now that you know how to manage your message notifications, here's the scoop on what happens after you swipe the Slide to Reply slider and have the message on your screen.

To read or reply to the message, tap Reply.

To read or reply to a message after you've tapped the Close button, tap the Messages icon. If a message other than the one you're interested in appears on the screen when you launch the Messages app, tap Messages in the top-left corner of the screen, and then tap the sender's name; that person's messages appear on the screen.

To reply to the message on the screen, tap the text-entry field to the left of the Send button, and the keyboard appears. Type your reply and then tap Send. Those of you with an iPhone 4S or 5 can tap the microphone key and speak your reply to Siri, who will translate it into text and type it for you. (To find out more about Siri, your intelligent assistant, see Chapter 7.)

Your SMS conversation is saved as a series of text bubbles. Your messages appear on the right side of the screen in green bubbles; the other person's messages appear on the left in gray bubbles, as shown in Figure 5-5.

You can delete a conversation in two ways:

- **If you're viewing the conversation:** Tap the Edit button at the top-right of the conversation screen and a circle appears to the left of each text bubble. Tap a text bubble and a red check mark appears in the circle. When you've added a red check mark to all the text bubbles you want to delete, tap the red Delete button at the bottom-left of the screen. Or, to delete the entire conversation in one fell swoop, tap the Clear All button in the top-left corner of the screen.

  If you want to forward all or part of a conversation to another mobile phone user (as an SMS, MMS, or iMessage message), follow the same procedure (that is, tap the Edit button, then tap the text bubbles you want to forward so that the red check mark appears in a circle to the left). Now, instead of tapping the red Delete button at the bottom-left of the screen, tap the blue Forward button at the bottom-right of the screen. The contents of the text bubbles with check marks will be copied to a new text message; specify a recipient and then tap Send.

- **If you're viewing the list of text messages:** Tap the Edit button at the top-left of the Messages list, and a red – icon appears to the left of the person's name. Tap the red – icon and then tap the Delete button that appears to the right of the name to delete the entire conversation with that person.

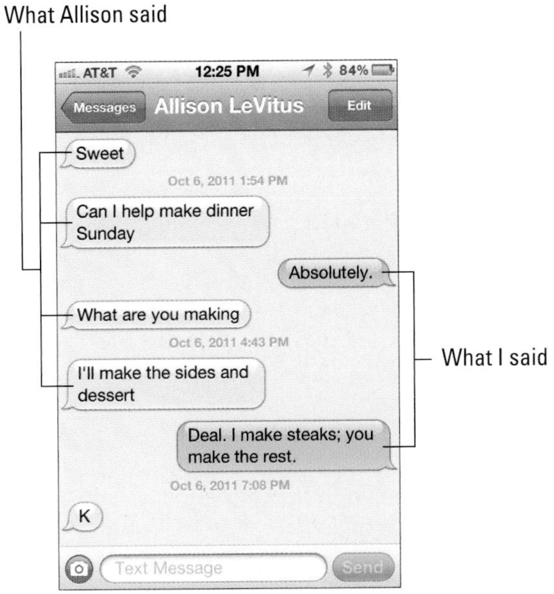

What Allison said

Figure 5-5: This is what an SMS conversation looks like.

MMS: Like SMS with media

To send a picture or video in a message, follow the instructions for sending a text message and then tap the camera icon to the left of the text-entry field at the bottom of the screen. You'll then have the option of using an existing picture or video or taking a new one. You can also add text to photos or videos. When you're finished, tap the Send button.

If you *receive* a picture or video in a message, it appears in a bubble just like text. Tap it to see it full-screen.

Tap the action icon in the upper-right corner (as shown in the margin) for additional options, which include Email, Twitter, Facebook, Save to Camera Roll, and Print. If you don't see the action icon, tap the picture or video once and the icon will magically appear.

Smart messaging tricks

Here are some more things you can do with messages:

✓ To search your messages for a word or phrase, type the word or phrase in the Search field at the very top of the main Messages screen.

✔ To use a Bluetooth keyboard instead of the on-screen keyboard, follow the instructions in Chapter 14 to pair your Bluetooth keyboard with your iPhone.

The Apple Wireless Keyboard ($69) works great with the iPhone (and iPad and iPod touch devices, too).

✔ To send a message to someone in your Favorites or Recents list, tap the Phone icon on the Home screen, and then tap Favorites or Recents, respectively. Tap the blue > icon to the right of a name or number, and then scroll down and tap Text Message at the bottom of the Info screen.

✔ To call, e-mail, or start a FaceTime video chat (as discussed in Chapter 4) with someone to whom you've sent a message in the past, tap the Messages icon on the Home screen, and then tap the person's name in the Messages list. Tap the Call or FaceTime button at the top of the conversation to call or start a FaceTime chat (respectively) with the person, or tap the Contacts button and then tap an e-mail address, and a new e-mail message addressed to that person appears. The last part will work only if you have an e-mail address for the contact.

✔ Did you send someone a message? Receive one from someone? You can add the person to your Contacts list by tapping the person's name or phone number in the Messages list and then tapping the Add to Contacts button. If the person is already in your Contacts list, the Add to Contacts button doesn't appear, so don't bother looking for it.

✔ If a message includes a URL, tap it to open that web page in Safari.

✔ If a message includes a phone number, tap it to call that number.

✔ If a message includes an e-mail address, tap it to open a pre-addressed e-mail message in Mail.

✔ If a message includes a street address, tap it to see a map in Maps.

And that's all there is to it. You are now an official messaging maven.

Taking Note of Notes

The Notes app creates text notes that you can save or send through e-mail. To create a note, first tap the Notes icon on the Home screen, and then tap the + button in the top-right corner to start a new note. The virtual keyboard appears. Type the note. When you're finished, tap the Done button in the top-right corner to save the note. (The Done button appears only when the virtual keyboard is on-screen, so you can't see it in Figure 5-6.)

After a note is saved, you can do the following:

- ✔ Tap the left or right arrow button at the bottom of the screen to read the preceding or next note, respectively.
- ✔ Tap the letter icon at the bottom of the screen to e-mail the note using the Mail app (see Chapter 12 for more about Mail).
- ✔ Tap the trash can icon at the bottom of the screen to delete the note.
- ✔ Tap the Notes button at the top-left corner of the screen to see a list of all your notes, as shown in Figure 5-7. Then just tap a note to open it for viewing or editing.

We'd be remiss if we didn't remind you that as long as you're running iPhone OS 3.0 or later, you can sync notes with your computer (see Chapter 3). And if you're running iOS 4 and have enabled note syncing for more than one account (tap Settings⇨Mail, Contacts, Calendars), you'll see an Accounts button at the top of the Notes list screen (refer to Figure 5-7). Tap Accounts and you can choose to display all your notes or only notes associated with a particular account.

Figure 5-6: The Notes app revealed.

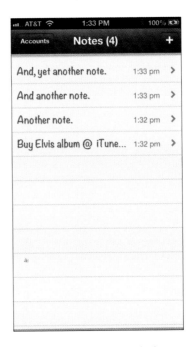

Figure 5-7: The list of notes in the Notes app.

An *account,* as mentioned in the preceding paragraph, refers to a Microsoft Exchange, iCloud, Apple ID, Gmail, Yahoo!, AOL, or other account that offers a notes feature.

One last thing: If you don't like the default font used in Notes (which is called Noteworthy), tap Settings⇨Notes, and then tap either Helvetica or Marker Felt, which are the only two other choices. After you choose the font, tap the Settings button to return to the main Settings screen or tap the Home button to return to your Home screen.

And that's all she, er, we, wrote. You now know everything there is to know about creating and managing notes with Notes.

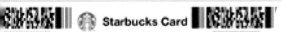 

6

Six Indispensible Utilities

In This Chapter

▶ Understanding the calendar's different views and functions
▶ Calculating with your iPhone
▶ Using the clock as an alarm, a stopwatch, and a timer too
▶ Leaving voice reminders
▶ Reminding yourself about reminders
▶ Managing Passbook

The iPhone is a smartphone. And, as a smart device, it can remind you of appointments, tell you the time (where you live or halfway around the world), and even help you perform arithmetic.

Over the next few pages, we look at a few of the iPhone's core — and, frankly, unsexy — apps. Indeed, we'd venture to say that no one bought an iPhone because of its calendar, calculator, clock, voice recorder, or Reminders app. And no one may not have bought it for the Passbook feature added with iOS 6 either. Just the same, it's awfully handy having these programs around.

NICKNAME
John's Card

Working with the Calendar

The Calendar program lets you keep on top of your appointments and events (birthdays, anniversaries, and the like). You open it by tapping the Calendar icon on the Home screen. The icon is smart in its own right because it changes daily, displaying the day of the week and the date.

You have three main ways to peek at your calendar: list, day, and month views. Choosing one is as simple as tapping on the List, Day, or Month button at the bottom of the Calendar screen. From each view, you can always return to the current day by tapping the Today button. Take a closer look in the following sections.

List view

List view, shown in Figure 6-1, isn't complicated. As its name indicates, list view presents current and future appointments in list format. You can drag the list up or down with your finger or flick to rapidly scroll through the list. List view compensates for the lack of week-at-a-glance view, though Apple certainly could add such a feature eventually.

If you rotate the iPhone to landscape mode, you can get a multiple day-at-a-glance view. You won't see the full week, but you can peek at a few days.

The iPhone can display the color-coding you assigned in Calendar in Mountain Lion (called iCal in older versions of iOS X on a Mac). Cool, huh?

If you're a Mac user who uses Calendar, you can create multiple calendars and choose which ones to sync with your phone (as described in Chapter 3). What's more, you can choose to display any or all of your calendars. You can also sync calendars with Microsoft Entourage or Outlook on a Mac or Microsoft Outlook 2003, 2007, or 2010 on a PC.

Be careful: To-do items created in Calendar aren't synced and don't appear on your iPhone.

Day view

Day view, shown in Figure 6-2, reveals the appointments of a given 24-hour period (scroll to see an entire day's worth of entries).

Month view

By now, you're getting the hang of these different views. When your iPhone is in month view, you can see appointments from January to December. In this monthly calendar view, a dot appears on any day that has appointments or events scheduled. Tap that day to see the list of activities the dot represents. The list of activities is just below the month in month view, as shown in Figure 6-3.

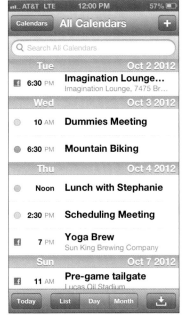

Figure 6-1: The Calendar list view.

Figure 6-2: The Calendar day view.

Figure 6-3: The Calendar month view.

Adding Calendar Entries

In Chapter 3, you discover pretty much everything there is to know about syncing your iPhone, including syncing calendar entries from your Windows machine (using the likes of Microsoft Outlook) or Mac (using iCal, Calendar, Microsoft Entourage, or Outlook).

As part of the Facebook integration that came as part of iOS 6, any calendar entries on the popular social network can automatically show up in the Calendar app. You will have to visit Settings, enter your username and password, and then make sure the Calendar app in the Facbook setting is turned on.

In plenty of situations, you enter appointments on-the-fly. Adding appointments directly to the iPhone is easy:

1. **Tap the Calendar icon at the top of the screen, and then tap the List, Day, or Month button.**

2. **Tap the + button in the upper-right corner of the screen.**

   The + button appears whether you're in list, day, or month view. Tapping it displays the Add Event screen, shown in Figure 6-4.

3. **Tap the Title/Location fields and finger-type as much (or as little) information as you feel is necessary or use dictation or Siri to employ your mouth and not your digits. Then tap Done.**

   Tapping displays the virtual keyboard (if it's not already shown).

4. **If your calendar entry has a start time or end time (or both):**

   a. **Tap the Starts/Ends/Time Zone field.**

   b. **In the bottom half of the screen that appears (see Figure 6-5), choose the time the event starts and then the time it ends.**

   Use your finger to roll separate wheels for the date, hour, and minute (in 5-minute intervals) and to specify AM or PM. It's a little like manipulating one of those combination bicycle locks or an old-fashioned date stamp used with an inkpad.

   c. **Tap Done when you're finished.**

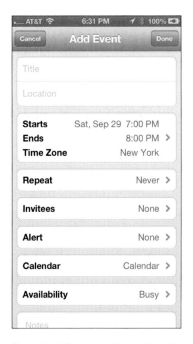

Figure 6-4: The screen looks like this just before you add an event to your iPhone.

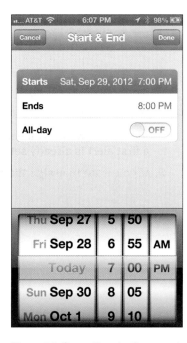

Figure 6-5: Controlling the Starts and Ends fields is like manipulating a bike lock.

5. **If you're entering an all-day milestone (such as a birthday), tap the All-Day button so that On (rather than Off) is showing. Then tap Done.**

Because the time is no longer relevant for an all-day entry, note that the bottom half of the screen now has wheels for just the month, day, and year.

6. **If you're setting up a recurring entry, such as an anniversary, tap the Repeat field. Tap to indicate how often the event in question recurs, and then tap Done.**

The options are Every Day, Every Week, Every 2 Weeks, Every Month, and Every Year.

7. **If you want certain people to join you, tap Invitees to specify who among your Contacts will be attending the event.**

8. **If you want to set a reminder or alert for the entry, tap Alert, tap a time, and then tap Done.**

Alerts can be set to arrive at the actual time of an event, or 2 days before, 1 day before, 2 hours before, 1 hour before, 30 minutes before, 15 minutes before, or 5 minutes before. If it's an all-day entry, you can request alerts 1 day in advance (at 9 AM), 2 days in advance (at 9AM), or 1 week in advance.

When the appointment time rolls around, you hear a sound and see a message like the one shown in Figure 6-6.

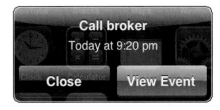

Figure 6-6: Alerts make it hard to forget.

If you're the kind of person who needs an extra nudge, set another reminder by tapping the Second Alert field (which you'll see only if a first alert is already set).

9. **If you want to assign the entry to a particular calendar, tap Calendar, and then tap the calendar you have in mind (Home or Work, for example). Then tap Done.**

10. **If you want to indicate whether you're busy or free, tap Availability (if it's shown on your phone). Then tap Done.**

11. **If you want to enter a web address, tap the URL field (at the bottom of the Add Event screen). Type the web address and then tap Done.**

12. **If you want to enter notes about the appointment or event, tap the Notes field (bottom of the screen). Type your note and then tap Done.**

A virtual keyboard pops up so that you can type the note.

13. **Tap Done after you finish entering everything.**

We mentioned that you can use Siri for your calendar entries. In fact, we can't think of any easier way to add an entry. You can instruct Siri along the lines of "Set a lunch appointment for tomorrow at noon with the Smiths." Siri is pleased to comply.

Choose a default calendar by tapping Settings➪Mail, Contacts, Calendars, and then flicking the screen until the Calendar section appears. Tap Default Calendar and select the calendar that you want to show up regularly.

If you travel long distances for your job, you can also make events appear according to whichever time zone you selected for your calendars. In the Calendar settings, tap Time Zone Support to turn it on, and then tap Time Zone. Type the time zone location using the keyboard that appears.

When Time Zone Support is turned off, events are displayed according to the time zone of your current location, and you won't see any reference to Time Zone in the Starts/Ends/Time Zone field.

To turn off a calendar alert, tap Settings➪Sounds, and then make sure that the Calendar Alerts button is turned off.

You can also set default alert times for birthdays, all-day events, or certain other events. Tap Settings➪Mail, Contacts, Calendars, and scroll down to Default Alert Times. For birthdays or all-day events specifically, you can choose to be alerted at 9 AM on the day of the event, at 9 AM one day before, at 9 AM two days before, or a week before.

Back in the Calendar app, if you want to modify an existing calendar entry, tap the entry, tap Edit, and then make whichever changes need to be made. To wipe out a calendar entry, tap Edit➪Delete Event. You have a chance to confirm your choice by tapping either Delete Event (again) or Cancel.

Calendar entries you create on your iPhone are synchronized with the calendar you specified in the iTunes Info pane.

Current and future Calendar events can be synchronized automatically through Apple's iCloud service. In Settings, you can also sync past events. Your options are to sync events 6 months back, 3 months back, 1 month back, or 2 weeks back. Or you can sync all your events.

You can use iCloud to keep your calendars updated as well and in sync across all your iOS devices and computers. Go to Settings➪iCloud and make sure the Calendars option is turned on.

Letting your calendar push you around

If you work for a company that uses Microsoft Exchange ActiveSync, calendar entries and meeting invitations from coworkers can be *pushed* to your device so that they show up on the screen moments after they're entered, even if they're entered on computers at work. Setting up an account to facilitate this pushing of calendar entries to your iPhone is a breeze, although you should check with your company's tech or IT department to make sure that your employer allows it. Then follow these steps:

1. **Tap Settings⇨Mail, Contacts, Calendars⇨Add Account.**

2. **From the Add Account list, tap Microsoft Exchange.**

3. **Fill in the e-mail address, username, password, and description fields, and then tap Next.**

4. **If required, enter your server address on the next screen that appears.**

   The iPhone supports something called the Microsoft Autodiscovery service, which uses your name and password to automatically determine the address of the Exchange server. The rest of the fields should be filled in with the e-mail address, username, password, and description you just entered.

5. **Tap Next.**

6. **Tap the On switch for each information type that you want to synchronize using Microsoft Exchange.**

   The options are Mail, Contacts, and Calendars. You should be good to go now, although some employers may require you to add passcodes to safeguard company secrets.

If you have a business-issued iPhone and it is lost or stolen — or it turns out that you're a double-agent working for a rival company — your employer's IT administrators can remotely wipe your device clean.

Responding to meeting invitations

The iPhone has one more important button, the Invitations button, located to the right of the Month button (and shown in the margin) — but you see it only under certain circumstances. For instance, you see the button when the Exchange calendar-syncing feature is turned on or when you have a calendar that adheres to the CalDAV Internet standard. You see the Invitations button also if you exploit iCloud, the free successor to Apple's once $99-per-year MobileMe set of online subscription services.

If you have any pending invitations, tap the Invitations button now to view them, and then tap any of the items in the list to see more details.

Suppose that a meeting invitation arrives from your boss. You can see who else is attending the shindig, check scheduling conflicts, and more. Tap Accept to let the meeting organizer know you're attending, tap Decline if you have something better to do (and aren't worried about upsetting the person who signs your paycheck), or tap Maybe if you're waiting for a better offer.

And if you do have a conflict, why not ask the Siri voice assistant to change your schedule? Visit Chapter 7 for more on this clever iPhone 4S and 5 feature.

You can choose to receive an alert every time someone sends you an invitation. In the Calendar settings, tap New Invitation Alerts so that the button displays On.

As mentioned, if you take advantage of iCloud, you can keep calendar entries synchronized between your iPhone, iPad, iPod touch, and Mac or PC. When you make a scheduling change on your iPhone, it's automatically updated on your computer and other devices, and vice versa. Choose iCloud from the Add Account screen to get started, assuming you didn't turn on iCloud when you first activated your phone.

You find out more about configuring iCloud when we discuss the iCloud setting in Chapter 14.

Subscribing to calendars

You can subscribe to calendars that adhere to the CalDAV and iCalendar (.ics) standards, which are supported by the popular Google and Yahoo! calendars and by the Mac's iCal and Calendar. Although you can read entries on the iPhone from the calendars you subscribe to, you can't create entries from the phone or edit the entries that are already present.

To subscribe to one of these calendars, tap Settings⇨Mail, Contacts, Calendars⇨Add Account⇨Other. You then choose Add CalDAV Account or Add Subscribed Calendar. Next, enter the server where the iPhone can find the calendar you have in mind, and if need be, a username, a password, and an optional description. Depending on the calendar you set up, you may have to dig into Advanced settings.

Searching calendars

You can search calendar entries, appointments, locations for events, and so on by using Spotlight search, a topic we address in Chapter 2. You can also search for events while in the calendar list view by typing text in the Search All Calendars field at the top of the screen.

Calculate This

Quick — what's 3,467.8 times 982.3? Why, the answer is 3,406,419.94 (of course). We can solve the problem quickly thanks to the iPhone calculator, buried (until it's needed) under another of those Home screen icons, Utilities.

Your handy iPhone calculator does just fine for adding, subtracting, multiplying, and dividing. Numbers and symbols (such as C for clear, and M+ for memory) are large and easy to see.

Are you thinking, "This isn't exactly the most advanced calculator I've ever used"? Well, you're right. The calculator can't handle a sine or a square root, much less more advanced functions.

Fortunately, the math whizzes at Apple were thinking right along with you. To see what they came up with, rotate the iPhone. As if by sleight of hand, your pocket calculator is now a full-fledged scientific calculator, capable of tackling dozens of complex functions. Take a gander at both calculators shown in Figure 6-7.

Isn't it nice to know just how much smarter a smartphone can make you feel?

Figure 6-7: Solving simple — and more complex — mathematical problems.

Punching the Clock

We hear you: "So the iPhone has a clock. Big whoop. Doesn't every cell phone have a clock?"

Well, yes, every cell phone does have a clock. But not every phone has a *world clock* that lets you display the time in multiple cities on multiple continents. And not every cell phone has an alarm, a stopwatch, and a timer to boot.

Let's take a moment in time to look at the time functions on your iPhone.

World clock

Want to know the time in Beijing or Bogota? Tapping World Clock (inside the Clock app) lets you display the time in numerous cities around the globe, as shown in Figure 6-8. When the clock face is dark, it's dark in the city you chose; if the face is white, it's light outside.

Tap the + button in the upper-right corner of the screen and use the virtual keyboard to start typing a city name. The moment you press the first letter, the iPhone displays a list of cities or countries that begin with that letter. So, as Figure 6-9 shows, typing *v* brings up both Caracas, Venezuela, and Hanoi, Vietnam, among myriad other possibilities. You can create clocks for as many cities as you like, though on a single screen you can see the time in only four cities on an iPhone 4 and 4S and five cities on an iPhone 5. To see times in other cities, scroll up or down.

To remove a city from the list, tap Edit and then tap the red circle with the white horizontal line that appears to the left of the city you want to drop. Then tap Delete.

You can also rearrange the order of the cities displaying the time. Tap Edit, and then press your finger against the symbol with three horizontal lines to the right of the city you want to move up or down in the list. Then drag the city to its new spot.

Alarm clock

Ever try to set the alarm in a hotel room? It's remarkable how complicated setting an alarm can be, on even the most inexpensive clock radio. Like almost everything else, the procedure is dirt-simple on the iPhone:

1. **Tap Clock on the Home screen to display the Clock app.**

2. **Tap the Alarm icon at the bottom of the screen.**

3. **Tap the + button in the upper-right corner of the screen.**

Figure 6-8: What time is it in Barcelona?

Figure 6-9: Clocking in around the world.

4. **Choose the time of the alarm by rotating the wheel in the bottom half of the screen.**

This step is similar to the action required to set the time that an event starts or ends on your calendar.

5. **If you want the alarm to go off on other days, tap Repeat and then tell the iPhone the days you want the alarm to be repeated, as in Every Monday, Every Tuesday, Every Wednesday, and so on.**

6. **Tap Sound to choose the ringtone (see Chapter 4) to use to wake you up. You can even use a custom ringtone you created or choose a song from your Music library.**

Your choice is a matter of personal preference, but we can tell you that the ringtone for the appropriately named Alarm managed to wake Ed from a deep sleep.

7. **Tap Snooze to display a Snooze button along with the alarm.**

Tap the Snooze button to shut down the alarm for nine minutes.

8. **If you want to call the alarm something other than, um, Alarm, tap the Label field and use the virtual keyboard to type another descriptor.**

9. **Tap Save when the alarm settings are to your liking.**

Simple stuff, really. But if you want really simple and have an iPhone 4S or 5, you can ask Siri to set the alarm for you.

You know that an alarm has been set and activated because of the tiny status icon (surprise, surprise — it looks like a clock) that appears in the upper-right corner of the screen.

An alarm takes precedence over any tracks you're listening to on your iPhone in Music. Songs momentarily pause when an alarm goes off and resume when you turn off the alarm (or press the Snooze button).

When your ring/silent switch is set to Silent, your iPhone doesn't ring, play alert effects, or make iPod sounds. But it *will* play alarms from the Clock app. That's good to know when you set your phone to Silent at a movie or the opera. And, although it seems obvious, if you want to *hear* an alarm, you have to make sure that the iPhone volume is turned up.

If you've set an alarm, it takes precedent over the Do Not Disturb feature we discuss in Chapters 4 and 14.

Not all phone carriers support the network time option in all locations, so an alarm may not sound at the correct time in a given area.

Stopwatch

If you're helping a loved one train for a marathon, the iPhone Stopwatch function can provide an assist. Open it by tapping Stopwatch in the Clock app.

Just tap Start to begin the count, and then tap Stop at the finish line. You can also tap a Lap button to monitor the times of individual laps.

Timer

Cooking a hard-boiled egg or Thanksgiving turkey? Again, the iPhone comes to the rescue. Tap Timer (in the Clock app) and then rotate the hour and minute wheels until the time you have in mind is highlighted. Tap When Timer Ends to choose the ringtone that will signify time's up.

After you set up the length of the timer, tap Start when you're ready to begin. You can watch the minutes and seconds wind down on the screen, if you have nothing better to do.

If you're doing anything else on the iPhone — admiring photos, say — you hear the ringtone and see a *Timer Done* message on the screen at the appropriate moment. Tap OK to silence the ringtone.

You can set a sleep timer in the iPhone to shut down music or video after you've shut down. Set the amount of time that you think you'll want the iPhone to be spitting out sound, and tap When Time Ends. Then tap Stop Playing. The iPhone will be silenced when the time you've set has been exhausted.

Voice Memos

Consider all the times you'd find it useful to have a voice recorder in your pocket — perhaps when you're attending a lecture or interviewing an important source (that's a biggie for us journalist types). Or maybe you just want to leave yourself a quickie reminder about something ("Pick up milk after work"). Well, you're in luck. Apple includes a built-in digital voice recorder.

A bunch of third-party apps add voice recording to the iPhone. Ed uses Recorder from Retronyms and Dictation from Dragon, and Bob uses iTalk Recorder from Griffin.

Making a recording

After you have that recorder in your pocket, how do you capture audio? When you tap the Voice Memos icon on the Home screen or in the Utilities folder, where it typically hangs out, up pops the microphone displayed in Figure 6-10. We'd tell you to talk right into that microphone, but it's mainly for show. The two real microphones on the iPhone 4 and 4S are on the top and bottom of the device and the three microphones on the iPhone 5 are on the front, back, and bottom left (as pictured in Chapter 1).

Tap the red record button in the lower-left part of the screen to start recording. You see the needle in the audio level meter move as Voice Memo detects sounds, even when you pause a recording by tapping the red button a second time. A clock at the top of the screen indicates how long your recording session is lasting. It's that easy.

The audio meter can help you determine an ideal recording level. Apple recommends that the loudest level on the meter be between –3dB and 0dB. We recommend speaking in a normal voice. To adjust the recording level, simply move the microphone closer or farther from your mouth.

Listening to recordings

After you capture your thoughts or musings, how do you play them back?

You can start playback in a couple of ways, and both involve tapping the same button:

- ✔ **Immediately after recording the memo, tap the button to the right of the audio level meter.** A list of all your recordings pops up in chronological order, as shown in Figure 6-11, with the most recent memo on top. That memo is the one you just recorded, of course, and it automatically starts to play.

- ✔ **If you haven't just recorded something, tapping the button to the right summons the same list of all your recordings.** However, nothing plays until you tap a recording in the list and then tap the little play button that appears to the left of the date and time that the recording was made (or to the left of the label you assigned to the recording, as we explain in the "Adding a label to a recording" section, later in this chapter).

You can drag the playhead along the scrubber bar to move ahead to any point in the memo.

If you don't hear anything after tapping play, tap the Speaker button in the upper-left corner of the screen. Sound will pump through the built-in iPhone speaker.

Figure 6-10: Leaving a voice memo.

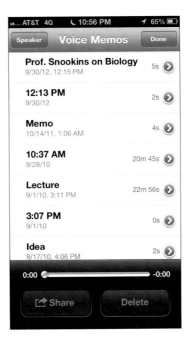

Figure 6-11: Tap the voice memo you want to play.

Trimming recordings

Maybe the person who left the recording rambled on and on. You just want to cut to the chase, for goodness' sake. Fortunately, you can trim the audio directly on the iPhone.

Tap the right-pointing arrow next to the memo you want to trim, and then tap Trim Memo. A narrow, blue tube representing the recording appears inside a yellow bar, as shown in Figure 6-12. Drag the edges of this *audio region* to adjust the start and end points of the memo. You can preview your edit before tapping the Trim Voice Memo button by tapping the little play button.

Your edits are permanent. Make sure that you're completely satisfied with your cuts before tapping Trim Voice Memo — or that you've synced the original back to iTunes on your computer so that you're working with a copy.

Figure 6-12: Trim a memo when someone says too much.

Adding a label to a recording

When a memo is added to your list of recordings, it just shows up with the date and time of the recording. You see no other identifier. As memos accumulate, you may have a tough time remembering which recording was made for which purpose. You can label a recording with one of the labels Apple has supplied or, better, create a custom label.

Here's how:

1. **From the list of recordings, tap the right-pointing arrow for the memo to which you want to add a label.**

   The Voice Memo information screen appears.

2. **Tap the right-pointing arrow in the box showing the date and time and the length of the video you just recorded.**

3. **Select a label from the list that appears.**

   Your choices are None, Podcast, Interview, Lecture, Idea, Meeting, Memo, and Custom.

4. **Choose Custom to type your own label (*Professor Snookins on Biology,* for example).**

   That's it. Your recording is duly identified.

You may want to share with others the good professor's wacky theories. Tap Share from either the main Voice Memos list or the information screen. You then have the option to e-mail the memo or send it as part of a message (an MMS message, text message, or an iMessage).

You can also sync Voice Memos to your Mac or PC by using iTunes, as described in Chapter 3.

When you have no further use for a recording, you can remove it from the Voice Memos app by tapping it in the list and then tapping the Delete button.

Remind me

Apple failed to provide a reminders or to-do app in its early iPhones, but fortunately several decent third-party apps helped fill the bill. With the iPhone 4S, however, Apple came to the realization that having a Reminders app of its own is a good thing. We agree.

The Reminders app isn't just any ordinary to-do list: Reminders on the iPhone can be tagged to your location, and it also works nicely with Calendar (iCal on older Macs) and Reminders on a Mac running Mountain Lion, and iCloud. iCloud can keep reminders in sync across all your iOS devices and computers.

Consider the power of tying a reminder to your location. You'll be notified of the items you must pick up at the supermarket at the moment you drive into the grocery parking lot. Or perhaps a reminder to call your spouse will pop up before you open your front door following a business trip.

Reminders are organized in lists, as shown in Figure 6-13. Apple supplies a general Reminders list, and a list that reveals the items you've completed. (We love the sense of accomplishment peeking at that list affords us.)

You can create your own lists, of course, perhaps one for groceries, another for the tasks you must do for the PTA. Lists show the due date or the location or both. You can swipe to the left or right to quickly jump from one list to another. In addition, tap any of the dates shown at the bottom of the list to reveal reminders due on that particular date.

To add a reminder to a given list, tap the list in question. (For example, we tapped the Groceries list and summoned the list shown in Figure 6-14.) Tap the + button at the upper right, and type the name of the reminder you have in mind. You can also just type the reminder directly in an available space on the list. Tap Edit if you want to remove any items on the list or change their order.

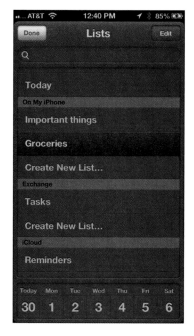

Figure 6-13: Listing your Reminders lists.

Figure 6-14: Remind me to get coffee.

To add or edit a list itself, tap the icon with the three bars at the upper-left of the Reminders screen to return to the list of lists. From the screen that appears, you can also search through all reminders.

To add or edit reminder details, tap the reminder itself. From the next screens, you'll be able to choose a date and time to be reminded. You can also request to be reminded at a given location. Choose Remind Me at a Location, select your current whereabouts, and then choose When I Leave or When I Arrive. To specify the location to use for the reminder, tap Current Location⇨Choose Address, and enter a new address or select a name from the iPhone Contacts list that appears. (Remember to turn on Location settings in Settings, if it's not already on.)

Please note that the location feature doesn't work with Microsoft Exchange or Outlook accounts or in every locale. And if your phone is locked, you may also experience Reminder delays.

Reminders are a great reason to call on Siri. Ask her to remind you of something and she will do your bidding.

You can view your reminders and see alerts in Notification Center. You can turn on Do Not Disturb in Settings (see Chapters 4 and 14) if you don't want to be nagged by a Reminder.

Passbook

We reckon most of you never leave the house without three things: your keys, your cell phone, and your wallet. That's a habit unlikely to change anytime soon. Nor do we expect most of you to ditch the plastic credit cards in your physical wallet for digital versions. That said, the tech and financial worlds are combining efforts to turn modern smartphones such as the iPhone into a version of a digital wallet.

Apple's own relatively early push in this area comes with the Passbook feature that arrived with iOS 6. Some people already use the iPhone to scan boarding passes at the airport or to pay for coffee in a Starbucks through a third-party app. Passbook provides a single repository for all these items, along with movie tickets, coupons, and gift cards. No more fumbling through printouts, apps, or e-mails to find the right ticket, coupon, or pass.

Moreover, Apple has made it so that Passbook is time and location based. In other words, the boarding pass appears when you get to the airport, even on the iPhone Lock screen, and you're notified of any gate changes. Or walk into the coffee shop and the appropriate gift card pops up.

Apple says you can find Passbook-capable apps in the App Store. Since this was all just getting started as we went to press, only a few Passbook apps were in place. That may no longer be the case by the time you're reading this.

You may also see an Add to Passbook link on a merchant's website — just make sure you're signed into your iCloud account to add passes to the Passbook app.

To use a given pass, tap it in the Passbook app, as shown in Figure 6-15, and then point it at the barcode reader or scanner at the terminal, neighborhood multiplex, hotel, department store, or whatever other place you frequent.

To show a pass on the Lock screen, tap the information button (a circled *i*) on the bottom-right front of the pass and make sure that the Show on Lock Screen switch is in the On position, as shown in Figure 6-16.

And with that, we remind you to proceed to the next chapter.

Figure 6-15: Tap an item in your Passbook to bring it out front and center.

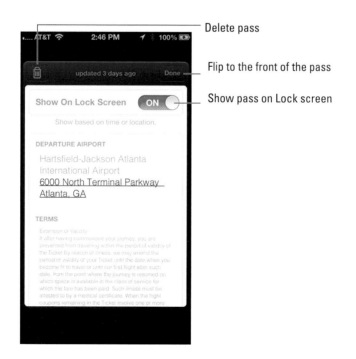

Delete pass

Flip to the front of the pass

Show pass on Lock screen

Figure 6-16: Show your passbook on the Lock screen.

7

Taking the iPhone Siri-ously

In This Chapter

▷ Calling Siri

▷ Determining what you can say

▷ Editing mistakes

▷ Dialing by voice

How could you not love Siri? The intelligent voice-activated virtual personal assistant living like a genie inside the iPhone 4S and iPhone 5 not only *hear*s what you have to say, but also attempts to figure out the intent of your words. Siri then does her darnedest to respond to your wishes. She — yes, it's a female voice (at least when you choose U.S. English as the default language) — can help you dictate and send a message, get directions, call a friend, discover who won the ball game, tell you when a movie is playing, arrange a wake-up call, search the web, find a decent place to eat, and lots more. Siri talks back, too, sometimes with humor and other times with attitude. When Ed told Siri he was tired, she responded with, "That's fine. I just hope you're not doing anything dangerous."

Siri used to be available as a free third-party app; Apple bought the startup company behind this neat technology and incorporated the magic inside the iPhone 4S and 5, as well as the third-generation iPad. Siri doesn't work on older iPhones or older iPads. And after Siri became the banner feature in the new iPhone 4S, Apple shut down the stand-alone app.

Apple concedes that Siri isn't perfect — the feature still carries that not quite finished beta tag. In our experience, Siri sometimes misheard us, occasionally more often than we'd like, and other times she didn't quite know what we had in mind. But blemishes and all, we think she's pretty special, and we think you'll agree.

Siri helps you get things done jus asking. You can make a phone call a message, dictate a note, or even restaurant.

About Siri and Privacy

Language English (United Stat

Feedback Al

Summoning Siri

When you first set up the iPhone 4S or iPhone 5, you have the option of turning on Siri. If you did so, you're good to go. If you didn't, tap Settings⟷General⟷Siri and flip the switch so that On is showing. (If you do turn Siri off on the 4S, it effectively turns on Voice Control.)

To call Siri into action, press and hold the Home button until you hear a tone and then start talking. Pretty simple, eh? At the bottom of the screen, you'll see a picture of a microphone inside a circle, as shown in Figure 7-1. The question, "What can I help you with?" appears on the screen. Alternatively, when the screen isn't locked, bring the phone up to your ear and wait for that same tone, and then talk. Siri responds also when you press a button on a Bluetooth headset.

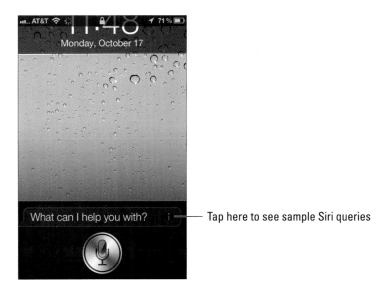

Tap here to see sample Siri queries

Figure 7-1: Siri is eager to respond.

What happens next is up to you. You can ask a wide range of questions or issue voice commands. If you didn't get your words out fast enough or you were misunderstood, tap the microphone icon and try again.

Siri relies on voice recognition and artificial intelligence. She'll respond in a conversational (if still slightly robotic) manner. But using Siri isn't entirely a hands-free experience. Spoken words are supplemented by information on the iPhone screen (as you see in the next section).

Making your iPhone (and other computers) really smart

Chances are you haven't heard of WolframAlpha. But if you want to know the gross domestic product of France or find events that happened on the day you were born, WolframAlpha can deliver such facts. You don't search the web per se on WolframAlpha as you would using a service such as Google. WolframAlpha describes itself as a "new way to get knowledge . . . by doing dynamic computations based on a vast collection of built-in data, algorithms, and methods." It taps into knowledge curated by human "experts." So you can get nutritional information for peanut M&Ms or compute a growth chart for your 4-foot, 7-inch, ten-year old daughter.

There's a reason why Siri relies on this "computational knowledge engine," which was driven over a period of nearly 30 years by really smart guy Stephen Wolfram. We also recommend checking out the $1.99 WolframAlpha app for your iPhone.

And just where does Siri get that information? She seeks answers from the web using sources such as Yelp, Yahoo!, Open Table, and WolframAlpha, which you can learn more about in the coming sidebar. She taps into Location Services on the phone.

And Siri, as of iOS 6, can open apps, Apple's own as well as third-party apps. Indeed, from your contacts, Siri might be able to determine who your spouse, coworkers, and friends are, as well as know where you live. You might ask, "How do I get home from here?" and Siri will fire up Maps to help you on your way. Or you can ask, "Find a good Italian restaurant near Barbara's house," and Siri will serve up a list, sorted by Yelp rating. She can even let you make a reservation (via Open Table).

Siri requires Internet access. In addition, many factors go into its accuracy, including surrounding noises and unfamiliar accents.

Figuring out what to ask

The beauty of Siri is that you don't have to follow a designated protocol when talking to her. Asking, "Will I need an umbrella tomorrow?" (which Siri heard as "Well I need . . ."), as shown in Figure 7-2, produces the same result as "What is the weather forecast around here?"

If you're not sure what to ask, tap the circled *i* to list sample questions or commands, as shown in Figure 7-3. You can tap on any of these examples to see even more samples.

Here are some of the ways Siri can lend a hand, um, voice:

✔ **Phone:** "Call my wife on her cell phone."

✔ **Music:** "Play Frank Sinatra."

✔ **Messages:** "Send a message to Nancy to reschedule lunch."

✔ **Calendar:** "Set up a meeting for 9 a.m. to discuss funding."

✔ **Reminders:** "Remind me to take my medicine at 8 a.m. tomorrow."

✔ **Maps:** "Find an ATM near here."

✔ **Mail:** "Mail the tenant about the recent check."

✔ **Stocks:** "What is the Dow at?"

✔ **Web search:** "Who was the 19th president of the United States?"

Figure 7-2: Siri can help you prepare for the weather.

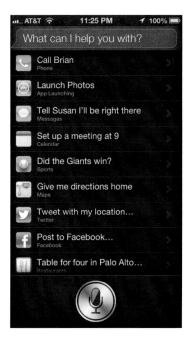

Figure 7-3: Siri can help out in many ways.

- **WolframAlpha:** "How many calories are in a blueberry muffin?"
- **Clock:** "Wake me up at 8:30 in the morning."
- **Sports:** "Who is pitching for the Yankees tonight?
- **Trivia:** "Who won the Academy Award for Best Actor in 2003?"
- **Twitter:** "Send Tweet, Going on vacation, smiley-face."

Using dictation

In many instances where you'd use the iPhone touchscreen keyboard, you can now use Siri instead. In lieu of typing, tap the microphone icon on the keyboard and speak. Tap Done when you're done. Dictation works as you search the web, take notes, compose messages, and so on. You can even update your Facebook status by voice.

Voice isn't the solution to everything. Putting Siri to work typically involves a combination of using voice, touch, and your eyes to see what's on the screen.

Correcting mistakes

As we've pointed out, Siri is good but sometimes needs to be put in her place. Fortunately, you can correct her mistakes fairly easily. The simplest way is to tap the microphone icon and try your query again. You can say something along the lines of, "I meant Botswana."

You can also tap the bubble showing what Siri thinks you said, and make edits by using the touch keyboard or by voice. If a word is underlined in blue, you can use the keyboard or your voice to make a correction.

Before Siri sends a dictated message, she seeks your permission. That's a safeguard you come to appreciate. If you need to modify the message, you can do so by saying such things as, "Change Tuesday to Wednesday" or "Add: I'm excited to see you, exclamation mark" — indeed, *I'm excited to see you* and *!* will be added.

Settings to make Siri smarter

From settings, you can tell Siri in which language you want to converse. Out of the gate, Siri was available in English (United States, United Kingdom, or Australian), French, and German. Versions in Chinese, Italian, Japanese, Korean, and Spanish were subsequently added.

You can also request voice feedback from Siri all the time or just when you're using a hands-free headset.

In the My Info field in Settings, you can tell Siri who you are. When you tap My Info, your Contacts list appears. Tap your own name in Contacts.

If you're concerned about Siri intruding when you raise the phone up to your ear to make a call, head to Settings as well to turn the Raise to Speak feature off.

As noted, you can call upon Siri even from the Lock screen. That's the default setting anyway. Consider this feature a mixed blessing. Not having to type a passcode to get Siri to do her thing is convenient. On the other hand, if your phone ends up with the wrong person, he or she would be able to use Siri to make a call, send an e-mail, or send a message in your name, bypassing whatever passcode security you thought was in place. We suspect Apple will close this loophole, perhaps even by the time you read this. But if they don't get around to it and you find this potential scenario scary, tap Settings➪General➪Passcode Lock. Then enter your passcode and switch the Siri option under Passcode Lock from Off to On. For more on Settings, read Chapter 14.

Voice Dialing

Several cell phones of recent vintage let you dial a name or number by voice. Bark out "Call Mom" or "Dial 212-555-1212," and such handsets oblige. Your engaging virtual personal assistant, Siri, can do that too.

But you can take advantage of voice calling (and some other functions too) with an older iPhone that doesn't have Siri. It's all part of a feature called Voice Control.

If you have an iPhone that predates the 4S, you have two ways to summon the Voice Control feature:

✔ Press and hold the Home button until the Voice Control screen shown in Figure 7-4 appears. The screen displays wavy lines that move as you speak. Scrolling in the background are some of the commands you can say out loud (*Play Artist, Previous Track,* and so on). Don't blurt out anything until you hear a quick double-beep. The iPhone will repeat the command it thinks it heard.

✔ Press and hold the center button on the wired headset. Once again, wait for an audible cue and then tell the iPhone what you have in mind.

Voice Control works quite nicely with the wired headset included with your iPhone. It works also with some Bluetooth headsets and car kits. If you use a wireless headset that's not supported, you'll have to hold the phone up to your lips if you want it to respond to voice commands.

Figure 7-4: Tell the iPhone to dial the phone or play a song.

You definitely want to wait for voice confirmation after you've spoken. In our experience, Voice Control isn't perfect, especially in a noisy environment. So if you're dialing a name or number, make sure the iPhone is indeed calling the person you had in mind. There's no telling what kind of trouble you might get into otherwise.

Wait for the tone and speak clearly, especially if you're in a noisy environment. You can dial by number, as in "Dial 202-555-1212." You can dial a name, as in "Call Bob LeVitus" or "Dial Ed Baig." Or you can be a tad more specific, as in "Dial Bob LeVitus mobile" or "Call Ed Baig home." Before actually dialing the phone, an automated female voice repeats what she thinks she heard.

If the person you're calling has multiple phone numbers and you fail to specify which one, the female voice will prompt you, "Ed Baig, home, mobile, or work?" Tell her which one to use, or say "Cancel" if you decide not to call or she offers the wrong name.

When the Voice Control screen appears, let go of the Home button before speaking a command. Otherwise, your thumb may cover the microphone, making it more difficult for the iPhone to understand your intent.

Voice Control need not be in Americanized English. From the Home screen, tap Settings⇨General⇨International⇨Voice Control. Then choose from nearly two dozen language options in the list. Choices include Australian English and English as spoken in the U.K., and versions of Chinese customized for Cantonese and Taiwan.

Part III
The Multimedia iPhone

The 5th Wave   By Rich Tennant

"Okay, the view's just up ahead. Everyone open up the Camera app and get ready to be dazzled."

*Y*our iPhone is arguably the best iPod in the world that can make and receive phone calls (with a tip of the hat to the iPad and iPod touch, the best iPods in the world that can't make and receive phone calls). So in this part, we look at the multimedia side of your phone — audio, video, and still pictures, too. There has never been a phone that was this much fun to use, and we show you how to wring the most out of every multimedia bit of it.

First we explore how to enjoy listening to music, podcasts, and audiobooks on your iPhone.

Then we move on to everything you always wanted to know about photos and iPhones: how to shoot them well, store them, sync them, and do all kinds of other interesting things with them.

We conclude this multimedia part by looking at some video, both literally and figuratively. We start with a quick segment about how to find good video for your iPhone, followed by instructions for watching video on your iPhone. Finally, we provide a delightful little epistle about shooting and sharing video with your iPhone.

Get in Tune(s): Audio on Your iPhone

As we mention elsewhere in this book, your iPhone is one of the best iPods ever — especially for working with audio and video. In this chapter, we show you how to use your iPhone to listen to audio; in Chapter 10, we cover video.

We start with a quick tour of the iPhone's Music app. Then we look at how to use your iPhone as an audio player. After you're nice and comfy with using it this way, we show you how to customize the listening experience so that it's just the way you like it. Then we offer a few tips to help you get the most out of using your iPhone as an audio player. Finally, we show you how to use the iTunes app to buy music, audiobooks, videos, and more, and how to download free content.

We assume that you already synced your iPhone with your computer or with iCloud and that your iPhone contains audio content — songs, podcasts, or audiobooks. If you don't have any audio on your iPhone yet, we humbly suggest that you get some (flip to Chapter 3 and follow the instructions for syncing or launch the iTunes app and buy a song or download a free podcast) before you read the rest of this chapter.

Okay, now that you have some audio content on your iPhone to play with, are you ready to rock?

Introducing the iPod inside Your iPhone

To use your iPhone as an iPod, just tap the Music icon in the lower-right corner of the Home screen. At the bottom of the screen that appears, you should see five icons: Playlists, Artists, Songs, Albums, and More.

If you don't see these icons, tap the back button in the upper-left corner of the screen (the one that looks like a little arrow pointing to the left).

Or, if you're holding your iPhone sideways (the long edges are parallel to the ground), rotate it 90 degrees so that it's upright (the short edges are parallel to the ground).

You'll understand why your iPhone's orientation matters when you read the later section "Go with the Cover (Flow)."

Playlists

Tap the Playlists icon at the bottom of the screen and a list of your playlists appears. If you have no playlists on your iPhone, don't sweat it. Just know that if you had some, this is where they'd be. (*Playlists* let you organize songs around a particular theme or mood: opera arias, romantic ballads, British invasion — whatever. Younger folks sometimes call them *mixes*.)

Tap a playlist and you see a list of the songs it contains. If the list is longer than one screen, flick upward to scroll down. Tap a song in the list and it plays. Or tap Shuffle at the top of the list to hear a song from that playlist (and all subsequent songs) at random.

That's all there is to selecting and playing songs from a playlist.

You find out how to create your own playlists on your iPhone a little later in this chapter.

Artistic license

Now we tell you how to find and play a song ordered by artist name rather than by playlist. Tap the Artists icon at the bottom of the screen and an alphabetical list of artists appears.

If the list is longer than one screen (which it probably is), you can, of course, flick upward to scroll down or flick downward to scroll up. But you have easier ways to find an artist.

For example, at the top of the screen, above the first artist's name, you see a search field. Tap it and type the name of the artist you want to find. Now tap the Search button to see a list of all matching artists.

Another way to find an artist is to tap one of the little letters on the right side of the screen, to jump directly to artists whose names start with that letter. In Figure 8-1, for example, that letter is *B*.

Notice that a magnifying glass appears above the *A* on the right side of the screen. Tap the magnifying glass to jump directly to the search field.

As you can see, those letters are extremely small, so unless you have tiny fingers, you may have to settle for a letter close to the one you want or else tap several times until you select the correct one.

Our technical editor, Dennis, suggests that using a stylus instead of your finger may help.

Tap an artist's name and one of two things occurs:

- ✔ **If you have songs from more than one album by an artist in your music library:** A list of albums appears, as shown in Figure 8-2. Tap an album to see a list of the songs it contains. Or tap the first item in the list of albums — All Songs — to see a list of all songs on all albums by that artist.
- ✔ **If all songs in your music library by that artist are on the same album or aren't associated with a specific album:** A list of all songs by that artist appears.

Either way, just tap a song and it begins to play.

Song selection

Now we tell you how to find a song by its title and play it. Tap the Songs icon at the bottom of the screen and a list of songs appears.

You find songs the same ways you find artists: Flick upward or downward to scroll; use the search field at the top of the list; or tap a little letter on the right side of the screen.

If you're not sure which song you want to listen to, try this: Tap the shuffle button at the top of the list between the search field and the first song title. Your iPhone will now play songs from your music library at random.

Magnifying glass   Little letters

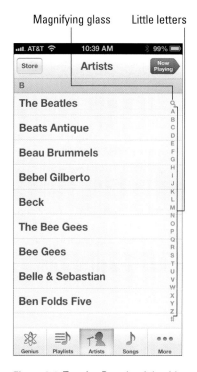

Figure 8-1: Tap the *B* on the right side of the screen to jump to artists with names that begin with a *B*.

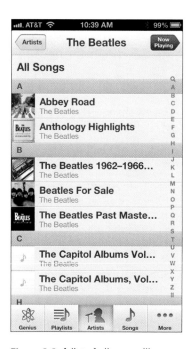

Figure 8-2: A list of albums will appear when you tap the artist's name.

You can also find songs (or artists, for that matter) by typing their names in a Spotlight search, as we mention in Chapter 2.

Share and share alike

One of our favorite features is Home Sharing, which lets you use your iPhone to listen to music and watch movies, TV shows, and other media content in your computer's iTunes library.

The gotcha is that Home Sharing is available only if your iPhone and your computer are on the same Wi-Fi network.

To make Home Sharing work for you, you have to enable it on your computer and on your iPhone. To set up Home Sharing on your computer, first launch iTunes and then Choose Advanced⟐Turn on Home Sharing. Type your Apple ID and password in the appropriate fields and click the Create Home Share button. As long as iTunes is open, your iTunes library will remain available for Home Sharing on your Wi-Fi network.

Now, to enable it on your iPhone, tap Settings⇨Music and type the same Apple ID and password you used to enable Home Sharing in iTunes. Tap the Home button when you're finished, tap Music⇨More⇨Shared, and tap the name of your iTunes library.

Here's the cool part: When you tap one of the icons at the bottom of the screen, rather than seeing the playlists, artists, songs, albums, and such that are stored on your iPhone, you instead see the playlists, artists, songs, albums, and so on in the iTunes library on your computer.

You'll continue to see the shared content in the Music app as long as your iPhone remains connected to the Wi-Fi network. If you want to switch back to the music stored on your iPhone, just reverse the process you used to select your iTunes library (tap More⇨Shared, and then tap My iPhone instead of the name of your iTunes library).

Home Sharing is simple, elegant, and free. If you've never used this feature, what are you waiting for?

Taking Control of Your Tunes

Now that you have the basics down, take a look at some other things you can do with the Music app.

Go with the (Cover) Flow

Finding tracks by playlist, artist, or song is cool, but finding them with Cover Flow is even cooler. Cover Flow lets you browse your music collection by its album artwork. To use Cover Flow, turn your iPhone sideways (long edges parallel to the ground) and Cover Flow will fill the screen, as shown in Figure 8-3.

The only time you won't see Cover Flow while your iPhone is turned sideways is after tapping the More icon, as described a little later in the chapter.

Flipping through your cover art in Cover Flow is simple. All you have to do is drag or flick your finger left or right on the screen and the covers go flying by. Flick or drag quickly and the covers whiz past; flick or drag slowly and the covers move leisurely. Or tap a particular cover on the left or right of the current (centered) cover and that cover jumps to the center.

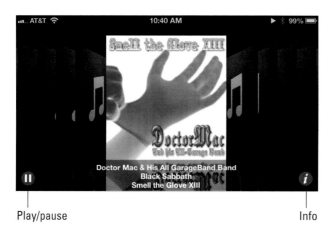

Play/pause   Info

Figure 8-3: Go with the Cover Flow.

Try it — you'll like it! Here's how to put Cover Flow to work for you:

- **To see tracks (songs) on an album:** Tap the cover when it's centered or tap the info button (the little *i*) in the lower-right corner of the screen. The track list appears.

- **To play a track:** Tap the track name in the list. If the list is long, scroll by dragging or flicking up and down on it.

- **To go back to Cover Flow:** Tap the title bar at the top of the track list or tap the little *i* button again.

- **To play or pause the current song:** Tap the play/pause button in the lower-left corner.

If no cover art exists for an album in your collection, the iPhone displays a plain-looking cover decorated with a single musical note. The name of the album appears below this generic cover.

And that, friends, is all there is to the Music app's cool Cover Flow.

Flow's not here right now

As you saw earlier in this chapter, when you hold your iPhone vertically (the short edges are parallel to the ground) and tap the Playlists, Artists, or Songs icon, you see a list rather than Cover Flow.

Along the same lines, when you're listening to music, the controls you see are different depending on which way you hold your iPhone. When you hold your iPhone vertically, as shown in Figure 8-4, you see controls that don't appear when you hold your iPhone sideways. Furthermore, the controls you see when viewing the Playlists, Artists, or Songs lists are slightly different from the controls you see when a song is playing.

Here's another cool side effect of holding your iPhone vertically: If you add lyrics to a song in iTunes on your computer (by selecting the song, choosing File➪Get Info, and then pasting or typing the lyrics into the Lyrics tab in the Info window), the lyrics are displayed along with the cover art.

Here's how to use the controls that appear when the iPhone is vertical:

- ✔ **Back button:** Tap to return to whichever list you used last — Playlists, Artists, or Songs.

- ✔ **Switch to track list button:** Tap to switch to a list of tracks.

- ✔ **Repeat button:** Tap once to repeat songs in the current album or list. The button turns blue. Tap the repeat button again to play the current song repeatedly; in this mode, the blue button displays the number 1. Tap the button again to turn off this feature. The button goes back to its original gray color.

Figure 8-4: Hold your iPhone vertically when you play a track and you see these controls.

If you don't see the repeat button, the scrubber bar, and the shuffle button, tap the album cover once to make them appear.

- ✔ **Scrubber bar:** Drag the little dot (the playhead) along the scrubber bar to skip to any point within the song.

- ✔ **Genius button:** Tap once and a Genius playlist appears with 25 songs that iTunes thinks will go great with the song that's playing.

The less popular the song, artist, or genre, the more likely the so-called Genius will choke on it. When that happens, you see an alert asking you to try again because this song doesn't have enough related songs to create a Genius playlist.

At the top of the Genius playlist, you find three buttons:

- **New:** Select a different song to use as the basis for a Genius playlist.

- **Refresh:** See a list of 25 other songs that go great with the song you're listening to, at least according to iTunes.

- **Save:** Save this Genius playlist so that you can listen to it whenever you like.

If you like the Genius feature, you can also create a new Genius playlist by tapping the Playlists icon at the bottom of the screen and then tapping Genius, which is the first item in the list of playlists.

✒ **Shuffle button:** Tap once to shuffle songs and play them in random order. The button turns blue when shuffling is enabled. Tap it again to play songs in order again. The button goes back to its original color — gray.

You can also shuffle tracks in any list of songs — such as playlists or albums — by tapping the word *Shuffle,* which appears at the top of the list. Regardless of whether the shuffle button has been tapped, this technique always plays songs in that list in random order. And, as you see later in this chapter, the Shake to Shuffle option, when enabled, lets you shake your iPhone from side-to-side to shuffle and play a different song at random.

✒ **Restart/previous track/rewind button:** Tap once to go to the beginning of the track. Tap this button twice to go to the start of the preceding track in the list. Touch and hold this button to rewind the song at double speed.

✒ **Play/pause button:** Tap to play or pause the song.

✒ **Next track/fast forward button:** Tap to skip to the next track in the list. Touch and hold down this button to fast-forward through the song at double speed.

✒ **AirPlay selector icon:** You may or may not see the AirPlay Selector icon on your screen (it's visible in Figure 8-4). AirPlay lets you stream content wirelessly over Wi-Fi from your iPhone to any AirPlay-enabled device. Check out the AirPlay sidebar for the details.

✒ **Volume control:** Drag the little dot left or right to reduce or increase the volume level.

If you're using the headset included with your iPhone, you can squeeze the mic to pause, and squeeze it again to play. You can also squeeze it twice in rapid succession to skip to the next song. Sweet!

When you tap the switch to track list button, the iPhone screen and the controls change, as shown in Figure 8-5.

Back   Current track

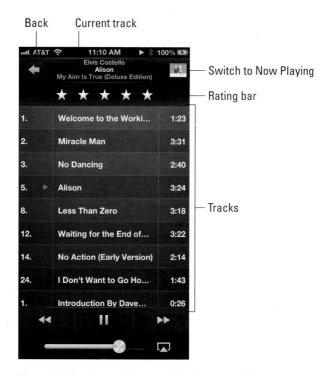

Switch to Now Playing

Rating bar

Tracks

Figure 8-5: Tap the switch to track list button and these controls appear.

Here's how to use *those* controls:

- **Switch to Now Playing button:** Tap to switch to the Now Playing screen for the current track (refer to Figure 8-4).
- **Rating bar:** Drag across the rating bar to rate the current track using zero to five stars. The track shown in Figure 8-5 has a five-star rating.

The tracks are the songs in the current list (Albums, Playlists, or Artists, for example). The current track indicator shows you which song is now playing (or paused). Tap any song in a track list to play it.

And that, gentle reader, is all you need to know to enjoy listening to music (and podcasts and audiobooks) on your iPhone.

Playing with AirPlay

AirPlay is a wicked cool bit of technology baked into every copy of iOS (version 4.2 or higher). It allows you to wirelessly stream music, photos, and video to AirPlay-enabled devices such as Apple's AirPort Express Wi-Fi base station and second-generation Apple TVs, plus certain third-party devices that have AirPlay technology, including (but not limited to) speakers and receivers.

The AirPlay Selector icon is quite shy. You'll see it only if your iPhone detects an AirPlay-enabled device on the same Wi-Fi network. Bob has a second-generation Apple TV in his den and an AirPort Express Wi-Fi base station on his back deck, so he sees the options in the figure when he taps his AirPlay selector icon.

Tapping Apple TV sends whatever is playing on the Music app to the Apple TV in his den. The Apple TV, in turn, is connected to his home theater audio system and HDTV via HDMI (an optical audio cable would suffice if you want to stream only audio, not video).

But wait — there's more! If you use an Apple TV as your AirPlay-enabled device, in addition to streaming music, video, or photos from your iPhone to your HDTV, you can also stream from your Mac, PC, iPad, or iPod touch.

Bob just loves his Apple TV and says it is one of his favorite Apple inventions and would be a bargain at twice its modest $99 price.

Customizing Your Audio Experience

In this section, we cover some Music features designed to make your listening experience more enjoyable.

Finding even more choices

If you prefer to browse your audio collection by criteria other than playlist, artist, or song, you can: Tap the More icon in the lower-right corner of the screen. The More list appears. Tap a choice in the list — albums, audiobooks, compilations, composers, genres, iTunes U, or podcasts — and your audio collection is organized by your criterion.

Wait — there's more. You can swap out the Playlists, Artists, Songs, and Albums icons for ones that better suit your needs. For example, if you listen to a lot of podcasts and rarely play entire albums, you can replace the Albums icon with a Podcasts icon.

Here's how:

1. **In the lower-right corner of the screen, tap the More icon.**

2. **In the upper-left corner of the screen, tap the Edit button.**

3. **Drag any icon on the screen right onto the button at the bottom of the screen that you want the icon to replace.**

   You can drag the Playlists, Artists, Songs, Albums, Audiobooks, Compilations, Composers, and Genres icons.

4. **(Optional) Rearrange the four icons by dragging them to the left or right (you can't move the More icon).**

5. **When you have everything just the way you like it, tap the Done button to return to the More list.**

If you replace one of the buttons this way, the item you replaced is available by tapping the More icon and choosing the item in the More list.

Setting preferences

You can change a few preference settings to customize your iPhone-as-an-iPod experience.

Play all songs at the same volume level

The iTunes Sound Check option automatically adjusts the level of songs so that they play at the same volume relative to each other. That way, one song never blasts out your ears even if the recording level is much louder than that of the song before or after it. To tell the iPhone to use these volume settings, you first have to turn on the feature in iTunes on your computer. Here's how to do that:

1. **Choose iTunes➪Preferences (Mac) or Edit➪Preferences (PC).**

2. **Click the Playback tab.**

3. **Select the Sound Check check box to enable it.**

Now you need to tell the iPhone to use the Sound Check settings from iTunes. Here's how to do *that:*

1. **On the iPhone's Home screen, tap the Settings icon.**

2. **In the list of settings, tap Music.**

3. **Tap Sound Check to turn it on.**

Choose an equalizer setting

An *equalizer* increases or decreases the relative levels of specific frequencies to enhance the sound you hear. Some equalizer settings emphasize the bass (low end) notes in a song; other equalizer settings make the higher frequencies more apparent. The iPhone has more than a dozen equalizer presets, with names such as Acoustic, Bass Booster, Bass Reducer, Dance, Electronic, Pop, and Rock. Each one is ostensibly tailored to a specific type of music.

The way to find out whether you prefer using equalization is to listen to music while trying out different settings. To do that, first start listening to a song you like. Then, while the song is playing, follow these steps:

1. **Press the Home button on the front of your iPhone.**

2. **On the Home screen, tap the Settings icon.**

3. **In the list of settings, tap Music.**

4. **In the list of Music settings, tap EQ.**

5. **Tap different EQ presets (Pop, Rock, R&B, or Dance, for example), and listen carefully to the way they change how the song sounds.**

6. **When you find an equalizer preset that you think sounds good, press the Home button and you're finished.**

If you don't like any of the presets, tap Off at the top of the EQ list to turn off the equalizer.

According to Apple's iPhone battery information page (www.apple.com/batteries/iphone.html), applying an equalizer setting to song playback on your iPhone can decrease battery life. So you need to decide which is more important to you: using equalization or maximizing battery life.

Set a volume limit for music (and videos)

You can instruct your iPhone to limit the loudest listening level for audio or video. To do so, here's the drill:

1. **On the Home screen, tap the Settings icon.**

2. **In the list of settings, tap Music.**

3. **In the list of Music settings, tap Volume Limit.**

4. **Drag the slider to adjust the maximum volume level to your liking.**

5. **(Optional) Tap Lock Volume Limit to assign a four-digit passcode to the setting so that others can't easily change it.**

The Volume Limit setting limits the volume of only music and videos. It doesn't apply to podcasts or audiobooks. And, although the setting works with any headset, headphones, or speakers plugged into the headset jack on your iPhone, it doesn't affect sound played on your iPhone's internal speaker.

Enable the Shake to Shuffle option

Shake to Shuffle does just what its name implies — plays a different song at random when you shake your iPhone. To enable this setting, here's what to do:

1. **On the Home screen, tap the Settings icon.**

2. **In the list of settings, tap Music.**

3. **Tap the Shake to Shuffle button to turn the feature on or off.**

From shake to shuffle — how can you not love that feature?

Make a playlist on your iPhone

Of course you can make playlists in iTunes and sync them with your iPhone, but you can also create playlists on your iPhone when you're out and about. Here's how:

1. **Tap the Music icon.**

2. **At the bottom of the screen, tap the Playlists icon.**

   If you've replaced Playlists with another icon as described previously, tap More, and then tap Playlists.

3. **Tap the second item in the list, Add Playlist.**

4. **Type a name for your new playlist, and then tap Save.**

   An alphabetical list of all songs on your iPhone appears. Note the little + that appears to the right of each song.

5. **Tap the + next to a song name to add the song to your playlist.**

   To add all these songs to your playlist, tap the + next to the first item in the list: Add All Songs.

6. **In the upper-right corner, tap the Done button.**

If you create a playlist on your iPhone and then sync with your computer, that playlist remains on the iPhone and will also appear in iTunes on your computer.

The playlists remain until you delete them in iTunes or on your iPhone. To remove a playlist in iTunes, select the playlist's name in the source list and then press Delete or Backspace; to remove a playlist on your iPhone, swipe from left to right across the playlist and then tap the red Delete button.

You can also edit playlists on your iPhone. To do so, tap the Playlists icon at the bottom of the screen (or tap More and then tap Playlists), and then tap the playlist you want to edit. Three buttons appear near the top of the screen — Edit, Clear, and Delete — with the songs in the playlist listed below them.

Tap Clear to remove all the songs from this playlist; tap Delete to delete this playlist from your iPhone. Or tap Edit to do any (or all) of the following:

- **To move a song up or down in the playlist:** A little icon with three gray bars appears to the right of each song. Drag the icon up to move the song higher in the list or drag down to move the song lower in the list.

- **To add more songs to the playlist:** Tap the + button in the upper-left corner.

- **To delete a song from the playlist:** Tap the – sign to the left of the song name. Note that deleting a song from the playlist doesn't remove the song from your iPhone.

When you finish editing, tap the Done button near the top of the screen. And that's all there is to creating and managing playlists on your iPhone.

Set a sleep timer

If you like to fall asleep with music playing but don't want to leave your iPhone playing music all night long, you can turn on its sleep timer.

Here's how:

1. **On the Home screen, tap the Clock icon.**

2. **In the lower-right corner, tap the Timer icon.**

3. **Set the number of hours and minutes you want music to play, and then tap the When Timer Ends button.**

4. **Tap the last item in the list, Sleep iPod.**

If you don't see the Sleep iPod item, don't be alarmed (semi-clever wordplay intended). You're simply looking at the middle (or the beginning) of the list of available alert sounds. To scroll to the bottom of the list and find the elusive Sleep iPod item, flick upward on the list a few times.

5. **In the upper-right corner, tap the Set button.**

6. **Tap the big, green Start button.**

That's it! If you have music playing already, you're finished. If not, press the Home button, tap the Music button, and select the music you want to listen to as you fall asleep. When the specified time period elapses, the music stops playing and your iPhone goes to sleep. By then, we hope you're in slumberland as well.

Use your voice to control your music

Here's something cool: You can boss around your music by using nothing but your voice, even if you don't have an iPhone with Siri. Just press and hold down the Home button (or the equivalent button on a headset) and, after you hear the tone, you can:

- **Play an album, an artist, or a playlist:** Say "Play" and then say "album," "artist," or "playlist" and the name of the album, artist, or playlist, respectively. You can issue these voice commands at any time except when you're on a phone call or having a FaceTime video chat. In other words, you don't have to have music playing for these voice commands to work.

- **Shuffle the current playlist:** Say "Shuffle." This voice command works only if you're listening to a playlist.

- **Find out more about the song that's playing:** Ask "What's playing?" "What song is this?" "Who sings this song?" or "Who is this song by?" Again, these commands work only if you're already listening to music.

- **Use Genius to play similar songs:** Say "Genius," "Play more like this," or "Play more songs like this." If your iPhone has no Genius playlists and you say "Genius," your iPhone will politely inform you that "Genius is not available." The same thing happens if you say "Play more like this" or "Play more songs like this" when no song is playing.

And hey, because your iPod happens to be an iPhone, you won't look stupid talking to it!

Although we found that controlling your music by speaking aloud works most of the time, in noisy environments the iPhone may mishear your verbal request and start playing the wrong song or artist or try to call someone on the phone. Using the wired headset helps. And syntax counts, so remember to use the exact wording in the list.

Shopping with the iTunes app

Last but certainly not least, the iTunes app lets you use your iPhone to download, buy, or rent just about anything you can download, buy, or rent with the iTunes application on your Mac or PC, including music, audiobooks, and videos. And, if you're fortunate enough to have an iTunes gift card or gift certificate in hand, you can redeem it directly from your iPhone.

If you want to do any of those tasks, however, you must first sign in to your iTunes Store account:

1. **On the Home screen, tap the Settings icon.**

2. **Tap Store in the list of settings.**

3. **Tap Sign In.**

4. **Type your username and password, and then tap OK.**

Or, in the unlikely event that you don't have an iTunes Store account:

1. **On the Home screen, tap the Settings icon.**

2. **Tap Store in the list of settings.**

3. **Tap Create New Account.**

4. **Follow the on-screen instructions.**

After the iTunes Store knows who you are (and, more importantly, knows your credit card number, gift card balance, or PayPal info), tap the iTunes icon on your Home screen and shop until you drop.

"Smile": Taking Pictures with Your iPhone

In This Chapter

▶ Taking pictures
▶ Focusing your shot
▶ Importing your pictures
▶ Viewing and admiring pictures
▶ Using Photo Stream and Shared Photo Stream
▶ Creating a slideshow
▶ Finding pictures by face, event, and place

Camera phones may outsell dedicated digital cameras nowadays, but — with exceptions — camera phones are mediocre picture takers.

One of the biggest of those exceptions is the iPhone. The device you have recently purchased (or are lusting after) is a spectacular photo viewer. And though its built-in digital camera isn't the one we'd rely on for snapping pictures during an African safari or perhaps even your kid's fast-paced soccer game, the iPhone in your steady hands can produce perfectly acceptable, if not really good, photos.

What's more, the picture keeps getting better and better. The iPhone 4 has not one camera, but two: a 5-megapixel autofocus camera on the rear, and a VGA camera on the front. The latter is used for FaceTime video (see Chapter 4) and for taking, dare we say, rather snappy self-portraits. The iPhone 4 also has an LED flash, the first iPhone with such a built-in nicety. Good as that sounds, the even fresher 8-megapixel iPhone 4S has one-upped its predecessor. It makes what was a pretty darn impressive camera phone even better.

But Apple didn't stop there. The 8-megapixel iSight camera on the iPhone 5 represents another leap ahead. With it, you can fire off pictures really fast, and capture splendid images, even in low light. And Apple added a cool panorama feature we get to in the coming pages. Meanwhile, the front-facing 1.2-megapixel camera on the iPhone 5 can handle high-definition video, up to the 720p video standard. For more on using the iPhone for video capture, though, you'll have to check out the next chapter.

You can launch the camera on all recent iPhones right from the Lock screen, by double-tapping the Home button and dragging the camera icon that appears in an upwards motion until you're in the app. This feature is a boon to parents who fumble with the phone trying to open the Camera app, missing that fleeting, never-to-be-seen again shot of both kids smiling simultaneously.

Over the next few pages, you discover how best to exploit the iPhone's cameras. We then move on to the real magic — making the digital photos that reside on the iPhone come alive — whether you imported them from your computer, received them via an e-mail or a text message, downloaded them from the Internet, or captured them with the iPhone's camera.

Taking Your Best Shot

As with many apps on the iPhone, you find the Camera app icon on the Home screen. Unless you moved things around, the Camera app is positioned on the upper row of icons, all the way to the right and adjacent to its next of kin, the Photos icon. You tap both icons throughout this chapter.

Might as well snap an image now:

1. **On the Home screen, tap the Camera app icon. Or from the Lock screen, double-tap Home and then flick the Camera icon on the bottom-right corner of the screen in an upward motion.**

   These actions turn the iPhone into the rough equivalent of a Kodak Instamatic, minus the film, of course.

2. **Keep your eyes fixed on the iPhone display.**

   The first thing you notice on the screen is something resembling a closed camera shutter. But that shutter opens in about a second on the iPhone 4 and in a snap (couldn't resist) on the 4S and 5, revealing a window into what the camera lens sees.

3. **Aim the camera at whatever you want to shoot, using the iPhone's display as your viewfinder.**

   You get a brilliant 3½-inch display on older models, or a widescreen 4-inch display on the iPhone 5.

We marvel at the display throughout this book; the Camera app gives us another reason to do so.

Make sure the switch at the bottom-right corner of the screen is set to camera mode rather than video mode. (The switch appears in the upper-right corner of the screen if you orient the iPhone in landscape, or a sideways, position). The on-screen switch is under the little picture of a camera rather than the little picture of a video camera.

4. **When you're satisfied with what's in the frame, do one of the following to snap the picture:**

   • **Tap the icon that resembles a camera at the bottom of the screen (see Figure 9-1) to snap the picture.** The camera icon is on the right if you hold the iPhone sideways. As we show you in a moment, you'll be able to change the point of focus if necessary.

   Preview of last picture taken   Camera/video switch

   Camera icon

   Figure 9-1: Say "Cheese."

   If you have trouble keeping the camera steady, try this trick. Rather than tap the camera icon at the bottom of the screen, keep your finger pressed against the icon and *release* it only when you're ready to snap an image.

   Be careful. The camera icon is directly above the Home button. We've seen more than one iPhone user erroneously press the Home button instead.

   • **Press the volume up button.** We generally consider this method a better way of shooting because it mimics the experience of capturing photos with a regular camera. If you're an iPhone traditionalist, however, don't let us stop you from continuing to use the on-screen camera button method.

On the iPhone 4, you may experience momentary shutter lag, so be sure to remain still. On the iPhone 4S and 5, thanks partly to their zippier chips, shutter lag is no longer something to worry about. When the shutter reopens, you see the image you shot, but just for a sec. The screen again functions as a viewfinder so that you can capture your next image. That's it: You've snapped your first iPhone picture.

5. **Repeat Steps 3 and 4 to capture additional images.**

If you position the iPhone sideways while snapping an image, the picture is saved in landscape mode.

In our experience, the iPhone camera button on the screen is supersensitive. We have accidentally taken a few rotten snapshots because of it. Be careful: A gentle tap is all that's required to snap an image.

Keeping Things in Focus

When composing your shot, you can take advantage of the Tap to Focus feature. Normally, the camera focuses on a subject in the center of the display, which you're reminded of when you momentarily see a square appear in the middle of the screen, as shown in Figure 9-2. But if you tap elsewhere in the frame, perhaps on the face of your kid in the background, the iPhone accordingly shifts its focus there, adjusting the exposure and what photographers refer to as the white balance. For another moment or so, you see a new, smaller square over your dog's face.

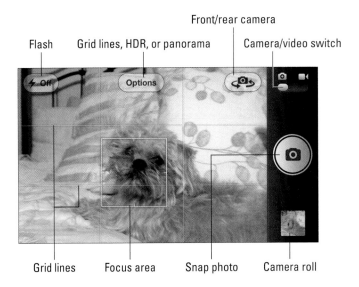

Front/rear camera

Flash   Grid lines, HDR, or panorama   Camera/video switch

Grid lines   Focus area   Snap photo   Camera roll

Figure 9-2: Squaring up for a focused photo.

If you want to lock the focus and exposure settings while taking a picture, press and hold your finger against the screen until the rectangle pulses. *AE/AF Lock* will appear on the screen. Tap the screen again to make *AE/AF Lock* disappear.

You can also exploit a feature known as *HDR,* or *high dynamic range,* photography. Tap the Options button (labeled in Figure 9-2) to turn on HDR. The HDR feature takes three separate exposures and then blends them into a single image. In Settings (under Photos & Camera), you can choose to keep the "normal" photo along with your HDR result or just hang onto the latter.

From the front to the rear — and back

We figure that most of the time, you'll use the main rear camera while shooting pictures (or video). But you may want to capture a shot of your own pretty face to post, say, on a social networking site such as Facebook. Not a problem. Just tap the front/rear camera button at the upper-right corner of the screen (labeled in Figure 9-2) to toggle between the front and rear cameras.

Firing up the flash

The iPhone 4, 4S, and 5 are the only models with an LED (light-emitting diode) flash — or any kind of flash — so they're the only iPhones with a flash button (labeled in Figure 9-2). Because no flash is associated with the front-facing camera, you won't see the button when you're using that camera. When the button is available, tap it to change the setting to On, Off, or Auto. We suggest using the Auto setting, which lets the iPhone decide when it's a good idea to fire up the flash.

Using the digital zoom

In iOS 4, you tap the screen to summon the zoom slider, and drag the slider to the right to get closer to a subject or to the left to zoom back out. In later versions of iOS, you pinch to zoom. So now when you spread your fingers or bring them back closer together, the zoom slider appears. Continuing to pinch or unpinch has the same effect of dragging the slider to the right or left.

You may not always love the results you get when zooming in close. The iPhone has a digital zoom, not an optical zoom, and the quality distinction is enormous. Using digital zoom, you can get closer to your subject by zooming in up to 5x, but it effectively crops and blows up part of the image, which can result in fuzziness or blurring. Not to sound harsh, but a subject's imperfections — and any inadequacies on the photographer's part — may come to light.

Capturing pleasing panoramas

In San Francisco, you want a picture of the magnificent span that is the Golden Gate Bridge. In the Himalayas, you want to record a visual memory of Mt. Everest. For posterity, you want that perfect image of your entire clan at a family reunion.

In these situations, you need the panorama feature in iOS 6 (iPhone 4S and 5 only). This feature lets you shoot up to 240 degrees and stitch together a high-resolution image of up to 28 megapixels.

Tasty pixels and other digital camera treats

The original iPhone and the iPhone 3G were 2-megapixel digital cameras. The iPhone 3GS increased that number to 3 megapixels, and the iPhone 4 raised the ante to 5 megapixels. The iPhone 4S jumped even higher, to 8 megapixels, matched by the iPhone 5.

If you've been shopping for a digital camera of any type, you're aware that megapixels are marketed like chocolate chips: The more of them, the better. But that may not always be true (for cameras, not cookies). Although the number of megapixels matters, so do a bevy of other factors, including lens quality and shutter lag.

Megapixels measure a camera's *resolution,* or picture sharpness, which is particularly important to folks who want to blow up prints well beyond snapshot size. For example, you probably want at least a 4-megapixel stand-alone digital camera if you hope to print decent 8-x-10-inch or larger photos. From a camera phone perspective, 2 or 3 megapixels are barely acceptable nowadays. Fortunately, more and more, you find cell phones with higher megapixel counts, including the recent iPhones. The iPhone 4 uses the same pixel size as the 3GS, while increasing the number of megapixels.

According to Apple, the ⅓-inch sensor in the iPhone 4S can capture 73 percent more light than its predecessor, to produce stunning 8-x-10-inch or smaller prints. And the iPhone 4S has five custom lens elements instead of the four lens elements in the iPhone 4. Having five lens elements helps to reduce distortion. Meanwhile, the larger f/2.4 aperture lets more light in than its immediate predecessor. The 4S also adds a feature found on many common point-and-shoots, called *face detection*. The feature helps the camera figure out whether you're shooting a portrait or taking a picture of a whole bunch of folks at once. Taken in tandem, such optical improvements mean that the camera in the 4S rivals many decent stand-alone point-and-shoot models.

And then there's iPhone 5. Apple says the new Camera app includes a dynamic low-light mode that can detect dim surroundings. When that's the case, it switches the sensor context to combine 4 pixels into 1, creating an additional two f-stops of brightness and sensitivity. According to Apple, the iPhone 5 can also examine surrounding pixels and deduce when pixels may be out of place, such as an image of the sky with a single green pixel in a sea of blue pixels.

This all sounds great in theory, but the bottom line is your satisfaction with the images you shoot. And yes, we think most of you will be more than satisfied most of the time, especially if you have an iPhone 4S or 5. Still, keep your expectations in check and don't expect to produce poster-size images.

Most camera phones can't hold a candle to the iPhone when it comes to showing off images, as the rest of this chapter proves. The iPhone exploits something Apple marketers call retina display, leading to the sharpest characters you've ever seen on a smartphone. The backlit 3.5-inch displays on the iPhone 4 and 4S boast 960-x-640 pixels. On the 4-inch iPhone 5, we're talking 1,136-by-640-pixel resolution at 326 ppi (points per inch).

Similar panorama features have been available on some point-and-shoot cameras and even rival smartphones. And it was possible to shoot panoramas on the iPhone 4 and 4S too via third-party apps. But now that the feature is baked into the Camera app, shooting panoramas is a veritable pleasure.

To summon a panorama:

1. **Tap Camera⇨Options⇨Panorama.**

2. **Position the phone so that it's at a proper starting point, and tap the Camera button when you're ready.**

3. **Steadily pan in the direction of the arrow, as shown in Figure 9-3, left.**

   Tap the arrow if you prefer panning in the opposite direction. As you move methodically — if you go too fast, the iPhone will advise you to slow down — try and keep the arrow just above the horizontal line.

4. **When the task is complete, tap Done and admire your handiwork (see Figure 9-3, right).**

Figure 9-3: Steadily follow the arrow to produce a panorama like this one captured on New York's Park Avenue.

Importing Pictures

You needn't use only the iPhone's digital camera to get pictures onto the device. You can also synchronize photos from a PC or Mac by using the Photos tab on the iTunes iPhone page, which is described in Chapter 3. (We assume that you already know how to get pictures onto your computer.)

Quickie reminder: On a Mac, you can sync photos via iPhoto software version 4.03 or later and Aperture. On a PC, you can sync with Adobe Photoshop Elements 3.0 or later. Alternatively, with both computers, you can sync with any folder containing pictures.

When the iPhone is connected to your computer, click the Photos tab on the iTunes iPhone page. Then select the appropriate check boxes to specify the pictures and photos you want to synchronize. Or choose All Photos and Albums if you have enough storage on the iPhone to accommodate them.

Syncing pictures is a two-way process, so photos captured with the iPhone's digital camera can also end up in the photo library on your computer.

Mac users: Connecting the iPhone with photos in the camera roll usually launches iPhoto in addition to iTunes. (The When a Camera Is Connected setting in Image Capture preferences controls what is launched.)

Tracking Down Your Pictures

So where exactly do your pictures hang out on the iPhone? The ones you snapped on the iPhone itself end up in a photo album appropriately dubbed the *camera roll* and — if you're taking advantage of iCloud — in another destination called Photo Stream, which we discuss later in this chapter. The photos you imported are readily available too (and grouped in the same albums they were on the computer). We show you not only where they are, but also how to display them and share them with others — and how to dispose of the duds that don't measure up to your lofty photographic standards.

Get ready to literally get your fingers on the pics (without having to worry about smudging them). You can get to your pictures from the Photos app or the Camera app. However, in the Camera app, you can see only the pictures and videos stored on the camera roll; in the Photos app, you can view all the pictures and videos you've imported as well.

Let's start with the procedures for the Photos app:

1. **Tap the Photos icon on the Home screen, and then tap the camera roll album or any other album that appears in the list of photo albums.**

   Doing so displays a thumbnail of all the photos and videos in the selected album, such as the one shown in Figure 9-4. (The process of shooting videos is described in the next chapter.)

2. **Browse through the thumbnail images in the album until you find the picture or video you want to display.**

   You'll know when a thumbnail represents a video rather than a still image because the thumbnail displays a tiny movie camera icon and the video length. If the thumbnail you have in mind doesn't appear on this screen, flick your finger up or down to scroll through the pictures rapidly or use a slower dragging motion to pore through the images more deliberately. Buttons at the bottom of the screen let you view photos and videos by albums, Photo Stream, events, faces, or places, as described later in this chapter.

3. **Tap the appropriate thumbnail.**

   The picture or video you selected fills the entire screen.

4. **Tap the screen again.**

   The picture controls appear, as shown in Figure 9-5. We discuss later what they do.

See action options and add photo to new album

Return to Album list

View albums

View Photo Stream

View events

View photos and videos by location

View photos and videos by subject

Figure 9-4: Your pictures at a glance.

5. To make the controls disappear, tap the screen again. Or just wait a few seconds and they go away on their own.

Trash image

Slideshow   Display image on TV through AirPlay

Use image as wallpaper, e-mail it, send it via Messages, assign it to a contact, Tweet it, add to Facebook or Photo Stream, copy or print it

Figure 9-5: Picture controls differ slightly depending on how you got there.

If you instead want to start from the Camera app, do the following:

1. Tap the Camera icon on the Home screen, and then tap the camera roll button at the bottom-left corner of the display.

Note that the camera roll button displays a thumbnail of your last shot taken in the camera roll (refer to Figure 9-2).

The shutter closes for just an instant, the last shot you took slides up onto the screen, and you see the camera controls (refer to Figure 9-5). Note that these controls differ slightly depending on whether you got to the picture through the Camera app or the Photos app. If you started in the Camera app, you see a camera icon at the bottom-left corner of the screen. Tapping that icon readies you for the next shot.

If you started in Photos instead, the leftmost icon is the action icon for using the photo as wallpaper, e-mailing the photo, sending it via Message, assigning it to a contact, Tweeting it, adding it to Facebook, adding it to Photo Stream, copying it, or printing it.

If you don't see any camera controls (they disappear after a few seconds), tap the screen again. You can drag your finger from left to right to bring up earlier shots stored in the camera roll.

2. **To transform the iPhone back into a picture taker rather than a picture viewer, make sure that the picture controls are displayed, and then tap the Camera icon in the bottom-left corner.**

   Again, this option is available only if you arrived at the camera roll from the Camera app. If you started in the Photos app instead, you have to back out of the app altogether by pressing the Home button. Then tap the Camera app icon on the Home screen to call the iPhone's digital camera back into duty.

Swimming in the Photo Stream

As part of the iCloud service, any photos you take with the iPhone, or other iOS 5 or iOS 6 devices such as the iPad, are automatically pushed to all your other devices, specifically, your PC, Mac, iPad, iPod touch, Apple TV, or another iPhone. The transfer takes place through the magic of *Photo Stream,* the antidote to the endless of problem of "I've snapped a picture, now what?"

You need not fret about storage space using Photo Stream either. The last 1,000 pictures you've taken over 30 days are held in a special Photo Stream album for 30 days — enough time, Apple figures, for all your devices to connect and grab those images, because a Wi-Fi connection is your only requirement. All the pictures you've taken remain on your PC or Mac, because those machines have more capacious storage. You can always manually move images from the Photo Stream album into other albums on your iPhone or other iOS devices and computers.

Photos taken on the iPhone aren't whisked away into the Photo Stream until you leave the Camera app. In that way, you get a chance to delete pictures that you'd rather not have turn up everywhere.

 If for some reason the pictures you snap on the iPhone are not being uploaded, go to Settings, scroll down and tap Photos, and make sure Photo Stream is turned on.

Sharing Photo Streams

The Photo Stream feature is a generally terrific and hassle-free way for you to make sure the pictures you shoot end up on your devices without you fretting about how they land there. But Apple in its infinite wisdom recognizes that you also might want to share your best images with friends and family and have those pictures automatically show up on their devices. An impressive and aptly named solution called Shared Photo Streams arrived on the iPhone with iOS 6 (and a bit earlier on Macs running OS X Mountain Lion). The feature lets you share pictures with other folks and also subscribe to the shared photo streams that they make available to you.

Here's how to create a shared photo stream for the first time:

1. **On the Home screen, tap Settings.**

2. **Scroll down and tap Photos & Camera.**

3. **Tap the Shared Photo Streams option so that On is showing.**

4. **Display your photos by opening the Photos app or the Camera app. Then do one of the following:**

   • From the view showing thumbnails of all your pictures in the camera roll or another album, tap the Photo Stream icon at the bottom of the screen.

   • Tap an individual photo to select it. In the picture controls, tap the action icon (shown in the margin) and then tap the Photo Stream option. (If you don't see the picture controls, tap the image.)

5. **Because this is the first time you'll be creating a photo stream, type a name for it in the name field that appears (see Figure 9-6, left).**

   If you've already created one or more shared photo streams, you'll have the option to add the picture or pictures you've selected to an existing photo stream. To create a new photo stream, tap the New Photo Stream option.

6. **Type the e-mail addresses of each person to whom you want to send your photo stream or tap the + button and add names from your contacts. Then tap Next.**

   Your friends will get an e-mail inviting them to view the shared photo stream, as shown in Figure 9-6, right.

   You can share your photo stream with everyone through a public gallery on iCloud.com. To do that, flip the Public Website switch to On (refer to Figure 9-6, left).

7. **If you want, enter a comment. Then tap Post.**

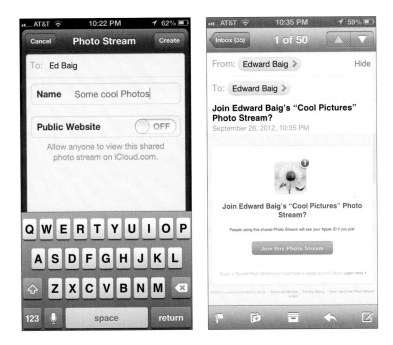

Figure 9-6: Stream pictures to chosen friends.

Admiring Your Pictures

Photographs are meant to be seen, of course, not buried in the digital equivalent of a shoebox. The iPhone affords you some neat ways to manipulate, view, and share your best photos.

You may already know (from previous sections in this chapter) how to find a photo and view it full-screen and display picture controls. But you can do a lot of picture maneuvering without summoning those controls. Here are some options:

- **Skip ahead or view the preceding picture:** Flick your finger left or right.

- **Landscape or portrait:** The iPhone's wizardry (or, more specifically, the device's accelerometer sensor) is at work. When you turn the iPhone sideways, the picture automatically reorients itself from portrait to landscape mode, as the images in Figure 9-7 show. Pictures shot in landscape mode fill the screen when you rotate the iPhone. Rotate the device back to portrait mode and the picture readjusts accordingly.

Figure 9-7: The same picture in portrait (left) and landscape (right) modes.

- ✔ **Zoom:** Double-tap to zoom in on an image and make it larger. Do so again to zoom out and make it smaller. Alternatively, on the photo, pinch your thumb and index finger together to zoom in, or unpinch them to zoom out.

- ✔ **Pan and scroll:** This cool little feature is practically guaranteed to make you the life of the party. After you zoom in on a picture, drag it around the screen with your finger. Besides impressing your friends, you can bring front and center the part of the image you most care about. That lets you zoom in on Fido's adorable face as opposed to, say, the unflattering picture of the person holding the dog in his lap.

Launching Slideshows

Those of us who store a lot of photographs on computers are familiar with running slideshows of those images. It's a breeze to replicate the experience on the iPhone:

1. **Choose your camera roll or another album from the Photo Albums list.**

   To do so, tap the Photos icon from the Home screen or tap the camera roll button in the Camera app.

2. **Do one of the following:**

   - **In the Photos app,** select a picture and then tap the play icon at the bottom of the picture.

   - **In the Camera app,** tap the image in the lower-left corner of the screen to display the most recent image in the camera roll, then tap the play icon at the bottom of the image. If you want to start the slideshow with a different image rather than the picture that is now visible, tap the camera roll button at the upper-left corner of the screen. You now see a thumbnails screen. Tap the play icon.

   You are taken to the Slideshow Options screen.

3. **Choose transition effects and the music (if any) that you'd like to accompany the slideshow.**

   You have five transitions choices (cube, dissolve, ripple, wipe across, wipe down). Why not try them all, to see what you like?

4. **Tap Start Slideshow.**

   Unless you've set the slideshow to repeat, as explained in the next chapter, the slideshow ends automatically. Tap the screen to end it prematurely.

That's it! Enjoy the show.

Special slideshow effects

You can alter the length of time each slide is shown, change the transition effects between pictures, and display images in random order.

From the Home screen, tap Settings and then scroll down and tap Photos & Camera. Then tap any of the following to make changes:

- ✔ **Play Each Slide For:** You have five choices (2 seconds, 3 seconds, 5 seconds, 10 seconds, 20 seconds). When you're finished, tap the Photos button to return to the main Settings screen for Photos.

- ✔ **Repeat:** If this option is turned on, the slideshow continues to loop until you stop it. If it's turned off, the slideshow for your camera roll or album plays just once. The Repeat control may seem counterintuitive. If Off is showing, tap it to turn on the Repeat function. If On is showing, tap it to turn off the Repeat function.

- ✔ **Shuffle:** Turning on this feature plays slides in random order. As with the Repeat feature, tap Off to turn on shuffle or tap On to turn off random playback.

Press the Home button to leave the settings and return to the Home screen.

Touching up photos

The iPhone is never going to serve as a substitute for a high-end photo-editing program such as Adobe Photoshop. But you can do some relatively simple touch-ups, right from inside the Photos app.

Choose an image and tap Edit. At the bottom of the screen are four icons, shown in Figure 9-8 and described next:

- ✓ **Rotate:** Rotate the image counterclockwise.

- ✓ **Auto-enhance:** Let the iPhone take a stab at making your image look better. Apple lightens or darkens the picture, tweaks color saturation, and more. Tap Save if you like the result.

- ✓ **Remove red-eye:** Get rid of that annoying red-eye. Tap each eye; tap again to undo.

- ✓ **Crop:** Crop the image. By tapping the Constrain button, you can choose to crop the image through many different aspect ratio options.

Figure 9-8: Who says you can't improve the quality of the picture?

Deleting pictures

We told a tiny fib by intimating that photographs are meant to be seen. We should have amended that statement by saying that *some* pictures are meant to be seen. Others you can't get rid of fast enough. Fortunately, the iPhone makes it a cinch to bury the evidence:

1. **From the camera roll, tap the objectionable photograph.**

2. **Tap to display the picture controls, if they're not already displayed.**

3. **Tap the trash can icon.**

4. **Tap Delete Photo (or Cancel, if you change your mind).**

   The photo gets sucked into the trash can and mercifully disappears.

More (Not So) Stupid Picture Tricks

 You can take advantage of the photos on the iPhone in a few more ways. In each case, you tap the picture and make sure the picture controls are displayed. Then tap the action (or share) icon, at the bottom-left (and shown in the margin) to display the nine choices shown in Figure 9-9.

Here's what each choice does:

- ✓ **Mail:** Some photos are so precious that you just have to share them with family members and friends. When you tap the Mail icon, the picture is automatically embedded in the body of an outgoing e-mail message. Use the virtual keyboard to enter the e-mail addresses, Subject line, and any comments you want to add — you know, something profound, like "Isn't this a great-looking photo?"

  After tapping Send but before the picture and accompanying message are whisked away, you have the option to reduce the image size (small, medium, or large) or keep the actual size. Consider the trade-offs: A smaller-sized image may get through any limits imposed by your or the recipient's Internet provider or company. But if you can get the largest image through, you will give the recipient the full picture (forgive the pun) in all its glory. (Check out Chapter 12 for more info on using e-mail.)

  You can also press and hold on the screen until a Copy button appears. Tap that button, and now you can paste the image into an e-mail, a text, or an iMessage message. But there's another easier way to send a picture via Message, as you're about to find out.

- ✓ **Message:** Apple and your provider support picture messaging through what's called MMS (Multimedia Messaging Service). Tap the Message icon, and the picture is embedded in your outgoing message; you merely need to enter the phone number or name of the person to whom you're sending the picture. If that person is also using an iOS 5 or iOS 6 device, or a Mac running OS X Mountain Lion, the photo will be sent as an iMessage, which doesn't count against your texting allotment.

- ✓ **Photo Stream:** As we describe earlier in this chapter, Photo Stream is a neat way for anyone exploiting iCloud to have pictures automatically show up in a special Photo Stream album. Tap Photo Stream to add the image to a particular photo stream.

✔ **Twitter:** Lots of people send pictures via Twitter these days. The iPhone makes it breeze. Tap the Twitter icon and your picture is embedded in an outgoing Tweet, as shown in Figure 9-10. Just add your words, sticking to Twitter's character limit of 140. You can also add your location to the Tweet by tapping the Add Location option that appears. Oh, and remember to enter your Twitter handle in Settings.

✔ **Facebook:** Tap the Facebook icon to add your picture to the world's most popular social network. At your discretion, you can add your location. And remember to add your Facebook credentials in Settings.

✔ **Assign to Contact:** If you assign a picture to someone in your Contacts list, the picture you assign pops up whenever you receive a call from that person. Tap Assign to Contact. Your list of contacts appears on the screen. Scroll through the list to find the person who matches the picture of the moment. As with the Use as Wallpaper option (described later), you can drag and resize the picture to get it just right. Then tap Set Photo.

As Chapter 4 explains, you can also assign a photo to a contact by starting out in Contacts. As a refresher, start by tapping Phone⇨Contacts. From Contacts, choose the person and tap Edit⇨Add Photo. At that point, you can take a new picture with the iPhone's digital camera or select an existing portrait from one of your onboard picture albums.

Figure 9-9: Look at what else I can do!

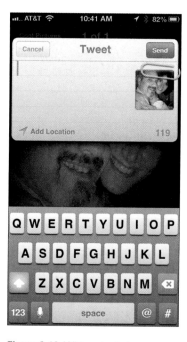

Figure 9-10: With a single tap, you can add a picture to your Tweet.

To change the picture you assigned to a person, tap his or her name in the Contacts list, tap Edit, and then tap the person's thumbnail picture, which also carries the label Edit. From there, you can take another photo with the iPhone's digital camera, select another photo from one of your albums, edit the photo you're already using (by resizing and dragging it to a new position), or delete the photo you no longer want.

✏ **Print:** If you have a wireless AirPrint-capable printer, tap Print to print the photo. You can choose how many copies of the print you want to duplicate.

✏ **Copy:** Tap this option to make a copy of an image that you can embed in an outgoing text message.

✏ **Use as Wallpaper:** The default background image on the iPhone when you unlock the device is a gray background with raindrops. Dramatic though it may be, you probably have an even better photograph to use as the iPhone's wallpaper. A picture of your spouse, your kids, or your pet, perhaps?

When you tap the Use as Wallpaper icon, you see what the present image looks like as the iPhone's background picture. And, as Figure 9-11 shows, you're given the opportunity to move the picture around and resize it, through the now familiar action of dragging or pinching against the screen with your fingers. When you're satisfied with how the wallpaper looks, tap the Set button. Options appear that let you use the photo as wallpaper for the Lock screen, the Home screen, or both. Per usual, you also have the option to tap Cancel. (You find out more about wallpaper in Chapter 14.)

You can also share, copy, add to a new album, or delete in bulk. Here are the general steps:

1. **From a thumbnails view of your pictures (refer to Figure 9-4), tap the Edit button at the upper-right.**

   The Share, Add To, and Delete buttons appear at the bottom of the page.

2. **Tap each image in the thumbnails view that you want to share, copy, add to an album, or delete so that a check mark appears.**

3. **Tap Share, Copy (an option under Share), Add To, or Delete, depending on what you want to do.**

   If you tap Share from here, you have the option to Tweet the photo, add it to Facebook, or print it. If you tap Share⊅Copy, you can paste images into an outgoing e-mail, text or iMessage message. If you tap Add To, choose the album you want to add the picture to. If you tap Delete, you get the chance to change your mind.

Organizing Your Places, Faces, and Events

We've already showed you how pictures on the iPhone can be organized into albums. Apple has also added iPhone support for the nifty Places, Faces, and Events features, which are familiar to Mac owners who use iPhoto software.

Consult Chapter 3, on syncing, for a refresher on getting data to and from a computer to your iPhone and back, a process that is even simpler since the presence of iCloud. When the iPhone is connected to a Mac, you can sync photo events (pictures taken around birthdays, anniversaries, and so on) or faces (all the shots taken with a particular person in them). In Figure 9-12, all the pictures have Ed's mug in them. Meanwhile, as you'll soon see, the Places feature is all about where pictures were taken.

The Faces feature requires that you sync to the iPhone with iPhoto or Aperture on a Mac and that you turn on Faces in the syncing options.

We think you'll be jazzed by the Places feature. All the images taken with the iPhone can be geotagged with the location where they were shot. The first few times you use the iPhone's Camera app, it asks for your permission to use your current location. Similarly, third-party apps ask whether it's okay to use your location, perhaps so a friend hanging out in the same area can find you on a social networking site.

Figure 9-11: Beautifying the iPhone with wallpaper.

Figure 9-12: Facing Ed in Faces.

To access the Places feature, tap Places from the thumbnails view (refer to Figure 9-4). You could instead tap Events to view pictures by occasion or tap Faces to view all the pictures containing a particular person.

If you tap Places, a map with red pushpins similar to the one shown in Figure 9-13 will appear. Tap a pushpin to see how many pix were shot in that area. You can pinch or unpinch the map to zoom in or out and find pictures by town or neighborhood. We think Places is really cool and gives you a nice sense of where you've been and whom you've been there with.

Before leaving this photography section, we want to steer you to the App Store, which we explore in greater depth in Chapter 15. Hundreds of photography-related apps, many free, are available. These apps come from a variety of sources and range from Omer Shoor's Photogene (a 99¢ suite of photo-editing tools) to Color Splash from Pocket Pixels, Inc., a 99¢ program that lets you convert color photos to black-and-white while keeping certain details in color. You can even try a free version.

You have just passed Photography 101 on the iPhone. We trust that the coursework was, forgive the pun, a snap.

Tap to find pictures taken in this area

Tap to reveal pictures in this area

Figure 9-13: Finding pictures by location.

You Oughta Be in Pictures: Video on Your iPhone

In This Chapter

▶ Finding videos

▶ Playing videos on your iPhone

▶ Shooting video

▶ Editing footage

*P*icture this scene: The smell of popcorn permeates the room as you and your family congregate to watch the latest Hollywood blockbuster. A motion picture soundtrack swells up. The images on the screen are stunning. And all eyes are fixed on the iPhone.

Okay, here's the reality check. The iPhone is not going to replace a wall-sized high-definition television as the centerpiece of your home theater, even on the larger 4-inch screen of the iPhone 5. But we want to emphasize that on that glorious widescreen display, as well as the 3½-inch displays on older models, watching movies and other videos on the iPhone can be a cinematic delight.

As you discover later in this chapter, you can even shoot your own blockbuster footage. And the iPhone 4S and 5 are capable of capturing video in the top 1,080p high-definition video standard. Let's get on with the show!

Are we compatible?

Sidebars in this book are considered optional reading, but we secretly hope you digest every word because you may discover something, or be entertained, or both. But you can safely skip the material contained herein — no matter how much you want to curry favor with your teachers, um, authors.

Still, we present this list of video formats supported by the iPhone as a courtesy to those with geek aspirations (you know who you are). And just to point out how absurd the world of tech can sound sometimes — even from a consumer-friendly company such as Apple — we are quoting this passage from Apple's website verbatim:

"Video formats supported: H.264 video up to 1080p, 30 frames per second, High Profile level 4.1 with AAC-LC audio up to 160 Kbps, 48kHz, stereo audio in .m4v, .mp4, and .mov file formats; MPEG-4 video up to 2.5 Mbps, 640 by 480 pixels, 30 frames per second, Simple Profile with AAC-LC audio up to 160 Kbps per channel, 48kHz, stereo audio in .m4v, .mp4, and .mov file formats; Motion JPEG (M-JPEG) up to 35 Mbps,

1280 by 720 pixels, 30 frames per second, audio in ulaw, PCM stereo audio in .avi file format."

Got all that? Here's the takeaway message: The iPhone works with a whole bunch of video, but not everything you'll want to watch will make it through. And you may not know if the video will play until you try. Indeed, several Internet video standards — most notably Adobe Flash, which the late Apple CEO Steve Jobs had publicly denigrated — are not supported. Then again, even Adobe is no longer supporting mobile Flash. And we should probably point out that some video that will play on an iPod Classic or iPod Nano might not play in the iPhone for technical reasons we won't bore you with right now.

Armed with the appropriate utility software, you may be able to convert some nonworking video to an iPhone-friendly format. If something doesn't play now, it may well in the future — because Apple has the capability to upgrade the iPhone through software.

Finding Stuff to Watch

The video you'll watch on the iPhone generally falls into one of four categories:

- **Movies, TV shows, and music videos that you've downloaded directly to your iPhone or that reside in iTunes software on your PC or Mac that you synchronize with your iPhone:** You can watch these by tapping the Videos icon on the Home screen, and then tapping the Store button at the upper-left side of the screen, or by tapping the iTunes button on the Home screen, and then tapping Videos at the bottom of the screen. For more on synchronization, check out Chapter 3.

Apple's own iTunes Store features dedicated sections for purchasing episodes of TV shows (from *Modern Family* to *Hawaii Five-O*) and movies (such as *The Avengers* or *Citizen Kane*). The typical price as of this writing is $1.99 per episode for TV shows. You can also buy complete seasons of certain series. For example, *Dexter, Season 6* costs $34.99 in high definition and $22.99 in standard definition. Movies generally fetch between $9.99 and $14.99, at least for features, though you'll find bargains below these, um, ticket prices, some for as little as 99¢.

You can also rent some movies, typically for $2.99 or $3.99, but again sometimes for less and sometimes more. You'll have 30 days to begin watching a rented flick, and 24 hours to finish once you've started. Such films appear in their own Rented Movies section in the video list, which you get to by tapping iTunes⇔Videos⇔Library, or by tapping the Video app directly on the Home screen. The number of days before your rental expires is displayed.

✔ **The boatload of video podcasts and courseware, featured in the free Podcasts and iTunes U apps, both from Apple:** Podcasts started out as another form of Internet radio, although instead of listening to live streams, you downloaded files onto your computer or iPod to take in at your leisure. Lots of audio podcasts are still available, but the focus here is on video. You can watch free episodes that cover *Sesame Street* videos, sports, investing, political shows, and much more. And you can take a seminar at Harvard, Stanford, and other prestigious institutions. Indeed, iTunes U boasts more than 250,000 free lectures from around the world, many of them videos. Better still: no homework, no grades, and no tuition.

✔ **Homegrown videos from the popular YouTube Internet site or the third-party YouTube app:** Apple used to think so highly of YouTube that it devoted a dedicated Home screen icon to the site. But Apple ditched YouTube when iOS 6 came along. As readers of the business pages know, Apple and Google, which owns YouTube, are major rivals. You can still fetch a free YouTube app from Google for free in the iTunes Store.

✔ **The movies you've created on your iPhone, iPod touch, or iPad, in iMovie software or other software on the Mac or, for that matter, other programs on the PC:** Plus all the other videos you may have downloaded from the Internet.

You may have to prepare these videos so that they'll play on your iPhone. To do so, highlight the video in question after it resides in your iTunes library. Go to the Advanced menu in iTunes on your computer, and click Create iPod or iPhone Version.

For more on compatibility, check out the "Are we compatible?" sidebar in this chapter (but read it at your own risk).

Playing Video

Now that you know what you want to watch, here's how to watch it:

1. **On the Home screen, tap the Videos icon.**

   Your list of videos typically pops up (though what appears may differ depending on your setup). Videos are segregated by category — Movies, TV Shows, Music Videos, as shown in Figure 10-1 — although other categories such as Rented Movies and Podcasts may also appear. Listings are accompanied by thumbnail images and the length of the video.

2. **Flick your finger to scroll through the list, and then tap the video you want to play.**

   You may see a spinning circle for just a moment and then the video will begin. But on the most recent iPhones, especially the snappy 4S and the 5, the video starts playing without any noticeable delay.

3. **Turn the device to its side because the iPhone plays video only in landscape, or widescreen, mode.**

   For movies, this is a great thing. You can watch flicks as the filmmaker intended, in a cinematic aspect ratio.

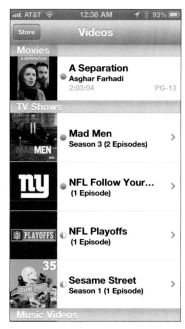

Figure 10-1: Choosing the video to watch.

4. **Now that the video is playing, tap the screen to display the controls shown in Figure 10-2.**

5. **Tap the controls that follow, as needed:**

   - To play or pause the video, tap the play/pause button.

   - Drag the volume slider to the right to raise the volume and to the left to lower it. Alternatively, use the physical volume buttons to control the audio levels. If the video is oriented properly, the buttons will be on the bottom-left of the iPhone.

   - Tap the restart/rewind button to restart the video or tap and hold the same button to rewind.

   - Tap and hold the fast forward button to advance the video. Or skip ahead by dragging the playhead along the scrubber bar.

- Tap the scale button to toggle between filling the entire screen with video or fitting the video to the screen. (You won't see this button in every movie.) Alternatively, you can double-tap the video to go back and forth between fitting and filling the screen.

Fitting the video to the screen displays the film in its theatrical aspect ratio. But you may see black bars above or below the video (or to its sides), which some people don't like. *Filling* the entire screen with the video may crop or trim the sides or top of the picture, so you aren't seeing the complete scene that the camera operator shot.

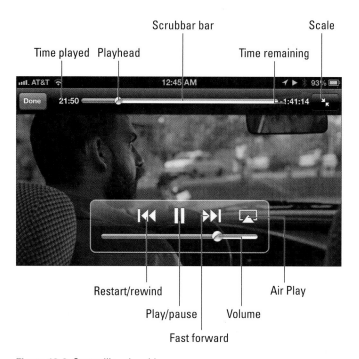

Figure 10-2: Controlling the video.

6. **Tap the screen again to make the controls go away (or just wait for them to go away on their own).**

7. **Tap Done when you've finished watching. (You have to summon the controls back if they're not already present.)**

   You return to the iPhone's video menu screen.

On some movies, you can tap a control to summon a film's Chapter guide (it's not shown in Figure 10-2). The control resembles three bars, one on top of another, each with a period to the left of the bar.

To delete a video manually, swipe left or right over the video listing. Then tap the small red Delete button that materializes. To confirm your intention, tap the larger Delete button that appears.

Shooting Video

The 3GS was the first iPhone to let you shoot video. Then the iPhone 4 joined the video party. More recently, the iPhone 4S and the iPhone 5 took the device to new heights.

Both the 4S and 5 produce high-definition video at what techies refer to as *1,080p*. The iPhone 5's front-facing camera plays in the high-def league, too, but at the lower *720p* video resolution standard. The front camera on the 4S does not do high-def. And neither do either of the cameras on the iPhone 4.

Moreover, the iPhone 5 made further improvements to the video stabilization feature introduced in the 4S. And through a process known as temporal noise reduction, you can shoot terrific video even in dim light.

Here's how to shoot video on these latest phone models. Note that you can capture video in portrait or landscape mode:

1. **Tap the Camera icon on the Home screen.**

2. **Drag the little on-screen button at the bottom-right corner of the display from the camera position to the video camera position, as shown in Figure 10-3.**

3. **Tap the big round button with the smaller red circle at the bottom center to begin shooting a scene.**

   The red circle blinks and you see a counter timing the length of your video at the bottom left if you hold the phone in portrait mode or bottom right in landscape.

4. **When you're finished, tap the red circle again to stop recording.**

   Your video is automatically saved to your camera roll, alongside any other saved videos and still pictures.

Flash   Front/rear camera

Camera roll   Camera/video switch

Start or stop capturing video

Figure 10-3: Lights, camera, action!

You can tap the LED flash button to shine a light while you record video. And, as with taking digital stills, you can switch from the front to the rear camera before starting to shoot video. But you can't switch from the front to back camera while you're capturing video. Remember too that the flash is available only with the rear camera.

You can capture still images while you're shooting video. Tap the camera icon that appears when you're shooting video.

Editing what you shot

We assume that you captured some really great stuff — as well as some footage that belongs on the cutting room floor. That's not a problem because you can perform simple edits right on your iPhone. Just do the following:

1. **Tap a video recording to display the on-screen controls shown in Figure 10-4.**

Tap to trim clip or create newly trimmed video

Drag either edge to trim

Figure 10-4: Trimming video.

2. **Drag the start and end points along the timeline to select only the video you want to keep.**

   Hold your finger over the section to expand the timeline to make it easier to apply your edits. You can tap the play button to preview the edit.

3. **Tap Trim.**

4. Decide what to do with your trimmed clip.

You can tap Trim Original to permanently remove scenes from the original clip. Or tap Save as New Clip to create a newly trimmed video clip; the original video is unaffected and the new clip is stored in the Camera Roll. Or tap Cancel to start over.

If you want to do more ambitious editing, check out iMovie for iPhone, a $4.99 app that resembles an ultralite version of iMovie for Mac computers.

After loading the video clips you've shot on the phone, iMovie lets you go Hollywood, within limits. Apple supplies eight custom themes — Modern, Bright, Travel, Playful, Neon, Simple, CNN iReport, and News — for adding titles and transitions to your budding masterpiece. Custom soundtracks are available, though you can also select a tune from your own music library. But what's really cool are the movie trailers you can make, with a dozen possible styles: Adrenaline, Bollywood, Coming of Age, Expedition, Fairy Tale, Narrative, Retro, Romance, Scary, Superhero, Swashbuckler, and Teen. When you've finished editing, you can export the movie in one of three file sizes and send the project to iTunes. Or you can send it to your camera roll, Facebook, Vimeo, CNN iReport, or YouTube.

Sharing video

 Unlike other video on your iPhone, you can play back what you've just shot in portrait or landscape mode. And if the video is any good (and why wouldn't it be), you're likely going to want to share it with others. To do so, display the playback controls by tapping the screen, and then tap the icon almost all the way to the left of the screen (the icon is shown in the margin). You can e-mail the video, include it in a message, or send it to YouTube. And speaking of YouTube, read on.

Watching video on TV

The Retina display on the iPhone is worth boasting about, but sometimes you want to watch videos on your iPhone on a larger screen television. Apple affords you several ways to do so:

✔ **Add a cable:** Apple is all too happy to sell you a cable to connect the iPhone to a TV. The cable you choose depends on your TV setup, the available ports, and the iPhone model you own. Wired choices from Apple include a digital A/V adapter and HDMI cable (iPhone 4 or 4S only); a composite A/V cable; and a VGA adapter and VGA cable. The 5 is the first iPhone to use Apple's new Lightning connector. At press time, no special accessories were available for iPhone 5, but we're hopeful that Apple and its partners would likely have delivered Lightning versions of these A/V cables by the time you read this.

✔ **Use wireless streaming:** You've heard us mention AirPlay, a wonderful feature for people who have iPhones and Apple TV boxes. As you're watching video, tap the AirPlay icon (labeled in Figure 10-2), and then choose an Apple TV unit from the list of AirPlay devices that shows up. If all goes well, the video you're watching now appears like magic on your TV set. If all doesn't go well, make sure the Apple TV is tapping into the same wireless network as your phone.

If you have an iPhone 4S or 5, you can take AirPlay streaming one step further and exploit the new AirPlay Mirroring feature. It lets you share or mirror to a TV anything on the iPhone screen — not just videos or music, but also games, pictures, web pages, and so on. As you rotate the iPhone from portrait to landscape or back, AirPlay Mirroring follows suit on the big screen. We think you'll agree that the feature is cool and useful, especially if you want to share what you're watching or doing with a larger audience. Note, however, that the quality of the experience is related to the quality of your Internet connection.

Restricting video (and other) usage

If you've given an iPhone to your kid or someone who works for you, you may not want that person spending time watching videos. You want him or her to do something more productive, such as homework or the quarterly budget.

That's where parental (or might we say "Mean Boss") restrictions come in. Please note that the use of this iron-fist tool can make you unpopular.

Tap Settings➪General➪Restrictions. Then tap Enable Restrictions. You'll be asked to establish or enter a previously established passcode. Twice. Having done so, in the Allowed Content section, tap Movies, TV Shows, and any other content you want to restrict. Choose the Don't Allow option for each, or choose a movie or TV show rating (PG or whatever) or both that you feel comfortable having the youngsters watch. If you made any specific app a no-no, the icon for that app is missing in action when you return to the Home screen. Same goes for any other restricted activities. To restore privileges, go back into Restrictions and tap Disable Restrictions. You'll have to reenter your passcode.

You can apply restrictions also to Safari, the Camera app, FaceTime, iTunes, iBookstore, Siri, and more, as you see when we delve into Settings further (see Chapter 14).

With that, let's roll the closing credits to this chapter.

Part IV
The Internet iPhone

The commercials for the iPhone used to say that it provides you with the real Internet — and, for the most part, it does. This part looks at the Internet components of your phone, starting with a chapter covering the best web browser ever to grace a handheld device, Safari. We reveal how to take advantage of links and bookmarks and how to open multiple web pages at the same time. We show you how to run a web search on an iPhone. And we spend time discussing two, three, and four-letter acronyms such as EDGE, 3G, 4G, LTE, and Wi-Fi — the wireless networks that are compatible with the device.

Then we visit the Mail program and see how easy it is to set up e-mail accounts and send and receive real honest-to-goodness e-mail messages and attachments.

Finally, we examine four superb web-enabled applications. In Maps and in Compass, you discover your location and orientation, determine the businesses and restaurants you'd like to visit, get driving directions and the traffic en route, and take advantage of the iPhone's capability to find you. In Stocks, you get the lowdown on how well the equities in your portfolio are performing. And in Weather, you get the forecast for the city you live in and those you plan on visiting.

11

Going On a Mobile Safari

*"T*he Internet in your pocket."

That's what Apple promised the iPhone would bring to the public when the product was announced in January 2007. In the years since, Apple has come tantalizingly close to delivering on that pledge.

For years, the cell phone industry offered a watered-down mobile version of the Internet, but their approaches typically fell far short of what people had come to experience while sitting in front of a computer.

Apple, however, has managed for the most part to replicate the real-deal Internet with the iPhone. Web pages on an iPhone look like web pages on a Windows PC or Mac, right down to swanky graphics and pictures — and at least some video and web-based games.

In this chapter, you find out how to navigate through cyberspace on your iPhone.

 **Reading List**

 **History**

iCloud Tabs

Surfin' Dude

A version of the Apple Safari web browser is a major reason that the Net on the iPhone is very much like the Net you've come to expect on a computer. Safari for the Mac (and for Windows) is one of the best web browsers in the computer business. And in our view, Safari is one of the very best cell phone browsers.

Exploring the browser

We start our cyberexpedition with a quick tour of the Safari browser. Take a gander at Figure 11-1: Not all browser controls found on a PC or Mac are present. Still, Safari on the iPhone has a familiar look and feel. We describe these controls and others throughout this chapter.

Address field

Navigation bar   Reload web page

Search

Bookmarks

Pages

Mail, Message, Twitter, Facebook, Add to Home screen, Print, Copy, Bookmark, Add to Reading list

Next web page

Previous web page

Figure 11-1: The iPhone's Safari browser.

Before plunging in, we recommend a little detour. Read the "Living on the EDGE" sidebar to find out more about the wireless networks that let you surf the web on the iPhone in the first place.

Blasting off into cyberspace

We told you how great web pages look on the iPhone, so we bet you're eager to get going. We won't hold you back much longer.

When you tap the address field (as you will in a moment), the virtual keyboard appears. You may notice one thing about the keyboard right off the bat: Because so many web addresses end with the suffix .com (pronounced "dot com"), the virtual keyboard has a dedicated .com key. For other common web suffixes — .edu, .net, .us, and .org — press and hold the .com key and choose the relevant suffix.

Of equal importance, both the period (.) and the slash (/) are on the virtual keyboard because you frequently use them when you enter web addresses. And because spaces aren't allowed in URLs, the keyboard does not have a space bar.

The moment you tap a single letter, you see a list of web addresses that match those letters. For example, if you tap the letter *s* (as we did in the example in Figure 11-2, left), you see web listings for CNN Sports Illustrated (`http://sportsillustrated.cnn.com`) and CBS SportsLine (`http://cbsportsline.com`), among others. Tapping *U* or *H* instead may display listings for *USA TODAY* or the *Houston Chronicle* (shameless plugs for the media properties where Ed and Bob are columnists). Scroll to see more suggestions and the virtual keyboard slides out of view, as shown in Figure 11-2, right.

Figure 11-2: Web pages that match your search letter.

TECHNICAL STUFF

Living on the EDGE

You can't typically make or receive phone calls on a wireless phone without tapping into a cellular network. And you can't prowl the virtual corridors of cyberspace (or send e-mail) on a mobile phone without accessing a wireless *data* network. In the United States, the iPhone works with Wi-Fi, AT&T EDGE, AT&T 3G, and an AT&T network called HSDPA, which is an even faster network that many consider 4G, or fourth generation. The iPhone also works with an advanced variant DC-HSDPA.

Few dispute that the even speedier LTE (Long Term Evolution) network is 4G. And the iPhone 5 is the first model to tap into LTE, from AT&T, Sprint, and Verizon Wireless. Verizon has the most built-out LTE network in the U.S. by a long shot, as of this writing, followed by AT&T. Sprint is still a relative LTE newbie.

The iPhone is also compatible with slower Verizon and Sprint 3G CDMA networks. (And it works also with another wireless technology, Bluetooth, but that serves a different purpose and is addressed in Chapter 14.)

The iPhone automatically hops onto the fastest available network, which is almost always *Wi-Fi,* the friendly moniker applied to the far geekier 802.11 designation. And "eight-oh-two-dot-eleven" (as it's pronounced) is followed by a letter — typically, *b, g,* or *n.* So you see it written as 802.11b, 802.11g, and so on. The letters relate to technical standards that have to do with the speed and range you can expect from the Wi-Fi configuration. But we don't want you to lose sleep over this issue if you haven't boned up on this geeky alphabet.

For the record, because the iPhone adheres to the 802.11a, 802.11b, 802.11g, and 802.11n standards — as well as the dual-band 2.4 GHz and 5 GHz spectrums — you're good to go pretty much anywhere you can find Wi-Fi. These days, Internet hotspots are in lots of places: airports, colleges, coffeehouses, libraries, public parks, and elsewhere. If you have to present a password to take advantage of a hotspot because it costs money or you have to authenticate your credentials, you can enter the password by using the iPhone's virtual keyboard.

Still, Wi-Fi isn't ubiquitous yet and neither is 4G, which leads us, at times, right back to CDMA or EDGE or 3G. EDGE is shorthand for Enhanced Datarate for GSM Evolution (good to know only if you're on a million-dollar game show) and is based on the global GSM phone standard. And 3G stands for third generation; 3G websites typically download two times faster than EDGE, in our experience, and sometimes even faster. But, again, Wi-Fi downloads are even zippier.

The bottom line is this: Depending on where you live, work, or travel, you may feel like you're teetering on the EDGE in terms of acceptable Internet coverage, especially if Wi-Fi or true 3G is beyond your reach. We've used the iPhone in areas where web pages load extremely slowly, not-so-vaguely reminiscent of dial-up telephone modems for your computer.

But the picture is indeed brightening. Wi-Fi and 3G are in more places than ever before. Better yet, the same can be said for 4G. The iPhone not only loads web pages a lot faster but also manages to do so with longer-lasting batteries.

The iPhone has two ways to determine websites to suggest when you tap certain letters. One method is the websites you already bookmarked from the Safari or Internet Explorer browser on your computer (and synchronized, as described in Chapter 3). More on bookmarks later in this chapter.

The second method iPhone uses when suggesting websites when you tap a particular letter is to suggest sites from the History list — those cyberdestinations where you recently hung your hat. Because history repeats itself, we also tackle that topic later in this chapter.

You might as well open your first web page now. It's a full HTML page, to borrow from techie lingo. Do the following:

1. **Tap the Safari icon at the bottom of the Home screen.**

   This icon is another member of the Fantastic Four (along with Phone, Mail, and Music).

2. **Tap the address field (refer to Figure 11-1).**

   If you can't see the address field, tap the status bar, or scroll to the top of the screen.

3. **Begin typing the web address on the virtual keyboard that slides up from the bottom of the screen.**

   The web address is also called the _URL_ (Uniform Resource Locator, for trivia buffs).

4. **Do one of the following:**

   - **To accept one of the bookmarked (or other) sites that show up on the list, merely tap the name.**

     Safari automatically fills in the URL in the address field and takes you where you want to go.

   - **Keep tapping the proper keyboard characters until you enter the complete web address for the site you have in mind, and then tap Go in the lower-right corner of the keyboard.**

     It's not necessary to type _www_ at the beginning of a URL. So, if you want to visit `www.theonion.com` (for example), typing _theonion.com_ or even just _onion.com_ is sufficient to transport you to the humor site.

To erase a URL you've erroneously typed, tap the address field and then tap the circled X to the right of the field.

When you rotate the iPhone sideways, you can tap the full-screen icon and display a web page in full-screen landscape mode. For example, check out Figure 11-3, which shows the landscape view of Figure 11-1.

Even though Safari on the iPhone can render web pages the way they're meant to be displayed on a computer, every so often you may run into a site that serves up the light, or mobile, version of the website, sometimes known as a WAP (Wireless Application Protocol) site. Graphics may be stripped down on these sites. Alas, the producers of these sites may be unwittingly discriminating against you for dropping in on them by using a cell phone. Never mind that the cell phone in this case is an iPhone. You have our permission to berate these site producers with letters, e-mails, and phone calls until they get with the program.

Full-screen mode

Figure 11-3: Tap the two opposite arrows to go full screen.

I Can See Clearly Now

If you know how to open a web page (if you don't, read the preceding section, "Blasting off into cyberspace"), we can show you how radically simple it is to zoom in on the pages so that you can read what you want to read and see what you want to see, without enlisting a magnifying glass.

Try these neat tricks:

- **Double-tap the screen so that the portion of the text you want to read fills up the entire screen:** It takes just a second before the screen comes into focus. By way of example, check out Figure 11-4. It shows two views of the same *Sports Illustrated* web page. In the first view, you see what the page looks like when you first open it. In the second one, you see how the picture takes over much more of the screen after you double-tap it. To return to the first view, double-tap the screen again.

- **Pinch the page:** Sliding your thumb and index finger together and then spreading them apart (or as we like to say, *unpinching*) also zooms in and out of a page. Again, wait just a moment for the screen to come into focus.

- **Press down on a page and drag it in all directions, or flick through a page from top to bottom:** You're panning and scrolling, baby.

- **Rotate the iPhone to its side:** Watch what happens to the White House website, shown in Figure 11-5. It reorients from portrait to a widescreen view. The keyboard is also wider, making it a little easier to enter a new URL.

Figure 11-4: Doing a double-tap dance zooms in and out.

Figure 11-5: Going wide.

Opening multiple web pages at a time

When we surf the web on a desktop PC or laptop, we rarely go to a single web page and call it a day. In fact, we often have multiple web pages open at the same time. Sometimes, several pages are open because we choose to hop around the web without closing the pages we visit. Sometimes, a link (see the next section) automatically opens a new page without shuttering the old one. (If these additional pages are advertisements, they aren't always welcome.)

Safari on the iPhone lets you open multiple pages simultaneously. Tap the Pages icon (refer to Figure 11-1), on the right side of the navigation bar at the bottom of the screen, and then tap New Page on the screen that pops up next. Tap the address field and then type a URL for your new page.

The number inside the Pages icon lets you know how many pages are open. To see the other open pages, flick your finger to the left or right, as shown in Figure 11-6, left. Tap a page to have it take over the full screen, as shown in Figure 11-6, right.

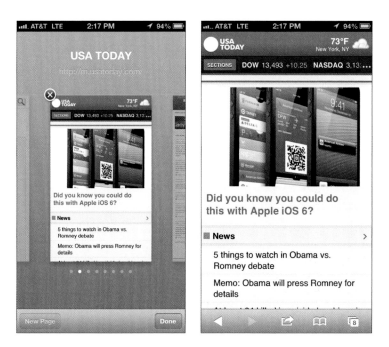

Figure 11-6: After tapping a web page, it appears full-screen.

To close one of your open web pages, tap the white X in the red circle, which appears in the upper-left corner of each open page in miniature (see figure on left).

Looking at lovable links

Surfing the web would be a real drag if you had to enter a URL every time you want to navigate from one page to another. That's why bookmarks are so useful. And, it's why handy links are welcome too. Because Safari functions on the iPhone the same way browsers work on your PC or Mac, links on the iPhone behave much the same way, too.

Text links that transport you from one site to another are underlined or appear in a different color from other text on the page. Merely tap the link to go directly to that site. But tapping on some other links (as well as pressing and holding) leads to different outcomes:

- ✐ **Open a map:** Tapping on a map launches the Apple Maps app that is, um, addressed in Chapter 13.

- ✐ **Prepare an e-mail:** Tap an e-mail address and the iPhone opens the Mail program (see the next chapter) and prepopulates the To field with that address. The virtual keyboard is also summoned so that you can add other e-mail addresses and compose a Subject line and message. This shortcut doesn't work in all instances in which an e-mail appears on the web.

- ✐ **Make a phone call:** Tap a phone number embedded in a web page and the iPhone offers to dial it for you. Just tap Call to make it happen, or tap Cancel to forget the whole thing.

To see the URL for a link, press and hold your finger against the link. Use this method also to determine whether a picture has a link. The window that slides up from the bottom of the screen to show you the URL gives you other options. You can tap to open the page (replacing the current one), open a link in a new page, or copy the URL so that you can, say, paste it in a note or in an outgoing e-mail. You can also add the page to a Reading list, as we discuss later in the chapter.

Not every web link cooperates with the iPhone. The iPhone doesn't support some common web standards — most notably sites, animations, and games that rely on Adobe Flash. Given the public stance against Flash by late Apple CEO Steve Jobs — and the fact that Adobe is no longer throwing its weight behind mobile Flash, this void seems unlikely to be addressed any time soon. If pigs start to fly and Apple changes its mind, it could magically distribute a software upgrade to remedy the situation. Don't bet on it. Apple is throwing its own weight behind another emerging video standard called HTML5. In the meantime, if you see an incompatible link, nothing may happen — or a message may appear that you need to install a plug-in, not that you could actually install it.

Book (mark) 'em, Dano

You already know how useful bookmarks are and how you can synchronize bookmarks from the browsers on your computer. It's equally simple to bookmark a web page directly on the iPhone:

1. **Make sure that the page you want to bookmark is open, and tap the action icon, in the bottom-middle area of the screen (as shown in the margin).**

   As you see in Figure 11-7, you have the opportunity to tap Mail, Message, Twitter, Facebook, Add to Home Screen, Print, Copy, Bookmark, and Add to Reading List. Figure 11-8 shows the screen that appears when you tap Bookmark. The Add Bookmark screen arrives with a default name and folder location.

2. **Decide whether to go with the default bookmark name and location:**

   • To accept the default bookmark name and default bookmark folder, tap Save, in the upper-right corner.

   • To change the default bookmark name, tap the X in the circle next to the name, and enter the new title (using the virtual keyboard). Tap Save unless you also want to change the location where the bookmark is saved.

   • To change the location, tap the > symbol in the Bookmarks field, tap the folder where you want the bookmark kept, and tap the Add Bookmark button in the upper-left corner of the screen. Then tap Save.

To open a bookmarked page after you set it up, tap the Bookmarks icon at the bottom of the screen (refer to Figure 11-1) and then tap the appropriate bookmark.

If the bookmark you have in mind is buried inside a folder, tap the folder name first, and then tap the bookmark you want.

The following is what happens if you tap another option instead of Bookmark (refer to Figure 11-7):

✓ **Tap Mail** and the Mail program opens, with a link for the page in the message and the name of the site or page in the Subject line.

✓ **Tap Message** and you can send a link to the web page in a text or an iMessage.

Figure 11-7: On your way to a bookmark or other options.

Figure 11-8: Turning into a bookie.

- ✔ **Tap Twitter** and the iPhone adds the web page to an outgoing Tweet. Of course, you must fill in the rest of the actual post, remembering that Twitter limits you to 140 characters max. Tap Add Location if you want to identify your location at the time you posted your Tweet. If this is your first time attempting to use Twitter on the iPhone, you will be prompted to go to Settings to enter your Twitter username and password.

- ✔ **Tap Facebook** to post the page — and whatever comments you choose to add — to the popular social network. Once again, you can tap Add Location to include your location.

- ✔ **Tap Add to Home Screen** and your iPhone adds the site's icon to your Home screen to let you quickly access the site. Note that the Add to Home Screen icon already shows the logo for the website you are adding or a small image of the page itself.

- ✔ **Tap Print** and the iPhone will search for an AirPrint printer. If you have one, you can choose the number of copies you want. Tap Print to complete the job.

✔ **Tap Copy** and you'll be able to paste a link to the page in question in another app. Just hold down your finger against the screen and then tap Paste.

✔ **Tap Add to Reading List** and you create a bookmark to pages that you want to read later. Then, when you want to access your Reading list, tap the bookmarks icon to summon your list of bookmarks. The Reading List entry sits at the top of your Bookmarks list. Through iCloud, you can keep this Reading list current across all your iOS devices, as well as your PC or Mac.

Altering bookmarks

If a bookmarked site is no longer meaningful, you can change it or get rid of it:

✔ To remove a bookmark (or folder), tap the bookmarks icon and then tap Edit, at the bottom-left corner of the display. Tap the red circle next to the bookmark you want to toss off the list, and then tap Delete.

✔ To change a bookmark's name or location, tap Edit and then tap the bookmark. The Edit Bookmark screen appears, with the name, URL, and location of the bookmark already filled in. Tap the fields you want to change. In the Name field, tap the X in the gray circle and then use the keyboard to enter a new title. In the Location field, tap the > symbol and scroll up or down the list until you find a new home for your bookmark. Tap that new destination.

✔ To create a new folder for your bookmarks, tap Edit and then tap the New Folder button. Enter the name of the new folder and choose where to put it.

✔ To move a bookmark up or down on a list, tap Edit and then drag the three bars to the right of the bookmark's name.

Viewing open pages on other devices

With the Safari version shipped in iOS 6, Apple introduced a feature called iCloud Tabs that lets you venture into cyberspace to look at web pages open on your other iOS devices and computers. Tap the bookmarks icon (refer to Figure 11-1), and tap iCloud Tabs. Up pops a screen like the one shown in Figure 11-9. Tap any listings to access that page.

Figure 11-9: Browsing from one device to another through iCloud.

If for some reason you don't see iCloud Tabs after tapping the bookmarks icon, head to Settings, tap iCloud, and make sure that the option for Safari is turned on.

Letting history repeat itself

Sometimes, you want to revisit a site that you failed to bookmark, but you can't remember the darn destination or what led you there in the first place. Good thing you can study the history books.

Safari records the pages you visit and keeps the logs on hand for several days. Tap the bookmarks icon, tap History, and then tap the day you think you hung out at the site. When you find the listing, tap it. You're about to make your triumphant return.

To clear your history so that nobody else can trace your steps — and just what is it you're hiding? — tap Clear at the bottom of the History list. Alternatively, on the Home page, tap Settings⇨Safari⇨Clear History. In both instances, per usual, you have a chance to back out without wiping the slate clean.

Launching a mobile search mission

Most of us spend a lot of time using search engines on the Internet. And the search engines we summon most often are Google, Yahoo!, and Microsoft Bing. So it goes on the iPhone.

Although you can certainly use the virtual keyboard to type *google.com, yahoo.com,* or *bing.com* in the Safari address field, Apple doesn't require that tedious effort. Instead, you tap into Google, Yahoo!, or Bing by using the search field (labeled in Figure 11-1). The default search engine of choice on the iPhone is Google. Yahoo! or Bing must come off the bench.

To conduct a web search on the iPhone, tap the search field. It expands and temporarily replaces the address bar at the top of the screen, and the virtual keyboard slides up from the bottom, as shown in Figure 11-10.

Enter your search term or phrase, and then tap the Search button in the lower-right corner of the keyboard to generate pages of results. You see search suggestions as you start tapping some letters. In Figure 11-10, for example, typing the letters *le* yields such suggestions as Lebron James and Lexus. Tap any search results that look promising or keep tapping out letters.

As you'll note in Figure 11-10, any On This Page matches will also be shown (though you may have to scroll down to see them).

To switch the search box from Google to Yahoo! to Bing or back, go to the Home page and tap Settings⇨Safari⇨Search Engine, and then tap to choose one search behemoth over the other.

As we point out in Chapter 2, you can search the web also through Spotlight. Merely enter your search term in the Spotlight search field and then tap Search Web. Doing so will initiate a Google search, even if you've chosen Yahoo! or Bing as your search engine. (To find Spotlight search, flick to the left of the first Home page.)

Saving web pictures

You can capture most pictures you come across on a website — but be mindful of any potential copyright violations, depending on what you plan to do with the image. To copy an image from a website, press your finger against the image and tap the Save Image button that slides up, as shown in Figure 11-11. Saved images end up in your camera roll, from which they can be synced back to a computer. If you tap Copy instead, you can paste the image into an e-mail or as a link in a program such as Notes.

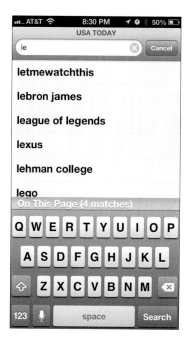

Figure 11-10: Running a Google search on the iPhone.

Figure 11-11: Hold your finger against a picture in Safari to save it to the iPhone.

Reading clutter-free web pages

It's all too easy to get distracted reading web pages nowadays, what with ads and other clutter surrounding the stuff you actually want to take in. So pay attention to the Reader button that often appears in the web address field, as shown in Figure 11-12 (left) next to the URL of this *USA TODAY* news article. Tap Reader to see the same article as it appears in Figure 11-12 (right), without the needless diversions.

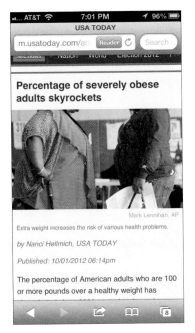 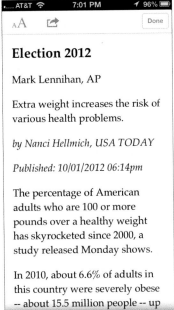

Figure 11-12: Reducing clutter when reading a web story.

 Tap the font icons (small a, big A) to adjust the font size. Tap the action icon (shown in the margin) to add the article as a bookmark or to your Reading list, mail it, Tweet it, print it, or summon other options.

Smart Safari Settings

Along with the riches galore found on the Internet are places in cyberspace where you're hassled. You might want to take pains to protect your privacy and maintain your security.

Return with us now to Settings, by tapping the Settings icon on the Home page. Now tap Safari.

You may have already discovered how to change the default search engine and clear the record of the sites you visited through Settings. Now see what else you can do:

- ✔ **Fill out forms with AutoFill:** When AutoFill is turned on, Safari can automatically fill out web forms by using your personal contact information, usernames, and passwords, or information from other contacts in your address book.

- ✔ **Open links:** You can determine whether links will open in a new page or in the background.

- ✔ **Browse privately:** Don't want to leave any tracks while you surf? Don't worry, we won't ask and we won't tell. Turn on Private Browsing, for a "what happens in Safari stays in Safari" type of tool. Those truly bent on staying private will also want to tap Clear History, as mentioned earlier in this chapter.

- ✔ **Cookies:** We're not talking about crumbs you may have accidentally dropped on the iPhone. *Cookies* are tiny bits of information that a website places on the iPhone when you visit so that the site recognizes you when you return. You need not assume the worst: Most cookies are benign and many are beneficial.

    If this concept wigs you out, you can take action: Tap Clear Cookies and Data and then tap it again (rather than tap Cancel). Separately, tap Accept Cookies and then tap Never. Theoretically, you will never again receive cookies on the iPhone. A good middle ground is to accept cookies only from the sites you visit. To do so, tap From Visited. You can also tap Always to accept cookies from all sites. Tap Safari to return to the main Safari settings page.

    If you don't set the iPhone to accept cookies, certain web pages don't load properly, and sites such as Amazon and organizations you belong to will no longer recognize you when you appear at their doors.

- ✔ **Use Cellular Data for Reading List:** When turned on, this option lets you use your cellular network to save Reading list items from iCloud so you can read them offline.

- ✔ **Turn JavaScript on or off:** This setting is on when you see the blue On button and off when you see the white Off button. Programmers use JavaScript to add various kinds of functionality to web pages, such as displaying the date and time or changing images when you access them. In the past, some security risks have also been associated with JavaScript, though none we know of affect mobile Safari.

✔ **Receive fraud warnings:** By turning this setting on, you'll be warned when you inadvertently visit a fraudulent website.

✔ **Block pop-ups:** Pop-ups are those web pages that show up whether you want them to or not. Often, they're annoying advertisements. But at some sites, you will welcome the appearance of pop-ups, so remember to turn off blocking under such circumstances.

✔ **Determine Advanced settings:** The Safari settings under Advanced aren't meant for regular folks. You'll find information here on website data, and a Web Inspector tool that can assist techies in resolving web page errors when your phone is connected by cable to a computer.

Taming Safari is just the start of exploiting the Internet on the iPhone. In upcoming chapters, you discover how to master e-mail, maps, and more.

12

The E-Mail Must Get Through

In This Chapter

▸ Setting up your accounts

▸ Reading and managing e-mail messages

▸ Searching for e-mail messages

▸ Sending e-mail messages

▸ Setting e-mail preferences

C hapter 5 shows you how well your iPhone sends SMS text messages, MMS messages, and iMessages. But such messages aren't the iPhone's only written communication trick, not by a long shot. One of the niftiest things your iPhone can do is send and receive real, honest-to-gosh e-mail, using Mail, its modern e-mail app. It's designed not only to send and receive text e-mail messages, but also to handle rich HTML e-mail messages — formatted e-mail messages complete with font and type styles and embedded graphics.

Furthermore, your iPhone can read several types of file attachments, including PDF, Microsoft Word, PowerPoint, and Excel documents, as well as stuff produced through Apple's own iWork software. Better still, all this sending and receiving of text, graphics, and documents can happen in the background so that you can surf the web or talk to a friend while your iPhone quietly and efficiently handles your e-mail behind the scenes.

The Mail app is compatible with the most popular e-mail providers: Yahoo! Mail, Gmail, AOL, and Apple's own iCloud service, a remnant of the now defunct online MobileMe service. As part of iCloud, Apple issues you a free, ad-free iCloud.com e-mail address.

ᴗool video anᴗ ᵢ

ᴗheck it out

Video.MOV

As you discover in this chapter, you can access a unified inbox of all your e-mail accounts (assuming you have multiple accounts). Moreover, you can organize messages by *thread,* or conversation. And you can bestow VIP status to your most important senders.

Prep Work: Setting Up Your Accounts

First things first. To use Mail, you need an e-mail address. If you have broadband Internet access (that is, a cable modem, FiOS, or DSL), you probably received one or more e-mail addresses when you signed up. If you're one of the handful of readers who doesn't already have an e-mail account, you can get one for free from Yahoo! (`http://mail.yahoo.com`), Google (`http://mail.google.com`), Microsoft (`www.outlook.com` or `www.hotmail.com`), AOL (`www.aol.com`), or one of many other service providers.

Many (if not all) free e-mail providers add a small bit of advertising at the end of your outgoing messages. If you'd rather not be a billboard for your e-mail provider, either use the address(es) that came with your broadband Internet access (*yourname*@comcast.net or *yourname*@att.net, for example) or pay a few dollars a month for a premium e-mail account that doesn't tack advertising (or anything else) onto your messages. As mentioned, you can get a free e-mail account as part of Apple's iCloud service.

Set up your account the easy way

Chapter 3 explains the option of automatically syncing the e-mail accounts on your computer with your iPhone. If you chose that option, your e-mail accounts should be configured on your iPhone already. You may proceed directly to the later section, "Darling, You Send Me (E-Mail)."

If you haven't yet chosen that option but want to set up your account the easy way now, go to Chapter 3 and read the section on syncing mail accounts with the iPhone. Then you, too, can proceed directly to the "Darling, You Send Me (E-Mail)" section.

Set up your account the less easy way

If you don't want to sync the e-mail accounts on your computer, you can set up an e-mail account on your iPhone manually. It's not quite as easy as clicking a box and syncing your iPhone, but it's not rocket science either.

If you have no e-mail accounts on your iPhone, the first time you launch Mail, you're walked through the following procedure. If you have one or more e-mail accounts on your iPhone already and want to add a new account manually, start on the Home screen by tapping Settings➪Mail, Contacts, Calendars➪Add Account.

Either way, you should now be staring at the Add Account screen, shown in Figure 12-1. Proceed to one of the next two sections, depending on your e-mail account.

Setting up an e-mail account with the Big Guys

If your account is with Apple's own iCloud service, Google's Gmail, Yahoo!, AOL, or Windows Live Hotmail, tap the appropriate button on the Add Account screen now. If you're setting up company e-mail through Microsoft Exchange, skip to the "Set up corporate e-mail" section. If your account is with a provider other than the ones listed, tap the Other button and skip to the next section.

Enter your name, e-mail address, and password, as shown in Figure 12-2. The description field is usually filled in automatically with the content you have in the address field, but you can replace that text with your own description (such as Work or Personal).

Tap the Next button in the upper-right corner of the screen. Your e-mail provider will verify your credentials. If you pass muster, that's all there is to setting up your account.

Figure 12-1: Tap a button to add an account.

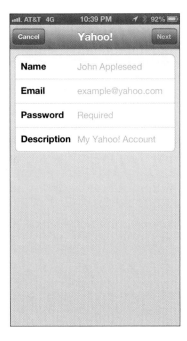

Figure 12-2: Just fill 'em in and tap Next, and you're ready to rock.

Setting up an account with another provider

If your e-mail account is with a provider other than iCloud, Gmail, Yahoo!, AOL, Hotmail, or Microsoft Exchange, you have a bit more work ahead of you. You're going to need a bunch of information about your e-mail account that you may not know or have handy.

We suggest that you scan the following instructions, note the items you don't know, and go find the answers before you continue. To find the answers, look at the documentation you received when you signed up for your e-mail account or visit the account provider's website and search there.

Here's how you set up an account:

1. **On the Add Account screen, tap the Other button.**

2. **Under Mail, tap Add Mail Account.**

3. **Fill in the name, address, password, and description in the appropriate fields, as if you were setting up an account for iCloud, Gmail, Hotmail, Yahoo!, or AOL. Tap Next.**

   With any luck, that's all you'll have to do, although you may have to endure a spinning cursor for awhile as the iPhone attempts to retrieve information and validate your account with your provider. Otherwise, continue with Step 4.

4. **Tap the button at the top of the screen that denotes the type of e-mail server this account uses: IMAP or POP, as shown in Figure 12-3.**

5. **Fill in the Internet host name for your incoming mail server, which should look something like mail.*providername*.com or mail.*providername*.net.**

6. **Fill in your username and password.**

7. **Enter the Internet host name for your outgoing mail server, which should look something like smtp.*providername*.com or smtp.*providername*.net.**

   You may have to scroll down to the bottom of the screen to see the outgoing mail server fields (refer to Figure 12-3, right).

8. **Enter your username and password in the appropriate fields.**

9. **Tap the Next button in the upper-right corner to create the account.**

Some outgoing mail servers don't need your username and password. The fields for these items on your iPhone note that they're optional. Still, we suggest that you fill them in anyway. That way, you won't have to add them later if your outgoing mail server *does* require an account name and password, which most do these days.

Figure 12-3: If you don't get your e-mail from iCloud, Gmail, Hotmail, Yahoo!, or AOL, you may have a few more fields to fill in before you can rock.

Set up corporate e-mail

The iPhone is friendly for business users, in large measure because it makes nice with the Microsoft Exchange servers that are a staple in large enterprises.

What's more, if your company supports something known as Microsoft Exchange ActiveSync, you can exploit push e-mail (messages are *pushed* to your iPhone automatically as opposed to being *pulled* in on a schedule) so that messages arrive pronto on the iPhone, just as they do on your other computers. (To keep everything up-to-date, the iPhone also supports push calendars and push contacts.) For push to work, your company must be simpatico with one of the last several iterations of Microsoft Exchange ActiveSync. Ask your company's IT or tech department if you run into an issue.

Setting up Exchange e-mail isn't particularly taxing, and the iPhone connects to Exchange right out of the box. However, you still might have to consult your employer's techie types for certain settings.

Start out by tapping the Microsoft Exchange button on the Add Account screen. Fill in what you can: your e-mail address, username (usually as *domain\user*), and password. Or call on your IT staff for assistance.

On the next screen, shown in Figure 12-4, enter the server address, assuming that the Microsoft Autodiscovery service didn't already find it. That address usually begins with *exchange.company.com.*

The company you work for doesn't want just anyone to have access to your e-mail — heaven forbid if your phone is lost or stolen. So your bosses may insist that you change the passcode lock inside Settings on the phone. (The passcode is different from the password for your e-mail account.) Skip over to Chapter 14 to find instructions for adding or changing a passcode. (We'll wait for you.) Now if your iPhone ends up in the wrong hands, your company can remotely wipe the contents clean.

After your corporate account is fully configured, you have to choose which information you want to synchronize through Exchange. You can choose Mail, Contacts, and Calendars by tapping each one. After you select an item, you see the blue On button next to it, as shown in Figure 12-5.

By default, the iPhone keeps e-mail synchronized for three days. To sync for a longer period, head to Settings and tap Mail, Contacts, Calendars, and then tap the Mail account that is using ActiveSync. Tap Mail Days to Sync, and then tap No Limit or choose another time frame (1 day, 1 week, 2 weeks, or 1 month).

If you're moonlighting at a second job, you can configure more than one Exchange ActiveSync account on your iPhone; there used to be a limit of just one such account per phone.

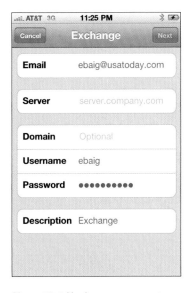

Figure 12-4: You're on your way to a corporate e-mail account.

Figure 12-5: Keeping Mail, Contacts, and Calendars in sync.

See Me, Read Me, File Me, Delete Me: Working with Messages

Now that your e-mail accounts are all set up, it's time to find out how to receive and read the stuff. Fortunately, you already did most of the heavy lifting when you set up your e-mail accounts. Getting and reading your mail is a piece of cake.

You can tell when you have unread mail by looking at the Mail icon at the bottom of your Home screen. The cumulative number of unread messages across all your e-mail inboxes appears in a little red circle in the upper-right area of the icon.

Reading messages

Tap the Mail icon now to summon the Mailboxes screen shown in Figure 12-6. At the top of the Inboxes section is the All Inboxes inbox, which as its name suggests is a repository for all the messages across all your accounts. The number to the right of All Inboxes should match the number in the Mail icon on your Home page. (If it doesn't, some fuzzy math is going on.) Again, it's the cumulative tally of unread messages across all your accounts.

Below the All Inboxes listing are the inboxes for your individual e-mail accounts. The tally this time is only for the unread messages in each account.

Scroll down toward the bottom of the Mailboxes screen and you'll find an Accounts section with a similar listing of e-mail accounts. But if you tap on the listings here, you'll see any subfolders for each individual account (Drafts, Sent Mail, Trash, and so on), as shown in Figure 12-7.

You can add new mailboxes by tapping Mailboxes⇨Edit⇨New Mailbox — if your e-mail provider allows you to add (and for that matter, delete) mailboxes. Not all do. Choose a name and location for the new mailbox. Or tap an existing mailbox, and then tap Delete Mailbox to get rid of it (and all its contents).

To read your mail, tap an inbox: either All Inboxes to examine all your messages in one unified view or an individual account to check out messages from just that account.

If you have just a single mail account configured on your iPhone, you'll see only that one inbox on the Mailboxes screen.

When you tap a mailbox to open it, Mail fetches the most recent messages and displays the total number of unread messages at the top of the screen.

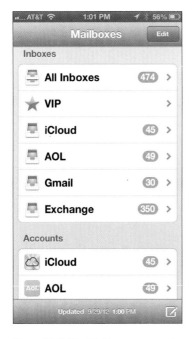

Figure 12-6: The Mailboxes screen is divided by inboxes and accounts.

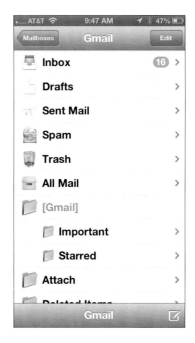

Figure 12-7: Tap one of your e-mail accounts to reveal its subfolders.

Now tap a message to read it. When a message is on the screen, buttons for managing incoming messages appear below it. These controls are addressed in the next section.

Managing messages

When a message is on your screen, you can do many tasks in addition to reading it. Check out Figure 12-8 for the location of the controls mentioned in this section.

You can perform the following actions:

✔ View the next message by tapping the next message arrow at the upper-right corner of the screen (it's the downward-pointing arrow).

✔ View the preceding message by tapping the previous message arrow (the one pointing upward).

✔ Flag the message to denote its importance or mark it as unread.

Previous message

Next message

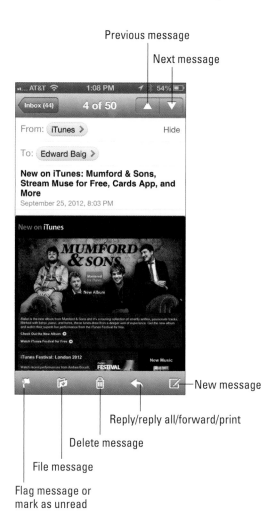

New message

Reply/reply all/forward/print

Delete message

File message

Flag message or
mark as unread

Figure 12-8: Reading and managing an e-mail message.

✔ File this message in another folder by tapping the file message icon.
   When the list of folders appears, tap the folder where you want to file
   the message.

✔ Delete this message by tapping the delete message icon. You have to dig
   in the trash to retrieve the message if you tap the delete message icon
   by mistake. Go to Mail Settings if you want the iPhone to ask you before
   deleting a message. As noted later in this chapter, in some instances you
   can archive mail instead of deleting it.

✔ Reply, reply to all, forward, or print this message by tapping the reply/reply all/forward/print icon.

✔ Create a new e-mail message by tapping the new message icon.

You can delete e-mail messages without opening them (see Figure 12-9).

Tap to select a message to remove

Number of messages read

Number of messages to remove

Number of messages to move

Figure 12-9: Wiping out or moving messages, en masse.

Delete your messages in two ways:

✔ Swipe left or right across the message, and then tap the red Delete button that appears to the right of the message. In some e-mail accounts, notably Google's Gmail, an Archive button may appear instead of Delete, depending on whether you turned on Archive Messages in Settings. In that case, tap the button to archive the message; it is not deleted.

✔ Tap the Edit button (in the upper-right corner of the Inboxes screen or a mail subfolder screen), and then tap the little circle to the left of each message you want to remove. Tapping that circle puts a check mark in it and brightens the red Delete button at the bottom of the screen. Tap that Delete button to erase all messages you selected. Deleted messages are moved to the Trash folder.

Threading messages

Apple lets you *thread* messages, or have Mail automatically group related missives. The beauty of this arrangement is that you can easily trace back an e-mail conversation. When you organize messages by a thread, the related messages show up as a single entry in the mailbox, with a number next to the right-pointing arrow in the entry indicating how many underlying messages are represented by the thread. So the number 6 next to Robert's message in Figure 12-10 (left) shows that six messages constitute this particular thread; when you tap that listing, the six threaded messages appear, as shown in Figure 12-10, right.

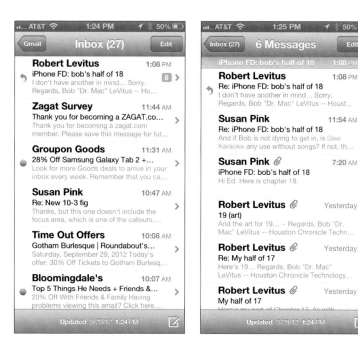

Figure 12-10: Your e-mails are hanging together by a thread.

You have to turn on threading in Settings. From the Home screen, tap Settings➪Mail, Contacts, Calendars➪Organize by Thread. Finally, tap the button so that it reads On, as shown in Figure 12-11. You may have to scroll down to see the Organize by Thread setting.

When you look at a message that's part of a thread, the numbers at the top of the screen tell you your location in the conversation. For example, in Figure 12-12, the message is number 1 of 6 in this thread.

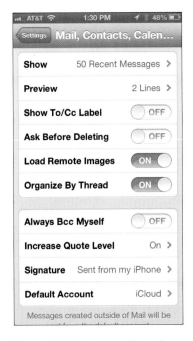

Figure 12-11: Organize by Thread keeps related messages together.

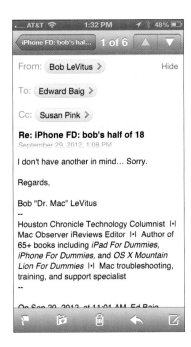

Figure 12-12: Reading a threaded message.

Searching e-mails

As part of Spotlight search, you can easily search through a bunch of messages to find the one you want to read right away — such as that can't-miss stock tip from your broker. Tap the status bar to scroll through the top of the inbox. You can type *stock* or whichever search term seems relevant. All matching e-mails that have already been downloaded appear. Or, by tapping in the search box itself, you can display tabs that let you narrow the search to the From, To, or Subject fields. You can also run a search to find words in the body of an e-mail message.

If you're using Exchange, iCloud, or certain IMAP-type e-mail accounts, you may even be able to search messages stored on the e-mail provider's servers or out in the Internet cloud. When available, tap Continue Search on Server, as shown in Figure 12-13.

The capability to search e-mails may vary by e-mail account. In some instances, you can search only whole words; in other cases, partial words may work.

You can delete messages in bulk. In much the same way, you can move them to another folder in bulk. Tap Edit and then tap the circle to the left of each message you want to move so that a check mark appears. Tap the Move button at the bottom of the screen (refer to Figure 12-9), and tap the new folder where you want those messages to hang out.

Don't grow too attached to attachments

Your iPhone can even receive e-mail messages with attachments in a wide variety of file formats. Here are some of the most common:

- **Apple Keynote:** .key
- **Apple Numbers:** .numbers
- **Apple Pages:** .pages
- **Contact information:** .vcf
- **Images:** .jpg, .tiff, .gif, .png
- **Microsoft Excel:** .xls, .xlsx
- **Microsoft PowerPoint:** .ppt, .pptx
- **Microsoft Word:** .doc, .docx
- **Preview and Adobe Acrobat:** .pdf
- **Rich Text:** .rtf
- **Text:** .txt
- **Web pages:** .htm, .html

The iPhone can also play many types of audio attachments that turn up in an e-mail, including MP3, AAC, WAV, and AIFF.

If the attachment is a file format not supported by the iPhone (for example, a Photoshop .psd file), you see the name of the file but you can't open it on your iPhone. In some other instances, you may see an Open In button if one of your apps can handle the file type.

Here's how to read an attachment:

1. **Open the mail message containing the attachment.**

2. **Tap the attachment.**

   You probably need to scroll down to see the attachment, which appears at the bottom of the message. The attachment, like the one shown in Figure 12-14, downloads to your iPhone and opens automatically.

3. **Read the attachment.**

4. **Tap the Message button in the upper-left corner of the screen to return to the message text.**

More things you can do with messages

Wait! You can do even more with your incoming e-mail messages:

- To see all recipients of a message, tap Details (displayed in blue) to the right of the sender's name.

  If all recipients are displayed, you see Hide in blue rather than Details. Tap Hide to hide all names except the sender's.

Figure 12-13: Your search doesn't end here.

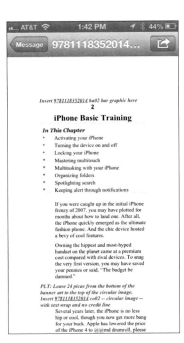

Figure 12-14: Text from a Microsoft Word file attached to an incoming e-mail message.

✏ To add an e-mail recipient or sender to your Contacts, tap the name or e-mail address at the top of the message and then tap either Create New Contact or Add to Existing Contact.

✏ To mark a message as unread or to flag it to call attention to it later, tap the icon that looks like a flag, at the lower-left corner of the screen. Tap either Mark As Unread or Flag, depending on your preference. If you choose the former, the message is again included in the unread message count on the Mail icon on your Home screen, and its mailbox again has a blue dot next to it in the message list for that mailbox. If you choose Flag, a flag will appear instead of the blue dot next to the message in the message list.

You can mark messages in bulk as unread by tapping the Edit button and then tapping the little circle next to each message you want to mark as unread. The Mark button (at the bottom right) brightens. You can then tap Mark As Unread. You're also presented with the option to Flag a message.

✏ **To make a sender a VIP,** tap the name or e-mail address at the top of the message and then tap Add to VIP. This tool is especially valuable considering that most of us deal with lots of unimportant e-mail, which tends to bury the important messages from the spouse, the kids, the boss, and key clients. A star appears next to any incoming messages from a VIP or threads in which the designated VIP is part of. You can summon mail from all your VIPs by tapping the VIP folder in the list of mailboxes (refer to Figure 12-6). To demote a VIP to what we jokingly refer to as an NVIP (translation: not very important person), tap the name or e-mail at the top of the message and then tap Remove from VIP. Don't worry; he or she will never know.

✏ To zoom in and out of a message, employ the pinch and unpinch gestures, which we suspect you excel at now.

✏ To follow a link in a message, tap the link. (Links are typically displayed in blue and may be underlined, but sometimes they appear in other colors.) If the link is a URL, Safari opens and displays the web page. If the link is a phone number, the Phone app opens and offers to dial the number. If the link is a map, Maps opens and displays the location. If the link is a day, date, or time, you can tap the item to create a calendar event. If the link is a shipper's tracking number, you may be able to get the status of a package. And last but not least, if the link is an e-mail address, a pre-addressed blank e-mail message is created.

If the link opens Safari, Phone, or Maps and you want to return to your e-mail, press the Home button on the front of your iPhone and then tap the Mail icon. You can also double-tap the Home button, tap Mail in the multitasking bar, or gesture your way back to the previous app, using a three-finger swipe.

Darling, You Send Me (E-Mail)

So now that you're a whiz at reading and organizing incoming messages, let's look at how to use your iPhone to send e-mail.

Makin' messages

Several subspecies of messages are available: pure text, text with a photo, a partially finished message (a *draft*) that you want to save and complete later, a reply to an incoming message, and a message you want to forward to someone else. The following sections examine these subsets one at a time.

Sending an all-text message

To compose a new e-mail message, tap Mail on the Home screen to open the Mailboxes screen (refer to Figure 12-6) or whichever screen was up when you last left the app.

Now, to create a new message, follow these steps:

1. **Tap the new message icon (refer to Figure 12-8), in the lower-right corner of the screen.**

   The icon appears on all the Mail screens, so don't worry if you're not at the main Mailboxes screen. A screen like the one shown in Figure 12-15 appears.

2. **Enter the names or e-mail addresses of the recipients in one of the following ways:**

   • Type the names or e-mail addresses of the recipients in the To field.

   • Tap the microphone icon on the virtual keyboard to dictate the names or e-mail addresses of the recipients in the To field.

   • Tap the + button to the right of the To field to select a contact or contacts from your iPhone's address book.

   You can rearrange names in the address field by dragging them around, moving, say, a name from the To field to the Cc field

3. **(Optional) Enter a name in the Cc field, Bcc field, or both fields. Or choose to send mail from a different account in the From field, as follows:**

   a. **Tap the field labeled Cc/Bcc, From.**

      Doing so breaks the single field into separate Cc, Bcc, and From fields. The Cc label stands for *carbon copy,* and *Bcc* stands for *blind carbon copy.* Bcc enables you to include a recipient on the message that other recipients can't see has been included. It's great for those secret agent e-mails!

b. Tap the respective Cc or Bcc field and type the name.

Or tap the + symbol that appears in one of those fields to add a contact.

If you start typing an e-mail address, e-mail addresses that match what you typed appear in a list, temporarily covering up the To, Cc, or Bcc field. If the correct one is in the list, tap it to use it.

c. Tap the From field to send the message from any of your e-mail accounts on-the-fly.

This step assumes that you have more than one account and want to send mail from an account different from the one already shown.

4. **Type a subject in the Subject field.**

The subject is optional, but it's considered poor form to send an e-mail message without one.

5. **Type your message in the message area.**

The message area is immediately below the Subject field.

6. **Tap the Send button in the upper-right corner of the screen.**

Begin typing

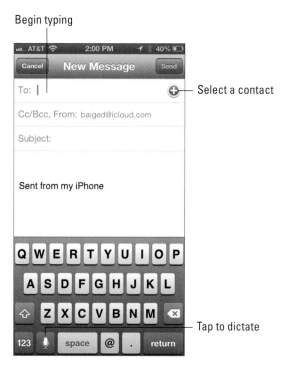

Select a contact

Tap to dictate

Figure 12-15: The New Message screen appears, ready for you to start typing the recipient's name.

Your message wings its way to its recipients almost immediately. If you aren't in range of a Wi-Fi network or a cellular data network when you tap Send, the message is sent the next time you're in range of one of these networks.

Apple includes a bunch of landscape orientation keyboards for various apps, including Mail. When you rotate the phone to its side, you can compose a new message using a wider-format virtual keyboard. Consult Chapter 2 for more on the various keyboards that may show up on your phone.

Sending a photo with a text message

Forgive the cliché, but sometimes a picture truly is worth a thousand words. When that's the case, here's how to send an e-mail message with a photo enclosed.

Apple made this process simpler with the iOS 6 upgrade. After addressing a message and perhaps composing a few words, press your finger against the screen and let go. At first you see options for Select, Select All, and Paste. Ignore these for now and instead tap on the right-pointing arrow. Doing so leads you to the Insert Photo or Video option, as shown in Figure 12-16, left. Tap that and you're transported to a list of your photo albums, from which you can select a picture or video. When you find the one you want, tap Choose.

If you selected a video, it will be compressed and an icon for the movie will be inserted into the body of the message, as shown in Figure 12-16, right. (The recipient would tap that icon to play the movie.)

If you choose a photo, you will see the actual picture inserted in the message body, as shown in Figure 12-17. When you're ready to send your e-mail off, tap Send and choose an appropriate file size for the image. Off it goes.

The alternate way to include pictures in an e-mail is the way it was done on the iPhone before the iOS 6 upgrade. If you're more comfortable doing it this way, so be it. Tap the Photos icon on the Home screen, and then find the photo you want to send. Tap the action icon (see the margin), in the lower-left corner of the screen, and then tap the Email Photo button.

An e-mail message appears on-screen with the photo already attached. The image appears to be embedded in the body of the message, but the recipient receives the image as a regular e-mail attachment. Just address the message and type whatever text you like, as you did for an all-text message in the preceding section, and then tap the Send button. You have the option to choose a file size for your picture: Small, Medium, Large, or Actual Size.

Figure 12-16: Inserting a video into an e-mail message.

Figure 12-17: You can admire an inserted picture before sending it in an e-mail.

Saving an e-mail message so that you can send it later

Sometimes you start an e-mail message but don't have time to finish it. When that happens, you can save it as a draft and finish it some other time.

Here's how: Start an e-mail message as described in one of the two preceding sections. When you're ready to save the message as a draft, tap the Cancel button in the upper-left corner of the screen and three buttons appear. Tap the Save Draft button if you want to save this message as a draft and complete it another time; tap the Delete Draft button to ditch your efforts; or tap Cancel to return to the message and continue crafting it to perfection.

If you tap the Delete Draft button, the message disappears immediately without a second chance. Don't tap Delete Draft unless you mean it.

To work on the message again, tap the Drafts mailbox for the account in question. All messages you saved as drafts hang out in that mailbox. Tap the one you want to resume working on so that it reappears on the screen. When you're finished, tap Send to send it or Cancel to go through the drill of saving it as a draft again.

The number of drafts appears to the right of the Drafts folder, the same way that the number of unread messages appears to the right of other mail folders, such as your inbox.

Formatting text in an e-mail

One of the goodies that arrived with iOS 5 is the capability to format e-mail text by underlining, bolding, or italicizing it. First you select the text by pressing your finger against the screen until you see the options shown in Figure 12-18, left. Next, tap the right-pointing arrow in that list of options to display the additional options shown in Figure 12-18, center. Then tap the BIU button. Apply whichever style (Bold, Italics, Underline) suits your fancy.

If you tap Quote Level, another option that appears when you tap the right-pointing arrow after selecting a word (it's not shown Figure 12-18), you can quote a portion of a message you're responding to. You can also increase or decrease the indentation in your outgoing message.

Replying to or forwarding an e-mail message

When you receive a message and want to reply to it, open the message and then tap the reply/reply all/forward/print icon (labeled in Figure 12-8). Then tap the Reply, Reply All, Forward, or Print button.

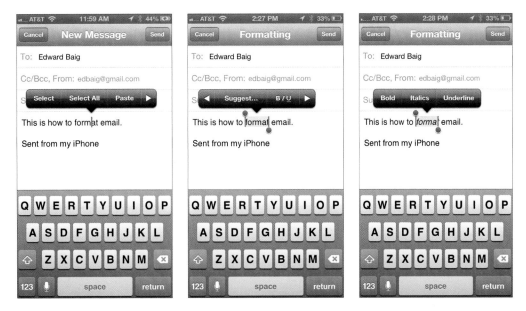

Figure 12-18: Select your text (left), tap the BIU button (center), and apply bold, italic, or underline (right).

The Reply button creates a new e-mail message addressed to the sender of the original message. The Reply All button creates an outgoing e-mail message addressed to the sender and all other recipients of the original message. In both cases, the Subject line is retained with a *Re:* prefix added. So if the original Subject line were *iPhone Tips*, the reply's Subject line would be *Re: iPhone Tips*. You also see text from the original message in the body of your reply (whether you are replying to one person or more than one person).

Tapping the Forward button creates an unaddressed e-mail message that contains the text of the original message. Add the e-mail address(es) of the person or people to whom you want to forward the message, and then tap Send. In this case, rather than a *Re:* prefix, the Subject line begins with *Fwd:*. So this time the Subject line reads *Fwd: iPhone Tips*.

You can edit the Subject line of a reply or a forwarded message or edit the body text of a forwarded message the same way you would edit any other text. It's usually considered good form to leave the Subject lines alone (with the *Re:* or *Fwd:* prefix intact), but you may want to change them sometimes. Now you know that you can.

To send your reply or forwarded message, tap the Send button as usual.

Printing requires an AirPrint printer. If you have one, tap the Print option.

Apple has included a Send Again option for a message you've already replied to but for some reason want to send again. Maybe you want to be doubly sure that the person sees the message.

Settings for sending e-mail

You can customize the mail you send and receive in lots of ways. In this section, we explore settings for sending e-mail. Later in this chapter, we show you settings that affect the way you receive and read messages. In each instance, you start by tapping Settings on the Home screen. Then:

- ✓ **To hear an alert when you successfully send a message:** Tap the Sounds option on the main Settings screen, and then turn on the Sent Mail setting. You choose what that alert sounds like, from a Suspense sound to Swoosh (the default). If you want to change other settings, tap the Settings button in the upper-left corner of the screen. If you're finished setting settings, press the Home button on the front of your iPhone.

  The instructions in the preceding paragraph are similar for all the settings we discuss in this section and later sections, so we won't repeat them. To summarize, if you want to continue using settings, you tap whichever button appears in the upper-left corner of the screen — it might be named Settings, Mail, Accounts, or something else. The point is that the upper-left button always returns you to the preceding screen so that you can change other settings. The same concept applies to pressing the Home button on the front of your iPhone when you're finished setting a setting. That action always saves the change you just made and returns you to the Home screen.

- ✓ **To add a signature line, phrase, or block of text to every e-mail message you send:** Tap Settings➪Mail, Contacts, Calendars➪Signature. (You may need to scroll down to see the Signature option.) The default signature is *Sent from my iPhone.* You can add text before or after it, or delete it and type something else, keeping your signature no longer than four lines max if you want to follow the unwritten rules of netiquette. Your signature is now affixed to the end of all your outgoing e-mail.

- ✓ **To have your iPhone send you a copy of every message you send:** Tap Settings➪Mail, Contacts, Calendars, and then turn on the Always Bcc Myself setting.

- ✓ **To add an indentation when you forward or reply to a message:** Tap Increase Quote Level and tap or slide the switch from Off to On.

✏ **To set the default e-mail account for sending e-mail from outside the Mail app:** On the Home screen, tap Settings⇨Mail, Contact, Calendars⇨ Default Account. Tap the account you want to use as the default. For example, when you want to e-mail a picture directly from the Photos app, this designated default e-mail account is used. Note that this setting applies only if you have more than one e-mail account on your iPhone.

That's what you need to know about the settings that apply to sending e-mail.

Setting your message and account settings

This final discussion of Mail involves more settings that deal with your various e-mail accounts.

Checking and viewing e-mail settings

Several settings affect the way you check and view e-mail. You might want to modify one or more, so we describe what they do and where to find them:

✏ **To specify how often the iPhone checks for new messages:** On the Home screen, tap Settings⇨Mail, Contacts, Calendars⇨Fetch New Data. You're entering the world of fetching and pushing. Check out Figure 12-19 to glance at your options. If your e-mail program supports push and you have it turned on (the On button is showing), fresh messages are sent to your iPhone automatically as soon as they reach the server. If you turned off push (Off is showing) or your e-mail program doesn't support it, the iPhone fetches data instead (that is, messages are batched before they are sent). Choices for fetching are Every 15 Minutes, Every 30 Minutes, Hourly, and Manually. Tap the one you prefer.

Figure 12-19: Fetch or push? Your call.

To determine these push and fetch settings for each account, tap Advanced at the bottom of the screen. Then tap the account in question. Push is shown as an option only if the e-mail account you tapped supports the feature.

As of this writing, Yahoo!, iCloud, Google, and Microsoft Exchange ActiveSync were among the pushy e-mail accounts (but only in a good way).

✒ **To hear an alert sound when you receive a new message:** Tap the Sounds option on the main Settings screen and then turn on the New Mail setting. Again, you can choose from a variety of sound effects. The Ding sound is the default.

✒ **To set the number of recent messages that appear in your inbox:** On the Home screen, tap Settings⇨Mail, Contacts, Calendars⇨Show. Your choices are 50, 100, 200, 500, and 1,000 recent messages. Tap the number you prefer.

You can see more messages in your inbox regardless of this setting by scrolling all the way to the bottom and tapping Load More Messages.

✒ **To set the number of lines of each message to be displayed in the message list:** On the Home screen, tap Settings⇨Mail, Contacts, Calendars⇨Preview, and then choose a number. Your choices are 0, 1, 2, 3, 4, and 5 lines of text. The more lines of text you display in the list, the fewer messages you can see at a time without scrolling. Think before you choose 4 or 5.

✒ **To specify whether the iPhone shows the To and Cc labels in message lists:** On the Home screen, tap Settings⇨Mail, Contacts, Calendars, and then turn on or off the Show To/Cc Label setting.

✒ **To turn on or off the Ask before Deleting warning:** On the Home screen, tap Settings⇨Mail, Contacts, Calendars, and then turn on or off the Ask before Deleting setting. If this setting is turned on, you need to tap the trash can icon at the bottom of the screen and then tap the red Delete button to confirm the deletion. When the setting is turned off, tapping the trash can icon deletes the message and you never see a red Delete button.

✒ **To archive messages rather than delete them:** Tap an e-mail account that presents this option — Gmail is one — and slide the switch so that On is showing. If selected, the trash can icon that you'd normally see in an e-mail is replaced by an icon showing an arrow pointing downward into what looks like a little file cabinet.

✒ **To specify whether the phone will automatically load remote images:** Tap Load Remote Images so that the On button is showing. If it's off, you can still manually load remote images.

Altering account settings

The next group of settings we explore in this chapter deals with your e-mail accounts. You most likely will never need most of these settings, but we'd be remiss if we didn't at least mention them briefly. So here they are, whether you need 'em or not:

✔ **To stop using an e-mail account:** Tap the Settings icon on the Home screen, tap Mail, Contacts, Calendars, and then tap the account name. Tap the Mail switch to turn off the account. Depending on the account, you might also turn off other settings. For example, in Gmail, you can turn off the Calendars and Notes settings but leave Mail turned on.

When you turn off an account, you don't delete it. You only hide the account from view and stop it from sending or checking e-mail until you turn it on again.

✔ **To delete an e-mail account:** Tap the Settings icon on the Home screen, tap Mail, Contacts, Calendars, and then tap the account name. Scroll to the bottom and tap the red button that reads Delete Account. You're given a chance to reconsider by tapping either Delete Account a second time or Cancel.

The last settings are reached the same way: On the Home screen, tap Settings↪ Mail, Contacts, Calendars, and then tap the name of the account with which you want to work. Next, tap the Account Info button and then tap Advanced. The settings you see under Advanced and how they appear vary a little by account. This list describes some of the ones you see:

✔ **To specify how long until deleted messages are removed permanently from your iPhone:** Tap Advanced and then tap Remove. Your choices are Never, After One Day, After One Week, and After One Month. Tap the choice you prefer.

✔ **Send signed and encrypted messages:** In an account that has an Advanced setting, tap S/MIME to turn on the setting and then indicate whether a message must be signed or require a certificate, which might be issued by a systems administrator at your job. This setting is under Advanced for a reason.

✔ **To choose whether drafts, sent messages, and deleted messages are stored on your iPhone or on your mail server:** Tap Advanced if this option is presented. Then, under the Mailbox Behaviors heading, choose various settings to determine whether you're storing such messages on the iPhone or on the server. Your options vary according to your e-mail account. If you choose to store any or all of them on the server, you can't see them unless you have an Internet connection (Wi-Fi or cellular). If you choose to store them on your iPhone, they're always available, even if you don't have Internet access.

We strongly recommend that you not change these next two items (again, assuming they are even presented) unless you know exactly what you're doing and why. If you're having problems with sending or receiving mail, start by contacting your ISP (Internet service provider), e-mail provider, or corporate IT person or department. Then change these settings only if they tell you to:

✓ **To reconfigure mail server settings:** Tap Host Name, User Name, or Password in the Incoming Mail Server or Outgoing Mail Server section of the account settings screen and make your changes.

✓ **To adjust Use SSL, Authentication, IMAP Path Prefix, or Server Port:** Tap Advanced, and then tap the appropriate item and make the necessary changes.

And that, as they say in baseball, retires the side. You're now fully qualified to set up e-mail accounts and send and receive e-mail on your iPhone.

13

Tracking with Maps, Compass, Stocks, and Weather

In This Chapter

▶ Mapping your route with Maps

▶ Course-setting with Compass

▶ Getting quotes with Stocks

▶ Watching the weather with Weather

*I*n this chapter, we look at four of the iPhone's Internet-enabled apps: Maps, Compass, Stocks, and Weather. We call them *Internet-enabled* because they display information collected over your Internet connection — whether Wi-Fi or wireless data network — in real time (or in the case of Stocks, near-real time).

Maps Are Where It's At

In the first edition of this book, we said that the Maps feature was one of the sleeper hits of our iPhone experience and an app we both use more than we expected because it's so darn handy. Since then, Maps has become better and more capable with each iOS update. Or at least that was the case until the release of iOS 6, when Apple jettisoned the Google Maps-powered Maps app we've known and loved since the first iPhone and replaced it with an Apple-powered Maps app.

Some people abhor the new Maps app; many don't notice much difference; and a (small) handful like it better. We think it's pretty good already and will only get better.

If your maps don't look like the ones you're about to see, chances are you're running iOS 5 or earlier. In any case, the new Maps app, like the one it supersedes, can quickly and easily discover exactly where you are; find nearby restaurants and businesses; get turn-by-turn directions for driving or walking from any address to any other address; and see real-time traffic information for many locations.

Unlike the old Maps apps, the Maps app in iOS 6 doesn't offer information about traveling via public transportation, or at least it didn't when we wrote this chapter, though it seems likely this feature will be added sometime in the future. On the flip side, the new Maps app delivers significantly improved overall performance, spoken turn-by-turn directions (iPhone 4S and 5 only), and a nifty 3D flyover view for many locations.

Finding your current location with Maps

Let's start with something supremely simple yet extremely useful: determining your current location. At the risk of sounding like self-help gurus, here's how to find yourself: Tap the Maps icon and then tap the show current location button, the little gray arrowhead shown in the margin and found in the lower-left corner of your screen.

A pulsating blue marker indicates your current location on the map when the phone's GPS is used to find your location. In addition, the Location Services indicator, an arrowhead, appears to the left of the battery indicator in the status bar, as shown in Figure 13-1.

If GPS is not being used because you're out of the satellite's sight line, a somewhat larger pale blue circle shows your approximate location. Either way, when you move around, the iPhone updates your location and adjusts the map so that the location indicator stays in the middle of the screen.

Current location indicator

Location Services indicator

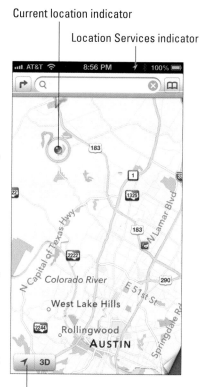

Show current location button

Figure 13-1: The blue marker shows your location; the arrowhead in the status bar means you're using Location Services.

If you tap or drag the map, your iPhone continues to update your location but won't recenter the marker, which means that the location indicator can move off the screen. Tap the show current location button in the lower-left corner again to move the current location marker back to the center.

When you tap the show current location button, it turns purple, which indicates that your current location is in the middle of the screen. If you tap, drag, rotate, or zoom the map (that is, do anything that moves the current location indicator from the center of the screen), the button turns gray. So, if the button is purple, your current location is currently in the middle of the screen; if the button is gray, your current location is anywhere except the middle of the screen.

Finding a person, place, or thing

To find a person, place, or thing with Maps, tap the search field at the top of the screen to make the keyboard appear. Now type what you're looking for. You can search for addresses, zip codes, intersections, towns, landmarks, and businesses by category and by name, or combinations, such as *New York, NY 10022, pizza 60645,* or *Auditorium Shores Austin TX.*

If the letters you type match names in your Contacts list, the matching contacts appear in a list below the search field. Tap a name to see a map of that contact's location. The Maps app is smart about it, too, displaying only the names of contacts that have a street address.

When you finish typing, tap Search. After a few seconds, a map appears. If you searched for a single location, it's marked with a single pushpin. If you searched for a category (*Pizza 60645,* for example), you see multiple pushpins, one for each matching location (pizza joints in or close to the 60645 zip code), as shown in Figure 13-2.

Figure 13-2: Search for *Pizza 60645* and you see pushpins for all nearby pizza joints.

How does it do that?

Maps uses iPhone's Location Services to determine your approximate location using available information from your wireless data network, local Wi-Fi networks (if Wi-Fi is turned on), and GPS. If you're not using Location Services, turning it off (tap Settings⇨General⇨Location Services) will conserve your battery. Don't worry if Location Services is turned off when you tap the show current location button — you'll be prompted to turn it back on. Note that Location Services may not be available in all areas at all times. One last thing: The purple arrowhead appears in the status bar whenever *any* app (not just Maps) is using Location Services and GPS to determine your current location.

You can search for all sorts of things, including intersections, neighborhoods, landmarks, restaurants, and businesses. Furthermore, you can combine several items, as with our pizza-with-a-zip-code example. The Maps app is quite adept at interpreting search terms and finding the right place. After you've used the app a few times, we're sure you'll be as addicted as we are.

Views, zooms, and pans

The preceding section talks about how to find just about anything with Maps. Now here's a look at some ways you can use what you find. But first, let's take a little detour and explore how to work with what's on the Maps screen.

Four views are available at any time: standard (map), satellite, hybrid, and list. Refer to Figure 13-2 for a standard view; Figure 13-3 shows the Satellite view. Select a view by first tapping the curling page in the lower-right corner of the screen. The map then curls back and reveals several buttons, as shown in Figure 13-4.

In standard (map), satellite, or hybrid view, you can zoom to see either more or less of the map — or scroll (pan) to see what's above, below, or to the left or right of what's on the screen:

- ✔ **To zoom out:** Pinch the map or double-tap using two fingers. To zoom out even more, pinch or double-tap using two fingers again.

    Double-tapping with two fingers may be a new concept to you: Merely tap twice in rapid succession with two fingers rather than the usual one finger. That's a total of four taps, input efficiently as two taps per finger.

- ✔ **To zoom in:** Unpinch the map or double-tap (the usual way — with just one finger) the spot you want to zoom in on. Unpinch or double-tap with one finger again to zoom in even more.

Figure 13-3: Satellite view of the map shown in Figure 13-2.

Figure 13-4: The map curls back to reveal these buttons.

An *unpinch* is the opposite of a pinch. Start with your thumb and a finger together and then flick them apart.

You can also unpinch with two fingers or two thumbs, one from each hand, but you'll probably find that a single-handed pinch and unpinch is handier.

✔ **To rotate:** Rotate two fingers on the screen. A compass appears in the upper-right corner of the screen to show the map's orientation as you rotate.

✔ **To scroll:** Flick or drag up, down, left, or right with one finger.

Maps and contacts

 Maps and contacts go together like peanut butter and jelly. For example, if you want to see a map of a contact's street address, tap the little bookmarks icon to the right of the search field, tap the Contacts button at the bottom of the screen, and then tap the contact's name. Or type the first few letters of the contact's name in the search field, and then tap the name in the list that automatically appears below the search field.

After you find a location by typing an address in Maps, you can add that location to one of your contacts. Or you can create a new contact with a location you've found. To do either, tap the location's pushpin on the map, and then tap the little > in a blue circle to the right of the location's name or description (shown for Gullivers in Figures 13-2 and 13-3) to display its Info screen, as shown in Figure 13-5.

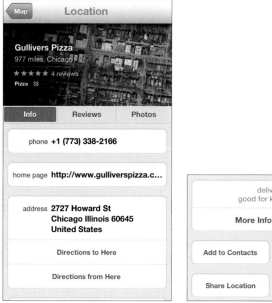
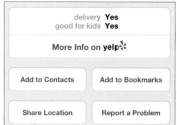

Figure 13-5: The Info screens for Gullivers Pizza.

Now tap the Add to Contacts button on the Info screen. You'll probably have to scroll to the bottom of the Info screen (see Figure 13-5, right) to see this button.

You work with your contacts in two ways. One way is to tap the Contacts icon, which is in the Utilities folder on the second page of icons on the Home screen. (Swipe from right to left on the Home screen to see this second page.) The other way is to tap the Phone icon on your Home screen, and then tap the Contacts icon in the Phone screen's dock.

You can also get driving directions from most locations, including a contact's address, to most other locations, including another contact's address. You see how to do that in the "Smart map tricks" section, later in the chapter.

Timesaving map tools: Bookmarks, Recents, and Contacts

The Maps app offers three tools that can save you from having to type the same locations over and over. All three are in the Bookmarks screen, which appears when you tap the little gray bookmarks icon on the right side of the search field.

At the bottom of the Bookmarks screen, you find three buttons: Bookmarks, Recents, and Contacts. The following sections give you the lowdown on these buttons.

Bookmarks

Bookmarks in the Maps app, like bookmarks in Safari, let you return to a location without typing a single character. To bookmark a location, tap the little > in a blue circle to the right of the location's name or description to display the Info screen for that location. Then tap the Add to Bookmarks button on the Info screen. (You may have to scroll down the Info screen to see the Add to Bookmarks button.)

You can also drop a *pin* (a kind of temporary bookmark) anywhere on the map by tapping the curling page button in the lower-right corner, and then tapping the Drop Pin button. After you've dropped a pin, you can press and drag it anywhere on the map. When the pin is where you want it, lift your finger to drop the pin and a banner with the location of the pin (if Maps can figure it out) and a little > in a blue circle appears. Tap the little > and the Info screen for the dropped pin appears. Now tap the Add to Bookmarks button on the Info screen.

The info screen for a dropped pin offers several buttons in addition to Add to Bookmarks, namely Directions to Here, Directions from Here, Add to Contacts, Share Location, Report a Problem, and Remove Pin.

After you add a bookmark, you can recall it at any time. To do so, tap the bookmarks icon to the right of the search field, tap the Bookmarks button at the bottom of the screen, and then tap the bookmark name to see it on a map.

The first things you should bookmark are your home and work addresses. You use these addresses all the time with Maps, so you might as well bookmark them now to avoid typing them over and over. Also create zip code bookmarks for your home, work, and other locations you frequently visit. Then when you want to find businesses near any of those locations, you can choose the zip code bookmark and type what you're looking for, such as *78729 pizza, 60645 gas station,* or *90201 Starbucks.*

To manage your bookmarks, first tap the Edit button in the top-left corner of the Bookmarks screen. Then:

> ✔ **To move a bookmark up or down in the Bookmarks list:** Drag the little icon with three gray bars that appears to the right of the bookmark upward to move the bookmark higher in the list or downward to move the bookmark lower in the list.

> ✔ **To delete a bookmark from the Bookmarks list:** Tap the – button to the left of the bookmark's name.

When you're finished using bookmarks, tap the Done button in the top-right corner of the Bookmarks screen to return to the map.

Recents

The Maps app automatically remembers every location you've searched for in its Recents list (unless you've cleared it, as described next). To see this list, tap the bookmarks icon to the right of the search field, and then tap the Recents button at the bottom of the screen. To see a map of a recent item, tap the item's name.

To clear the Recents list, tap the Clear button in the top-left corner of the screen, and then tap the Clear All Recents button. Sadly, removing a single entry is not possible; clearing the Recents list is an all-or-nothing deal.

When you're finished using the Recents list, tap the Done button in the top-right corner of the screen to return to the map.

Contacts

To see a map of a contact's location, tap the bookmarks icon to the right of the search field, and then tap the Contacts button at the bottom of the screen. To see a map of a contact's location, tap the contact's name in the list.

To limit the Contacts list to specific groups (assuming you have some groups in your Contacts list), tap the Groups button in the top-left corner of the screen and then tap the name of the group. Now only contacts in this group are displayed in the list.

When you're finished using the Contacts list, tap the Done button in the top-right corner of the screen to return to the map.

Smart map tricks

The Maps app has more tricks up its sleeve. This section lists a few nifty features you may find useful.

Get route maps and driving directions

You can get route maps and driving directions to any location from any other location in a couple of ways:

- **If a pushpin is already on the screen:** Tap the pushpin and then tap the little > in a blue circle to the right of the name or description. This action displays the item's Info screen. Now tap the Directions to Here or Directions from Here button to get directions to or from that location, respectively.

- **When you're looking at a map screen:** Tap the Directions button on the left of the search field. The Start and End fields appear at the top of the screen. Type the start and end points or select them from your bookmarks, recent maps, or contacts if you prefer. If you want to swap the starting and ending locations, tap the little swirly arrow button to the left of the Start and End fields.

  If you need to change the start or end location, tap the Clear button in the top-left corner and try again.

  When the start and end locations are correct, tap the Route button in the top-right corner of the screen and the route map appears.

  Maps will often suggest several routes. The number of suggestions appears at the top of the screen and the routes appear on the map in blue with cartoon balloons denoting their route number. Tap the blue line or cartoon balloon to select a route, as in Figure 13-6, where Route 2 is selected.

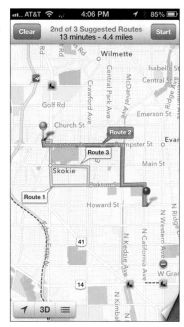

Figure 13-6: Route maps from Bob's first house in Skokie to Gullivers Pizza in Chicago.

Weird but true: If you type the end location, you'll have to tap the Route button before you can proceed; but if you select the end location from your Bookmarks, Contacts, or Recents list, you won't see the Route button and thus won't have to tap it before you proceed.

Tap the curling page button in the lower-right corner of the map you're viewing and then tap the Show Traffic button to help you decide which route will be most expedient.

The next step is to tap the Start button in the top-right corner to receive turn-by-turn driving directions, as shown in Figure 13-7. To see the next step in the directions, swipe the green instructional signs from right to left; to see the preceding step, swipe from left to right.

If you prefer your driving directions displayed as a list with all the steps, as shown in Figure 13-8, tap the curling page button in the lower-right corner (refer to Figure 13-6) and then tap the List Results button.

Older iPhones can speak directions if you purchase a third-party GPS app, such as TomTom U. S. A. ($39.99), Navigon ($24.99 and up), or MotionX GPS Drive (99¢ plus $2.99 per month or $9.99 per year for Live Voice Guidance), which are all decent. We advise plugging the iPhone into a power outlet if at all possible while driving because such apps can quickly drain the battery.

When you're finished with the step-by-step directions, tap the Search button at the bottom of the screen to return to the regular map screen and single search field.

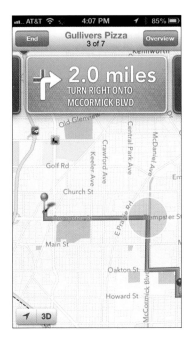

Figure 13-7: The third step in the step-by-step driving directions for the route to Gullivers.

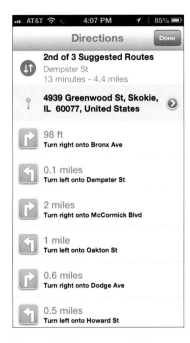

Figure 13-8: Step-by-step driving directions to Gullivers displayed as a list.

Get walking directions

For step-by-step directions for walking, tap the walking person icon above the Start and End fields that appear after you tap the Directions button. Walking directions generally look a lot like driving directions except for your travel time. For example, driving time in Figure 13-6 is approximately 13 minutes with traffic; walking time (not shown) is estimated at 1 hour and 24 minutes.

Get 3D and flyover views (iPhone 4S and 5)

New in iOS 6 are three-dimensional views for most metropolitan areas. You may have to zoom in to see the 3D or Flyover button, which appears on the right of the show current location button when available.

 In Standard view, the 3D button says (d'oh) 3D, as shown in the margin.

 In hybrid or satellite view, the Flyover button looks like a three-dimensional skyscraper, as shown in the margin.

Tap the 3D or Flyover button and the button turns blue while the map becomes three-dimensional, as shown on the right in Figures 13-9 and 13-10.

Figure 13-9: Downtown Austin in standard view (left) and with 3D enabled (right).

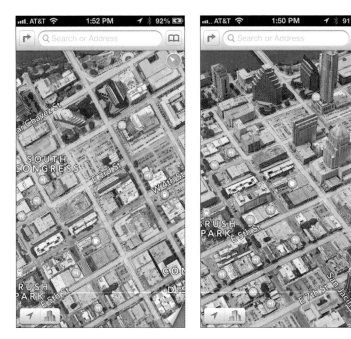

Figure 13-10: Downtown Austin in hybrid view (left) and with flyover enabled (right).

When 3D or flyover is enabled, you navigate and zoom as described earlier in the chapter. To change the camera angle, you drag up or down on the screen with two fingers.

Finally, note the compass in the upper-right corner of the screen when 3D or flyover is enabled. Tap it to return to north-facing orientation.

Get traffic info in real time

You can find out the traffic conditions for whatever map you're viewing by tapping the curling page button in the lower-right corner and then tapping the Show Traffic button. When you do this, major roadways are color-coded to inform you of the current traffic speed, as shown in Figure 13-11.

Figure 13-11: Traffic may be moving very slowly (red), kind of slowly (yellow), or nice and fast (green) in New York City.

Here's the key to those colors:

- ✔ **Green:** More than 50 miles per hour
- ✔ **Yellow:** 25 to 50 miles per hour
- ✔ **Red:** Under 25 miles per hour
- ✔ **Gray:** No data available at this time

Traffic info isn't available in every location, but the only way to find out is to give it a try. If no color codes appear, assume that traffic information doesn't work for that particular location.

Do more on the Info screen

If a location has a little > in a blue circle to the right of its name or description (refer to Figure 13-2), you can tap the > to see the location's Info screen.

As we explain earlier in this chapter, you can get directions to or from that location, add the location to your bookmarks or contacts, or create a new contact from it. But you can do three more things with a location from its Info screen:

- ✔ Tap the phone number to call it.
- ✔ Tap the e-mail address to launch the Mail app and send an e-mail to it.
- ✔ Tap the URL to launch Safari and view its website.

Contemplating the Compass

The Compass app works like a magnetic needle compass. Launch the Compass app by tapping its icon in the Utilities folder on the second Home screen. You see the direction you're facing, as shown in Figure 13-12.

But wait — there's more. If you were to tap the little arrowhead icon in the lower-left corner of the Compass screen, the Maps app launches. Now for the cool part: Tap the little arrowhead icon in the lower-left corner of the Maps app two times and the blue marker grows a little white cone that indicates the direction you're facing, as shown in Figure 13-13.

Also note that when the map is in compass mode, the little arrowhead icon in its lower-left corner grows a little white cone (shown in the margin) as well, letting you know that you're now using the compass mode.

Figure 13-12: The Compass app says I'm facing north.

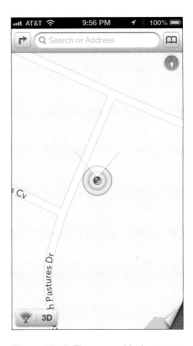

Figure 13-13: The map with the cone says I'm facing north, too.

If you rotate to face a different direction while Maps is in compass mode, the map rotates in real time. So the map always displays the direction you're currently facing, even if you've moved around a bit, which is pretty darn cool.

Taking Stock with Stocks

Stocks is another Internet-enabled app on your iPhone. It's kind of a one-trick pony, but if you need its trick — information about specific stocks — it's a winner.

Every time you open the Stocks app by tapping its icon (on the second Home screen by default), it displays the latest price for your stocks, with two provisos:

- ✔ The quotes are provided in real-time; in earlier versions of iOS, they were delayed by up to 20 minutes.
- ✔ The quotes are updated only if your iPhone can connect to the Internet via either Wi-Fi or a wireless data network.

So tap that Stocks icon and take a peek. The first time you open Stocks, you see information for a group of default stocks, funds, and indexes. You can't see them all on the screen at once, so flick upward to scroll down.

Your stocks also appear by default in Notification Center (swipe down from the top of the screen). If you don't see them in your Notification Center, tap Settings➪Notifications➪Stock Widget to enable them.

Adding and deleting stocks, funds, and indexes

Your chance of owning that exact group of stocks, funds, and indexes displayed on the screen is slim, so this section shows you how to add your own stocks, funds, or indexes and delete any or all default ones if you want.

Here's how to add a stock, a fund, or an index:

1. **Tap the *i* button in the bottom-right corner of the initial Stocks screen.**

   The *i* is for *info.*

2. **Tap the + button in the top-left corner of the Stocks screen.**

3. **Type the stock symbol or the name of the company, index, or fund.**

4. **Tap the Search button.**

   The Stocks app finds the company or companies that match your search request.

5. **Tap the stock, fund, or index that you want to add.**

6. **Repeat Steps 4 and 5 until you've finished adding stocks, funds, and indexes.**

7. **Tap the Done button in the top-right corner.**

And here's how to delete a stock (the steps for deleting a fund or an index are the same):

1. **Tap the *i* button in the bottom-right corner of the initial Stocks screen.**

2. **Tap the – button to the left of the stock's name.**

3. **Tap the Delete button that appears to the right of the stock's name.**

4. **Repeat Steps 2 and 3 until you've deleted all unwanted stocks.**

5. **Tap the Done button.**

That's all there is to adding and deleting stocks.

≡ To change the order of the list, tap the *i* button and then drag the three horizontal lines to the right of the stock, fund, or index up or down to its new place in the list.

Details, details, details

To see the details for an item, tap its name to select it and the lower portion of the screen will offer additional information. Note the three small dots under the words *Market Closed.* These dots tell you that three screens of information are available, all shown in Figure 13-14. To switch between these three screens, simply swipe to the left or the right on the lower part of the screen.

Three little dots

Yahoo.com button

Info button

Figure 13-14: The Stocks screens.

To look up additional information about a stock at Yahoo.com, first tap the stock's name to select it, and then tap the Y! button in the lower-left corner of the screen. Safari launches and displays the Yahoo.com finance page for that stock.

Charting a course

Referring to Figure 13-14, note the chart at the bottom of the middle image. At the top of the chart, you see a bunch of numbers and letters, namely 1d, 1w, 1m, 3m, 6m, 1y, and 2y. They stand for 1 day, 1 week, 1 month, 3 months, 6 months, 1 year, and 2 years, respectively. Tap one of them and the chart updates to reflect that period of time. (In Figure 13-14, 2y is selected.)

That feature is sweet but here's an even sweeter one: If you rotate your iPhone 90 degrees, the chart appears in full-screen, as shown in Figure 13-15. Here are three cool things you can do with full-screen charts:

- Touch any point in time to see the value for that day.
- Use two fingers to touch any two points in time to see the difference in values between those two days, as shown in Figure 13-15.
- Swipe left or right to see the chart for another stock, fund, or index.

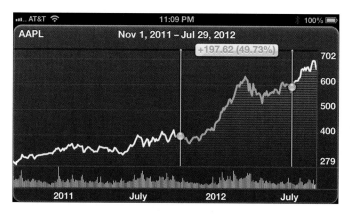

Figure 13-15: Use two fingers to see the difference in values ($197.62, or 49.73%) between two dates (November 1, 2011, and July 29, 2012).

By default, the Stocks app displays the change in a stock's price in dollars. You can instead see the change expressed as a percentage or as the stock's market capitalization. Simply tap the number next to any stock (green numbers are positive; red numbers are negative) to toggle the display for all stocks — dollar change, percent change, market cap. So if your stocks, funds, and indexes are currently displayed as dollars, tapping any one of them switches them all to percent — and tapping again switches them to market cap.

Another method requires more steps: Tap the *i* button in the bottom-right corner of the initial Stocks screen. Then tap the %, Price, or Mkt Cap button at the bottom of the screen. The values are then displayed in the manner you chose. Tap the Done button in the top-right corner when you're finished.

Weather Watching

Weather is a simple app that provides you with the current weather forecast for the city or cities of your choice. By default, you see a five-day forecast at the bottom of the screen, as shown in Figure 13-16, with the hourly forecast above.

Swipe right to display later hours.

To add a city, first tap the *i* button in the bottom-right corner to display the Info screen. Next, tap the + button in the upper-left corner, type a city and state or zip code, and tap the Search button in the bottom-right corner of the screen. Finally, tap the name of the found city. Add as many cities as you want this way.

To delete a city, tap the *i* button in the bottom-right corner. Tap the red – button to the left of its name, and then tap the Delete button that appears to the right of its name.

You can also choose between Fahrenheit and Celsius by first tapping the *i* button in the bottom-right corner and then tapping either the °F or °C button near the bottom of the screen.

Finally, if you enable local weather by tapping the on/off switch at the top of the Info screen, you'll always see the local weather for your current location when you launch the Weather app.

When you're finished, tap the Done button in the top-right corner of the screen.

If you've added one or more cities to Weather, you can switch between them by flicking your finger across the screen to the left or the right.

See the Location Services arrow and two little gray dots centered at the bottom of the screen in Figure 13-16? The white Location Services arrow means you're currently viewing the local weather; the two gray dots denote the two other cities we've added to the list as we've just described.

When the local weather is displayed, as it is in Figure 13-16, the words *Local Weather* appear above your current location (*Austin* in Figure 13-16). When you swipe across the screen to see cities you've added manually, as described a few paragraphs back, you see only the city name.

Last, but not least, to see even more detailed weather information about a city at Yahoo.com, tap the Y! button in the lower-left corner of the screen. Safari launches and then displays the Yahoo.com weather page for the current city, as shown in Figure 13-17.

Figure 13-16: The five-day and hourly local forecasts for Austin, TX.

Figure 13-17: Detailed weather on Yahoo.com is just a tap away.

Part V
The Undiscovered iPhone

This part is where we show you what's under the hood and how to configure your iPhone to your liking. Then we look at the things to do if your iPhone ever becomes recalcitrant.

We start by exploring every single iPhone setting that's not discussed in depth elsewhere in the book. iPhone offers dozens of different preferences and settings to make your iPhone your very own; by the time you finish with Chapter 14, you'll know how to customize every part of your iPhone that *can* be customized.

We love going on a shopping spree as much as the next guy. Chapter 15 is all about shopping in the App Store, an emporium replete with a gaggle of neat little programs and apps (more than 700,000 of them). Best of all, unlike most of the stores you shop in, a good number of the items can be had for free.

iPhones are well-behaved little beasts for the most part, except when they're not. Like the little girl with the little curl, when they're good they're very, very good, but when they're bad, they're horrid. So Chapter 16 is your comprehensive guide to troubleshooting for the iPhone. It details what to do when almost anything goes wrong, offering step-by-step instructions for specific situations as well as a plethora of tips and techniques you can try if something else goes awry. You may never need Chapter 16 (and we hope you won't), but you'll be very glad we put it here if your iPhone ever goes wonky on you.

14

Setting You Straight on Settings

re you a control freak? The type of person who must have it your way? Boy, have you landed in the right chapter.

Throughout this book, you have occasion to drop in on Settings, which is kind of the makeover factory for the iPhone. For example, we show you how to open Settings (by tapping its Home screen icon) to set ringtones and text tones, change the phone's background or wallpaper, and specify Google, Yahoo!, or Bing as the search engine of choice. We also show you how to alter security settings in Safari, tailor e-mail to your liking, and get a handle on how to fetch or push new data.

The Settings area on the iPhone is roughly analogous to the Control Panel in Windows and System Preferences on a Mac.

Because we cover some settings elsewhere, we don't dwell on every setting here. But you can still discover plenty to help you make the iPhone your own.

Sky-High Settings

When you first open Settings, you see the scrollable list shown in Figure 14-1. In all but airplane mode (at the top of the list), a greater-than symbol (>) appears to the right of each listing. This symbol tells you that the listing has a bunch of options. Throughout this chapter, you tap the > symbol to check out those options.

Figure 14-1: Presenting lists of settings.

If you scroll down towards the bottom of the Settings list, you will see settings that pertain to Twitter and Facebook, and settings that pertain to some of the specific apps you've added to the iPhone, as shown in Figure 14-1, right. (See Chapter 15 for the scoop on third-party apps.)

Airplane mode

Using a cell phone on an airplane is a no-no. But there's nothing verboten about using an iPod on a plane to listen to music, watch videos, and peek at pictures — at least, after the craft has reached cruising altitude.

So how do you take advantage of the iPhone's built-in Music player (among other capabilities) while temporarily turning off its phone, e-mail, and Internet functions? The answer is, by turning on airplane mode.

To do so, merely tap airplane mode on the Settings screen to display On (rather than Off).

That act disables each of the iPhone's wireless radios: Wi-Fi, EDGE, 3G, LTE (if applicable), and Bluetooth. While your iPhone is in airplane mode, you can't make or receive calls, surf the web, or do anything else that requires an Internet connection. The good news is that airplane mode keeps your battery running longer — particularly useful if your flight is taking you halfway around the world.

 The appearance of a tiny airplane icon on the status bar in the top-left corner reminds you that airplane mode is turned on. Just remember to turn it off when you're back on the ground.

 Since many flights now offer Wi-Fi, you can go into airplane mode and then separately turn on Wi-Fi, using the method addressed in the next section.

Wi-Fi

As we mention in Chapter 11, Wi-Fi is typically the fastest wireless network you can use to surf the web, send e-mail, and perform other Internet tricks on the iPhone. You use the Wi-Fi setting to determine which Wi-Fi networks are available to you and which one to exploit based on its signal.

Figure 14-2: Checking out your Wi-Fi options.

Tap Wi-Fi, and you see any Wi-Fi networks in range, as shown in Figure 14-2.

A signal-strength indicator can help you choose the network to connect to if more than one is listed; tap the appropriate Wi-Fi network when you reach a decision. If a network is password-protected, you see a lock icon.

You can also turn on or off the Ask to Join Networks setting. Networks that the iPhone is already familiar with are joined automatically, regardless of which one you choose. If the Ask feature is on, you're asked before joining a new network. If it's off, you have to select a network manually.

 If you used a particular network automatically in the past but no longer want your iPhone to join it, tap the > symbol next to the network in question (within Wi-Fi settings), and then tap Forget This Network. The iPhone develops a quick case of selective amnesia.

In some instances, you have to supply other technical information about a network you hope to glom on to. You encounter a bunch of nasty-sounding terms: DHCP, BootP, Static, IP address, Subnet Mask, Router, DNS, Search Domains, Client ID, HTTP proxy, and Renew Lease. (At least this last one has nothing to do with real estate or the vehicle you're driving.) Chances are that none of this info is on the tip of your tongue — but that's okay. For one thing, it's a good bet that you'll never need to know this stuff. What's more, even if you *do* have to fill in or adjust these settings, a network administrator or techie friend can probably help.

Sometimes, you may want to connect to a network that's closed and not shown on the Wi-Fi list. If that's the case, tap Other and use the keyboard to enter the network name. Then tap to choose the type of security setting the network is using (if any). Your choices are WEP, WPA, WPA2, WPA Enterprise, and WPA2 Enterprise. Again, it's not exactly the friendliest terminology, but we figure that someone nearby can provide assistance.

If no Wi-Fi network is available, you have to rely on a cellular network. If a cellular network isn't available either, you can't rocket into cyberspace until you regain access to a network.

Bluetooth

Of all the peculiar terms you may encounter in techdom, *Bluetooth* is one of our favorites. The name is derived from a tenth-century Danish king named Harald Blåtand, who, the story goes, helped unite warring factions. And, we're told, *Blåtand* translates to *Bluetooth* in English. (Bluetooth is all about collaboration between different types of devices — get it?)

Blåtand was obviously ahead of his time. Although he never dialed a cell phone, he now has an entire short-range wireless technology named in his honor. On the iPhone, you can use Bluetooth to communicate wirelessly with a compatible Bluetooth headset or hands-free car kit. These optional headsets and kits are made by Apple and numerous others. They've become more of a big deal as a number of states and municipalities around the United States make it illegal to hold a phone to your mouth and ear to gab while you're driving. To ensure that the iPhone works with one of these devices, it has to be wirelessly *paired,* or coupled, with the chosen device. With the optional iPhone Bluetooth headset that Apple sells, you can automatically pair the devices by placing the iPhone and headset in a *dual dock* (supplied with the headset), which you connect to your computer.

If you're using a third-party accessory, follow the instructions that came with that headset or car kit so that it becomes *discoverable,* or ready to be paired with your iPhone. Then turn on Bluetooth in Settings so that the iPhone can find such nearby devices and the device can find the iPhone. Bluetooth works up to a range of about 30 feet.

You know Bluetooth is turned on when you see the Bluetooth icon on the status bar. If the symbol is blue or white, the iPhone is communicating wirelessly with a connected device. (The color differences provide contrast to whatever is behind the icon.) If it's gray, Bluetooth is turned on in the iPhone *but* a paired device isn't nearby or isn't turned on.

Figure 14-3: Falling out of love — tap an item so you're no longer connected.

To unpair a device, tap it from the device list shown in Figure 14-3 so that the word *Connected* becomes *Not Connected.* Tap the device again to reconnect.

To divorce a Bluetooth device from the iPhone, tap the right arrow in the blue circle to the right of the Bluetooth device you're unceremoniously dumping. On the next screen, tap Forget This Device. At least you won't have to pay alimony.

The most recent iPhones support *stereo* Bluetooth headphones, car kits, and other accessories, so you can stream stereo audio from the iPhone to those devices. Sadly, stereo Bluetooth still doesn't work on the original iPhone.

The iPhone can tap into Bluetooth in other ways. One is through *peer-to-peer* connectivity, in which you can engage in multiplayer games with other nearby iPhone users. You can also do such things as exchange business cards, share pictures, and send short notes. And, you don't even have to pair the devices, as you do with a headset or car kit.

What's more, you can use an Apple Wireless Keyboard or other Bluetooth keyboard to more easily type on the iPhone.

 You can use Bluetooth to share data with certain apps, even when you're not using those apps. To see which app(s) have requested the capability to take advantage of Bluetooth, tap Settings from the Home screen and then tap Privacy⊅Bluetooth Sharing. If there's app on the list that makes you feel uncomfortable, tap the switch so that On becomes Off.

 You still can't use Bluetooth to exchange files or sync between an iPhone and a computer. Nor can you use it to print stuff from the iPhone on a Bluetooth printer. That's because the iPhone doesn't support any Bluetooth profiles (or specifications) required to allow such wireless stunts to take place. Of course, the iPhone does support Apple's wireless AirPrint technology.

Although you can't use Bluetooth to sync, you can take advantage of Wi-Fi sync, as Chapter 3 expounds on. A dedicated iTunes Wi-Fi Sync setting lets you sync wirelessly whenever you are on the same network as the iTunes installation with which you want to sync.

Settings for What iPhone Looks Like, Sounds Like, and Reports

The next bunch of settings control what the iPhone reports back to you, what the phone sounds like, and what it looks like.

Notifications

One of the biggest additions that came to the iPhone via the iOS 5 upgrade was Notification Center, discussed in Chapter 2. By swiping down from the top of the screen, you can receive a variety of notifications, from missed calls and texts to appointments.

Under Notifications Settings, you can choose which apps report information in Notification Center and choose whether these apps should be sorted manually or by time, that is, the order in which they come in. After you determine which apps belong in Notification Center, tap the app listing in the In Notification Center roster and choose an alert style (a banner that appears at the top of the screen momentarily before it disappears or an alert, which requires you to do something before it goes away).

App developers can send you alerts related to the programs you've installed on your iPhone by exploiting the Apple Push Notification service. Such alerts are typically in text form but may include sounds as well. Or they may appear in a little circle affixed to the app icon as numbered badges. You can receive such alerts even when the app isn't running.

You can turn off notifications for individual apps. Simply tap an app in the In Notification Center list, and turn on or off the app's sounds, alerts, or badges. Figure 14-4 shows available notification options for the Epicurious app.

You'll also find a setting here for the Do Not Disturb feature added in iOS 6. When turned on, the iPhone is respectful of your wishes to not be bothered by needless phone calls or alerts. The moon icon in the status bar reminds you that the feature is turned on. You can schedule the time that the Do Not Disturb edict is in effect and customize it to allow calls from your favorites or designated contacts. You can also turn on a Repeated Calls option that bypasses Do Not Disturb if the same caller rings you twice within three minutes. Read Chapter 4 for more about Do Not Disturb.

Meantime, for more on privacy, read the next section.

Privacy

Location, location, location. The iPhone makes good use of knowing where you are in the Maps app and several other apps and by geotagging photos taken with its camera. The iPhone exploits built-in GPS but can also find your general whereabouts by *triangulating* signals from Wi-Fi base stations and cellular towers.

If your iPhone knowing your location creeps you out a little, don't fret. To protect your right to privacy, individual apps pop up quick messages (similar to the one shown in Figure 14-5), asking whether you want them to use your current location. But you can also turn off Location Services by going to Settings⇨Privacy. Not only is your privacy shielded, but you also keep your iPhone battery juiced a little longer.

 You can also allow individual apps to determine your approximate location. Apps that are using location data are listed in Location Services. You can turn these on or off individually. If an app in Settings has a location icon (as shown in the margin), note the icon's appearance. If the icon is

- ✓ Purple: The app recently used your location.
- ✓ Gray: The app used your location within the past 24 hours.
- ✓ Outlined: The app is using a *geofence,* or virtual perimeter, around a location. The Reminders app, for example, uses geofencing to remind you when you arrive at or leave one of these locations.

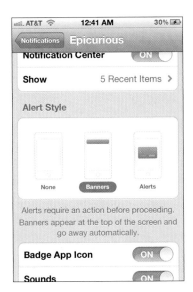

Figure 14-4: Notify the iPhone of your notification intentions.

Figure 14-5: The Maps app wants to know where you are.

If you scroll all the way down Location Settings and tap System Services, you'll see a bunch of location settings tied to your cell network, your compass calibration, diagnostics and usage, Genius for apps, location-based iAds, time zone settings, and traffic. You can turn any of these on or off as well.

When an app is using your location, you'll also see the location icon in the status bar at the top of the screen.

If you back out of the Location Services section of Privacy Settings to the main Privacy Settings screen (see Figure 14-6, left) you'll see a list for Contacts, Calendars, Reminders, Photos, Twitter, Facebook, and, as noted earlier in this chapter, Bluetooth Sharing. Tap any one of the items to see the other apps that have requested access to the selected app. In Figure 14-6, right, for example, you can see the apps requesting access to Photos.

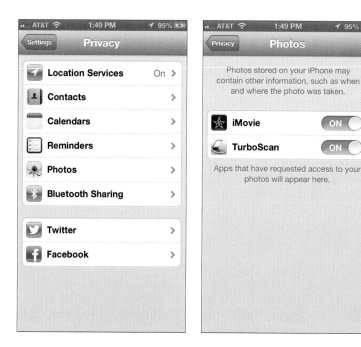

Figure 14-6: Tap an app in the Privacy list to see which apps are accessing it.

Sounds

Consider the Sounds settings area as the iPhone's soundstage. There, you can turn on or off audio alerts for a variety of functions: new voicemail messages, new text messages, new mail, sent mail, Tweets, Facebook posts, calendar alerts, and reminder alerts. You also set ringtones and text tones here (as described in Chapter 4).

That's not all. Want to hear lock sounds and keyboard clicks or not? The Sounds settings area is where you make that decision. In addition, you can determine whether the iPhone should vibrate when you receive a call. And you can drag the volume slider to determine the loudness of your ringer and alerts. Note that you can instead use the physical volume buttons on the side of the iPhone to change the volume of the ringer and alerts, as long as you're not already on a call or using the iPod to listen to music or watch video.

Brightening up your day

Who doesn't want a bright, vibrant screen? Alas, the brightest screens exact a trade-off: Before you drag the brightness slider shown in Figure 14-7 to the max, remember that brighter screens sap the life from your battery more quickly.

Figure 14-7: Sliding this control adjusts screen brightness.

We recommend tapping the Auto-Brightness control so that it's on. This control adjusts the screen according to the lighting conditions around the iPhone while being considerate of your battery.

Wallpaper

Choosing wallpaper is a neat way to dress up the iPhone according to your taste. You can sample the pretty patterns and designs that Apple has already chosen for you by tapping the thumbnails shown in Figure 14-8. But stunning as they are, these images may not hold a candle to the masterpieces in your own photo albums (more about those in Chapter 9). After making a selection, tap the image, and then tap Set. You can set wallpaper for the Home screen, the Lock screen, or both by tapping the appropriate button. The Home and Lock screens can have the same or different images.

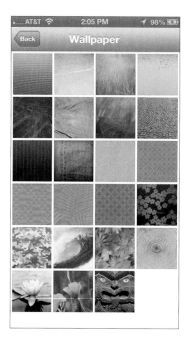 

Figure 14-8: Choosing a masterpiece background.

In General

Certain miscellaneous settings are difficult to pigeonhole. Apple wisely lumped many of these under the General settings moniker. Figure 14-9 gives you a look at them all.

About About

You aren't seeing double. This section is all about the setting known as About. And About is full of trivial (and not-so-trivial) information *about* the device. What you find here is straightforward:

- ✓ **Name of your network**
- ✓ **Number of songs stored on the device**
- ✓ **Number of videos**
- ✓ **Number of photos**
- ✓ **Number of apps**
- ✓ **Storage capacity used and available:** Because of the way the device is formatted, you always have a little less storage than the advertised amount of flash memory.

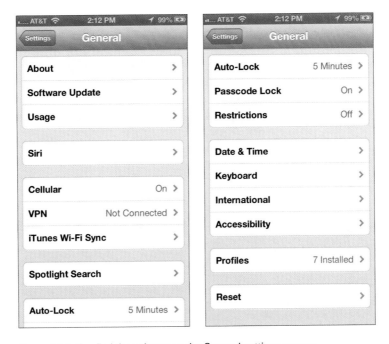

Figure 14-9: You find these items on the General settings screen.

✔ **Software version:** We were up to version 6.0 as this book was being published. But in parentheses next to the version number, you also see a number such as (10A405), which is the build number of the software version you have. The build number changes whenever the iPhone's software is updated.

✔ **Carrier:** Yep, in the United States, that's most likely AT&T, Sprint, or Verizon Wireless.

✔ **Model and serial numbers**

✔ **Wi-Fi address**

✔ **Bluetooth address**

✔ **IMEI, ICCID, and MEID:** Say what? These abbreviations stand for the International Mobile Equipment Identity, Integrated Circuit Card Identifier, and Mobile Equipment Identifier numbers, respectively. ICCID is for GSM type networks, and MEID pertains to CDMA networks. Hey, we warned you some of this was trivial — and geeky.

✔ **Diagnostics & Usage:** At your discretion, you can send daily diagnostic and usage data to help Apple out. This data may include location information.

✔ **Modern firmware:** It's not quite software and not quite hardware. But without it your phone wouldn't function.

- ✔ **Advertising:** Tap here to limit ad tracking via the Advertising Identifier introduced as part of iOS 6.

- ✔ **Legal and Regulatory:** You had to know that the lawyers would get their two cents in somehow. All the fine print is here, including license, warranty, regulatory, and even RF (radio frequency) exposure information. And *fine print* it is. Although you can flick to scroll these lengthy legal notices, you can't unpinch the screen to enlarge the text. (Not that we can imagine more than a handful of you will bother to read this legal mumbo jumbo.)

Software update

If there's a software update to be had, you can find it under the Software Update setting. Otherwise you'll be informed that your software is up to date.

Usage

Think of the Usage setting as one of the places to go on the iPhone for statistics about how you employ the device. You find other information in the About setting (under General on the Settings screen), described in the preceding section.

You can scroll up or down the Usage list to discover the following information:

- ✔ **Battery percentage:** How much of your battery is charged in percentage terms. The percentage appears just to the left of the battery gauge at the upper-right corner of the iPhone.

- ✔ **The amount of time since you last fully charged your iPhone:** Indicated in days and hours, for the time when the iPhone has been unlocked and in use and also when it has been in standby mode.

- ✔ **Call time:** Shown for the current period and for the lifetime of the product.

- ✔ **Cellular Network Data:** The amount of network data you sent and received over EDGE, CDMA, 3G, or 4G. You can reset these statistics by tapping the Reset Statistics button at the bottom of the screen.

- ✔ **Storage:** A list of all the apps taking space on your iPhone. Ask yourself if you really need all the apps that are hogging the most space. If not, tap the name of the app and then tap Delete App. You can always sync again if you find that you can't live without the bloat that the app provided. You also see your total iCloud storage and how much is available. If you need to buy more storage, tap Manage Storage⇨Buy More Storage. At the time this book was going to press, an additional 20GB of storage cost $40 a year, and an additional 50GB cost $100 a year. But remember that anything you buy through iTunes doesn't count against your storage limits.

Siri

Apple's voice assistant (see Chapter 7) gets its own dedicated place in Settings, at least on the only models as of this writing that have Siri. As you know by now those are the iPhone 4S and iPhone 5. Choose the language Siri works in (across an increasing number of countries), determine whether you always want voice feedback or only in a hands-free situation, let Siri know your own information, and decide whether Siri will kick in when you raise the phone to speak. We revisit another setting relevant to Siri later in this chapter, in the "Passcode" section.

Cellular

A few major controls appear under the Cellular setting: Cellular Data, Enable LTE (if you have an iPhone 5), Data Roaming, Set Up Personal Hotspot, and Use Cellular Data For. We tackle them one by one in this section.

Cellular Data

Turn off the Cellular Data option if you don't want to exhaust your cellular minutes. Of course, turning off this setting means you can access the Internet only through Wi-Fi.

Enable LTE

If you have an iPhone 5, you'll appreciate the zippy speeds that LTE (Long Term Evolution) is capable of delivering. But if you're concerned about consuming too much data or overtaxing the battery, you may want to turn off LTE sometimes. Here's where you flip the switch for that purpose.

Data Roaming

You may unwittingly rack up lofty roaming fees when using Safari, exchanging e-mails, and engaging in other data-heavy activities while traveling in a foreign country. Turn off data roaming to avoid those excess charges.

Set Up Personal Hotspot

If your provider offers tethering, when it's turned on you can share the iPhone's Internet connection with a PC and iOS devices via Bluetooth or USB. Typically, an extra fee is involved; check with your carrier for rates.

Use Cellular Data For

You can specify that you want to use cellular data for iCloud documents, iTunes, FaceTime (the capability to do this over cellular rather than just Wi-Fi is new to iOS 6), Passbook updates, and Reading List.

VPN

A *virtual private network,* or *VPN,* is typically a way for you to securely access your company's network behind the firewall — using an encrypted Internet connection that acts as a secure "tunnel" for data. The iPhone software supports the protocols *L2TP* (Layer 2 Tunneling Protocol), *PPTP* (Point-to-Point Tunneling Protocol), and Cisco *IPSec VPN,* which apparently provides the kind of security that satisfies network administrators.

You can configure a VPN on the iPhone by tapping VPN under Network, tapping Add VPN Configuration, and then tapping one of the aforementioned protocols. Then, using configuration settings provided by your company, fill in the appropriate server information, account, password, encryption level (if appropriate), and other information. Better yet, lend your iPhone to the techies where you work and let them fill in the blanks on your behalf.

After you configure your iPhone for VPN usage, you can turn that capability on or off by tapping (yep) the VPN On or Off switch under Settings.

iTunes Wi-Fi sync

Through the magic of wireless, you no longer have to connect a cable to a PC or Mac to sync your iPhone with your iTunes account. If you've set up Wi-Fi syncing with iTunes, you can click a Sync Now button here to commence a Wi-Fi syncing session. For more on syncing, consult Chapter 3.

Spotlight search

You can designate which apps on your phone are searched when you take advantage of Spotlight. (As a reminder, you initiate a Spotlight search by flicking to the left of the Home page, or pressing the Home button from the first Home screen).

By default, all the options on the list shown in Settings will be part of a search. Tap to remove the check mark next to any app that you don't want the iPhone to include in its search mission. You can also change the order in which items are searched. Press the three bars to the right any item and drag that item up or down the list.

Auto-lock

You can set the amount of time that elapses before the phone automatically locks or turns off the display. Your choices are 5 minutes before, 4 minutes before, and so on, all the way down to 1 minute. Or you can choose to have the iPhone never lock automatically.

If you work for a company that insists on a passcode (see the next section), the Never Auto-Lock option isn't on the list your iPhone shows you.

Don't worry if the iPhone is locked. You can still receive calls and text messages, adjust the volume, see notifications, take pictures, call upon Siri's services (if you have an iPhone 4S or 5), access Passbook, and reply with a message when you can't answer an incoming call.

Passcode lock

You can select a passcode to prevent people from unlocking the iPhone. Tap Passcode Lock, and then use the virtual keypad to enter a 4-digit code (or skip a few paragraphs to see how to set up a more complex code). During this setup, you have to enter the code a second time before it's accepted.

You can also determine whether a passcode is required immediately, after 1 minute, after 5 minutes, or after 15 minutes. Shorter times are more secure, of course. On the topic of security, the iPhone can be set to automatically erase your data if you (or someone else!) make ten failed passcode attempts. Your settings will be reset to their defaults and all your media and information might as well be dust.

You can also change the passcode or turn it off later (unless your employer dictates otherwise), but you need to know the present passcode to apply any changes. If you forget the passcode, you have to restore the iPhone software, as described in Chapter 16.

The iPhone has two kinds of passcodes. A simple passcode is a four-digit number. If you require a more stringent password — one that is much harder to guess — turn off the simple passcode and come up with something much more difficult to crack, a longer combination of letters, numbers, punctuation, and special characters.

Under Passcode Lock settings on the 3GS and 4, you have the option to turn voice dialing on or off by keeping Voice Control enabled. Choose your preference by tapping the Voice Dial switch. On the 4S and 5, you have the option to turn Siri on or off. Note that Voice Control is still available regardless of the setting for Siri.

Siri can send an e-mail, send a message, or dial the phone even from the Lock screen. In fact, having Siri at the ready from the Lock screen is the default. Although that's a convenience for some, others might construe this as a security risk because an intruder would not need to know the phone's passcode to make a call or send an e-mail or text. If this notion bothers you, turn off Siri.

Restrictions

Parents and bosses may love the Restrictions tools, but kids and employees usually think otherwise. You can clamp down, um, provide proper parental guidance to your children by preventing them at least some of the time from using the Safari browser, the camera, FaceTime, iTunes, iBookstore, and Siri. Or you might not let them remove old apps, install new apps, or make purchases in the apps you do allow. You can also try to avoid exposing them to explicit language. When restrictions are in place, icons for off-limit functions can no longer be seen.

For instance, you can allow Junior to watch a movie on the iPhone but prevent him from watching a flick that carries an R or NC-17 rating. You can also restrict access to certain TV shows and apps, based on age-appropriate ratings, and stop the kids from engaging in multiplayer games or adding friends in Game Center. You can also access the various Privacy settings we address earlier in this chapter, including settings for Location Services, here.

Don't feel guilty: You have your users' best interests at heart.

Date and time

In our neck of the woods, the time is reported as 11:32 PM (or whatever time it happens to be). But in some circles, it's reported as 23:32. If you prefer the latter format on the iPhone's status bar, tap the 24-Hour Time setting (under Date & Time) to turn on the setting.

This setting is just one that you can adjust under Date & Time. You can also have the iPhone set the time automatically, using the time reported by the cellular network (and adjusted for your time zone).

If you've turned off the option to set the time automatically, you're asked to select the time zone and then set the date and time. Here's how:

1. **Tap Set Automatically so that it's off.**

   You see fields for setting the time zone and the date and time.

2. **Tap the Time Zone field.**

   The current time zone and virtual keyboard are shown.

3. **Tap out the letters of the city or country whose time zone you want to enter until the one you have in mind appears. Then tap the name of that city or country.**

   The Time Zone field is automatically filled in for that city.

4. **Tap the Set Date & Time field so that the time is shown. Then roll the bicycle-lock-like controls until the proper time is displayed.**

5. **Tap the date shown so that the bicycle-lock-like controls pop up for the date. Then roll the wheels for the month, day, and year until the correct date appears.**

6. **Tap the Date & Time button to return to the main Date & Time settings screen.**

Keyboard

Under Keyboard settings, you can turn on or off autocapitalization and turn on or off Enable Caps Lock.

Autocapitalization, which the iPhone turns on by default, means that the first letter of the first word you type after ending the preceding sentence with a period, a question mark, or an exclamation point is capitalized.

If Cap Locks is enabled, all letters are uppercased LIKE THIS if you double-tap the shift key. (The shift key is the one with the arrow pointing up.)

You can also turn on a keyboard setting that inserts a period followed by a space when you double-tap the space key. Additionally, you can choose to use an international keyboard (as discussed in Chapter 2), which you select from the International setting — the next setting after Keyboard in the General settings area. You can also choose a foreign keyboard by tapping Keyboards under the Keyboard setting and then choosing Add New Keyboard.

As you might have surmised, this is also the area where you can turn on or off the keyboard's autocorrection smarts.

And you can add keyboard shortcuts such as *omw* for *On my way!* To do so, tap Shortcuts, and create a shortcut that will automatically expand into the word or phrase you have in mind as you type.

International

The iPhone is an international sensation. It's sold and used around the world by people of all nationalities. In the International section, you can set the language you type on (by using a custom virtual keyboard), the language in which the iPhone displays text, and the language in which it speaks through Voice Control. Heck, you can even select a different region format (from among numerous countries) and a different calendar type, among Gregorian, Japanese, and Buddhist.

Accessibility

The ever-comprehensive Accessibility tools are targeted at people with certain disabilities. The following tools are available:

✓ **VoiceOver:** A screen reader describes aloud what's on the screen. The screen reader can read e-mail messages, web pages, and more. As you dig into these settings, you'll see that you can use phonetics, change the pitch, alter the speaking rate, and more.

✓ **Zoom:** This tool is a screen magnifier for those who are visually challenged. To zoom, double-tap the screen with *three* fingers, and drag three fingers to move around the screen. Double-tap the screen with three fingers again to zoom back out.

✓ **Large text:** You can enlarge the text in Mail, Contacts, Calendars, Messages, and Notes from a range of 20pt (points) up to 56pt. Don't worry if you don't know exactly what these *point* sizes mean. You'll see a sample of the text on the screen.

✓ **Invert colors:** The colors on the iPhone can be reversed to provide a higher contrast for people with poor eyesight. The screen sort of resembles a film negative.

✓ **Speak selection and speak auto-text:** When the Speak Selection setting is on, you'll see a Speak button when you select text. The Speak Auto-Text option allows the iPhone to automatically speak autocorrections and capitalizations.

✓ **Hearing aids:** The iPhone can communicate with hearing aids through Bluetooth.

✓ **LED flash for alerts:** This tool lets those who are hard of hearing know when an alert arrives. The setting works only when the phone is locked or asleep.

✓ **Mono audio:** If you suffer hearing loss in one ear, the iPhone can combine the right and left audio channels so that both can be heard in both earbuds or earpods, or any speakers connected to the iPhone's audio jack. You can drag a volume slider left or right to raise or lower the volume, respectively, in one channel or the other.

✓ **Guided access:** Parents of autistic kids know how challenging it can be to keep the child focused on a given task. The Guided Access setting, new in iOS 6, can limit iPhone usage to a single app and also restrict touch input on certain areas of the screen. You actually circle the area of the screen that you want to restrict. You can turn the feature on or off by triple-pressing the Home button. You can also create a passcode to use when Guided Access is at work. By turning on Enable Screen Sleep, you can dim the screen after a period of inactivity. If you tap the sleep/wake button, the screen will take an immediate nap.

✓ **AssistiveTouch:** Turn on this setting if you need to use an adaptive accessory such as a joystick because of difficulties touching the screen. Plus, when this setting is on, you can create your own custom gestures.

✓ **Home-click speed:** Slow down the speed required to double or triple-click the Home button, which is next on the list of Accessibility options.

✔ **Triple-click the Home button:** As you know by now, double-pressing the Home button launches multitasking. But you can set up the iPhone so that triple-clicking the button (pressing three times really fast) turns on certain Accessibility features. By doing so, you can turn on or off VoiceOver, Invert Colors, Zoom, and AssistiveTouch.

✔ **Incoming calls:** You can route calls to come through a headset or the iPhone speaker.

Profiles

If you know an app developer who is willing to share an app with you before it is publicly made available, you'll see that app in the list. You'll also see when any of the prerelease apps on the list expire, and can manually remove them.

Reset

As little kids playing sports, we ended an argument by agreeing to a do-over. Well, the Reset settings on the iPhone are one big do-over. Now that we're (presumably) grown up, we're wise enough to think long and hard about the consequences before implementing do-over settings, which is probably why you must enter a passcode before proceeding. Regardless, you may encounter good reasons for starting over; some of these reasons are addressed in Chapter 16.

Here are your reset options:

✔ **Reset All Settings:** Resets all settings, but no data or media is deleted.

✔ **Erase All Content and Settings:** Resets all settings *and* wipes out all your data.

✔ **Reset Network Settings:** Deletes the current network settings and restores them to their factory defaults.

✔ **Reset Keyboard Dictionary:** Removes added words from the dictionary. As we point out early on, the iPhone keyboard is intelligent. And one reason it's so smart is that it learns from you. So when you reject words that the iPhone keyboard suggests, it figures that the words you specifically banged out ought to be added to the keyboard dictionary.

This option deletes *all* the words you've added to the keyboard dictionary, so it will make your keyboard stupider instead of smarter. We suggest that you think twice before you invoke this option.

✔ **Reset Home Screen Layout:** Reverts all icons to the way they were at the factory. This feature is useful if, as has happened to us, an icon that used to be where you expected it has gone AWOL.

✔ **Reset Location & Privacy:** Restores factory defaults.

Phoning In More Settings

We cover most of the remaining settings in earlier chapters devoted to e-mail, calendars, music, photos, Safari, and e-mail. Still, we didn't get to a few other settings — 'til now.

iCloud

The iCloud settings are where you let iCloud know which of your apps, plus Photo Stream, ought to be turned on or off. You can also check on your storage and iCloud Backup options here, and if worse comes to worst, delete your iCloud account.

Consider carefully before deleting your iCloud account. If you do decide to delete your account, all your Photo Stream photos and documents stored in iCloud will be removed from your phone.

Twitter

In Twitter settings, you can add a new Twitter account and update your contacts so that Twitter uses their e-mail addresses and phone numbers to automatically add their Twitter handles and photos. You also can choose yay or nay on whether you can use various apps with Twitter.

Facebook

Most of us know Facebook as a great service to help you stay in touch with relatives, associates, and old pals, rekindle those relationships, and make new friends. But some people collect Facebook friends like baseball cards. If it seems like you're acquainted with all 1 billion or so members of the mammoth social network, we know what you mean.

Fortunately, Apple kindly organizes your Facebook relationships on the iPhone. If you turn on the Calendar and Contacts settings under Facebook settings on the iPhone, your Facebook friends automatically populate your Contacts list, complete with their profile picture as well as their e-mail addresses and phone numbers (if they made them public on Facebook). Birthdays and calendar appointments appropriately turn up in the iPhone calendar app.

Think of these Facebook entries as live synced contact entries. If a person changes his or her phone number and e-mail address on Facebook, that change will be reflected on your iPhone, provided you have Wi-Fi or cellular coverage or the next time you do. And if your friends de-friend you — what did you do, anyway? — their contact info will disappear altogether.

If the iPhone can correctly match a Facebook friend entry with an existing contact entry, it will try to unify that contact under a single view. Meanwhile, the Update All Contacts option under Facebook settings on the iPhone serves a slightly different purpose. It tries to add Facebook profile information to your contacts who are on Facebook but are not among your Facebook friends.

Sorting and displaying contacts

Do you think of us as Ed and Bob or Baig and LeVitus? The answer to that question will probably determine whether you choose to sort your Contacts list alphabetically by last name or first.

Tap Mail, Contacts, Calendars; scroll down to the Contacts section; and peek at Sort Order. Then tap Last; First; or First, Last.

You can also determine whether you want to display a first name or last name first. Tap Display Order, and then choose First; Last; or Last, First.

In My Info, make sure your own name is chosen so that Siri knows where you live, among other reasons.

While you're at it, check out the Default Account setting under the Contacts settings. If you create new contacts outside a specific account, the default account you select here is the account to which the new contact will be added.

Nothing phone-y about these settings

In Chapter 4, we tip our hand and indicate that we save a few more phone tricks — those found in Phone settings — for this chapter.

Tap Phone now to review some of the choices we don't get to in that chapter. Be aware that you have to scroll down the screen to find Phone settings.

Call forwarding

If you expect to spend time in an area with poor or no cell phone coverage, you may want to temporarily forward calls to a landline or other portable handset. Here are the simple steps:

1. **On the Settings screen, tap Phone⇨Call Forwarding.**

2. **Tap to turn on Call Forwarding.**

3. **Use the virtual keypad to enter the number where you want incoming calls to ring.**

4. **Tap the Call Forwarding button to return to the main Call Forwarding screen.**

To change the forwarding number, tap the circle with the X in the Phone Number field to get rid of the old number, and then enter a new one.

Remember to turn off Call Forwarding to receive calls directly on your iPhone again.

You must have cellular coverage while setting the Call Forwarding feature.

Call waiting

Tap the Call Waiting button to turn the feature on or off. If Call Waiting is off and you're speaking on the phone, the call is automatically dispatched to voicemail.

Show my Caller ID

Don't want your name or number displayed on the phone you're calling? Make sure to tap Show My Caller ID and turn off the setting. If privacy isn't a concern, you can leave this setting on.

TTY

Folks who are hearing impaired sometimes rely on a teletype, or TTY, machine, to hold conversations. You can use the iPhone with standard TTY devices by plugging a cable from the TTY device into an optional $19 iPhone TTY adapter, and then plugging the adapter into the iPhone. Make sure the TTY setting on the phone is turned on.

SIM locking

The tiny SIM (Subscriber Identity Module) card inside your iPhone holds your phone number and other important data. Tap to turn on SIM PIN and enter a password with the keypad. Then, if someone gets hold of your SIM, he or she can't use it in another phone without the password.

Change voicemail password

This setting is straightforward enough. Tap Change Voicemail Password, type your old 4-digit password, and tap Done. Then type the new password and tap Done twice. Your new password is saved until, and if, you change it again.

If you assign a PIN to your SIM, you have to enter it to turn the iPhone off and on again.

Carrier services

A major difference between the iPhone and all the other Apple products you might buy is that you enter into a relationship with not only Apple but also the phone company when you have an iPhone. On your AT&T iPhone, for example, you can tap AT&T Services and then tap any of the following options for a shortcut phone call:

- **Check Bill Balance:** The phone dials *225# and, if all goes according to plan, you receive a text message with the due date and sum owed. This type of text message isn't counted against your messaging allotment.

- **Call Directory Assistance:** The phone dials 411.

- **Pay My Bill:** The iPhone dials *729 and you're connected to an automated voice system. You can pay your bill with a checking account, debit card, or credit card by following the voice prompts.

  You're billed for phone service *from AT&T,* not from Apple. Of course, charges for any music or other content purchased in iTunes from your computer are paid to Apple through whichever credit card you have on file, as with any iPod.

- **View My Data and Msg:** Find out if you're getting close to your data limits, messaging limits, or both. An incoming text supplies the answer. The phone dials *3282#.

- **View My Minutes:** This time, *646# is called. You again receive a text reply that doesn't count against your messaging allotment.

- **Voice Connect:** The iPhone dials *08 to connect you to automated news, weather, sports, quotes, and more. Just bark out the kind of information you're looking for, such as finance, and follow voice prompts for stock quotes and business news, for example. Or say "Sports" and follow the voice prompts to see the latest scores of your favorite team. Of course, in many instances Siri can deliver similar information.

Not all AT&T Services options make a phone call. If you tap the AT&T My Account button, Safari opens an AT&T account management page on the web.

Of course, if you have an iPhone from Verizon, Sprint, or another carrier, you'll see different shortcuts on their respective devices.

Nike + iPod

You're passionate about fitness. You're equally passionate about music. Apple has teamed up with the folks at Nike on a $29 wireless sports kit that lets runners place a sensor inside a Nike sneaker that can wirelessly communicate with a receiver connected to an iPod Nano. There's no need for a separate receiver in the iPhone; it can communicate with the Nike + sensor. As runners dash off, they can track time, distance, and calories burned on the iPhone (or Nano), receive vocal feedback, and upload results to a Nike website. Runners can even play a select "power song" on the iPod for that last push when they're feeling exhausted.

When you turn on the Nike + app in Settings, your iPhone can record every step you make. You don't have to connect a separate receiver, as you do on the Nano. By tapping Go to Nike + in Settings, you can see how well (or not) you're doing, as shown in Figure 14-10.

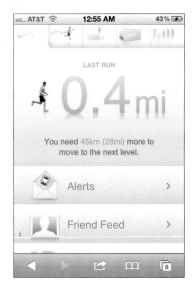

Figure 14-10: Born to run with your iPhone.

Find My iPhone

We hope you never have to use the Find My iPhone feature — though we have to say that it's pretty darn cool. If you inadvertently leave your iPhone in a taxi or restaurant, Find My iPhone may just help you retrieve it. It helped Ed retrieve a phone he left on a bus.

To turn on Find My iPhone, open Settings and tap iCloud. (You get an iCloud e-mail account when you join the free iCloud service.) Refer to Chapter 12 to see how to add an e-mail account to the iPhone. Make sure the Find My iPhone setting is turned on.

Now suppose that you lost your phone — and we can only assume that you're beside yourself. Log in to your iCloud account from any browser on your computer. Click Find My iPhone.

Apple now supplies a free Find My iPhone app in the App Store. So you could use an iPhone loaded with this app to locate another iPhone (or iPad or Mac computer).

Assuming that your lost phone is turned on and in the coverage area, its general whereabouts should appear on a map, as shown in Figure 14-11. In our tests, Find My iPhone found our iPhones quickly.

Figure 14-11: Locating a lost iPhone.

The truth is that even seeing your iPhone on a map may not help you much, especially if the phone is lost somewhere in midtown Manhattan. Take heart. At the Find My iPhone site, click Lost Mode to bang out a plea to the Good Samaritan whom you hope picked up your phone. The message appears on the lost iPhone's screen. You'll get to enter a phone number so that the person can reach you, as shown in Figure 14-12.

To get someone's attention, you click Play Sound to sound an alarm that plays for two minutes, even if the phone was in silent mode. Hey, that alarm may come in handy if the phone turns up under a couch in your house.

After all this labor, if the phone is seemingly gone for good, click Erase iPhone at the site to delete your personal data from afar and return the iPhone to its factory settings. And, if you ever get your phone back afterward, you can always restore the information with an iTunes or iCloud backup on your PC or Mac.

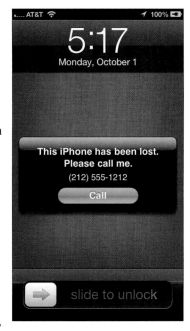

Figure 14-12: An appeal to return the phone.

We trust that you control freaks are satisfied with all the stuff you can manage in Settings. Still, the iPhone may not always behave as you want. For the times when things get *out* of control, we highly recommend Chapter 16.

15

Apps-O-Lutely!

In This Chapter

▶ Browsing for cool apps

▶ Searching for specific apps

▶ Getting apps onto your iPhone

▶ Deleting and organizing your iPhone apps

▶ Getting the scoop on newspapers, magazines, and books

*O*ne of the best things about the iPhone is that you can download and install apps created by third parties, which is to say not created by Apple (the first party) or you (the second party). At the time of this writing, our best guess is that there are more than 700,000 apps available and over 25,000,000,000 (yes, 25 billion) apps downloaded to date. Some apps are free, other apps cost money; some apps are useful, other apps are lame; some apps are perfectly well-behaved, other apps quit unexpectedly (or worse). The point is that of the many apps out there, some are better than others.

In this chapter, we take a broad look at iPhone apps. Don't worry: We have plenty to say about specific apps in Chapters 17 and 18.

You can obtain and install apps for your iPhone in three ways:

✔ On your computer

✔ On your iPhone

✔ By Automatic Download

To switch on Automatic Downloads on the iPhone, tap Settings⬦iTunes & App Store. After you do so, all apps you buy with iTunes on your computer or buy on other iOS devices will automagically appear on your iPhone.

To use the App Store on your iPhone, it must be connected to the Internet. And, if you obtain an app on your computer, it won't be available on your iPhone until you sync it with your computer — unless you've turned on Automatic Downloads as described in the preceding paragraph.

But before you can use the App Store on your iPhone or computer, you need an iTunes Store account. If you don't already have one, we suggest that you launch iTunes on your computer, click Sign In near the upper-right corner of the iTunes window, click Create New Account, and then follow the on-screen instructions. Or if you prefer to create your account on your iPhone rather than on your computer, follow the instructions near the end of Chapter 8.

Let's put it this way: If you don't have an iTunes Store account, you can't download a single cool app for your iPhone. Enough said.

Using Your Computer to Find Apps

Okay, start by finding cool iPhone apps using iTunes on your computer. Follow these steps:

1. **Launch iTunes.**

2. **In the source list on the left, click the iTunes Store.**

3. **Click the Apps link.**

   The iTunes App Store appears.

4. **Click the iPhone tab at the top of the screen (as opposed to the iPad tab).**

   The iPhone App section of the App Store appears, as shown in Figure 15-1.

Looking for apps from your computer

After you have the iTunes App Store on your screen and have clicked the iPhone tab so that you're looking at iPhone apps and not iPad apps, you have a few options for exploring its virtual aisles. Allow us to introduce you to the various "departments" available from the main screen.

Browsing the iPhone App Store screen

Like most retail stores, the iPhone App Store rearranges things in its windows (ha!) all the time. Names of departments and even the layout can change from week to week. For the most part, the main departments are down the middle of the screen (interspersed with some ads), with ancillary departments and the Top Paid, Free, and Grossing App lists appearing to the right of the main departments.

iTunes Store
in source list

Scroll bar for
Amazing Apps
on iPhone 5

iPhone tab

App Store link

iPad tab

Search iTunes
Store

Figure 15-1: The iTunes App Store, in all its glory.

We start with the middle:

  ✔ The **Amazing Apps on iPhone 5** department has six visible icons (from
    Foursquare to Catch Notes in Figure 15-1), representing apps that have
    been updated to take advantage of every pixel on the iPhone 5's new
    longer screen.

Only six icons are visible, but the Amazing Apps on iPhone 5 department has more than that. Look to the right of the words *Amazing Apps on iPhone 5.* See the words *See All?* That's a link; if you click it, you'll see *all* apps in this department on a single screen (though you may have to scroll to see them all). Or you can drag the scroll bar below the Amazing Apps on iPhone 5 section to the right to see more icons.

✔ The **Great Games on iPhone 5** department also displays six icons in Figure 15-1. These apps are games that have been updated for iPhone 5. Note the See All link and scroll bar for this department, either of which you can use to see more hot apps.

✔ The **New and Noteworthy** department has six visible icons in Figure 15-1. These represent apps that are — what else? — new and noteworthy.

Apple has a habit of redecorating the iTunes Store every so often, so allow us to apologize in advance if things aren't exactly as described here.

You also see a large display ad at the top of the screen (Games in Figure 15-1), with featured links (that is, ads) between the departments just described. Sometimes these link to specific apps; other times they link to groups of apps with a theme, such as Free Apps or Special Education.

Three Top departments appear to the right of the main ones: Top Paid Apps, Top Free Apps (one of our favorite departments), and Top Grossing Apps, which is not visible in Figure 15-1. The number-one app in each department is displayed with its icon; the next nine apps show text links only.

Finally, the black App Store tab near the top of the screen is also a drop-down menu (as are most of the other department links to its left and right). If you click and hold down on most of these department links, a menu with a list of the department's categories appears.

The menus won't work if you've disabled JavaScript in your browser.

For example, if you click and hold down the Apps link, as shown in Figure 15-2, you can choose specific categories such as Books, Business, Education, and Entertainment from the drop-down menu, allowing you to bypass the App Store home page and go directly to that category.

Using the Search field

Browsing the screen is helpful, but if you know exactly what you're looking for, we have good news and bad news. The good news is that there's a faster way than browsing: Just type a word or phrase in the Search Store field in the upper-right corner of the main iTunes window, and then press Enter or Return to initiate the search. Figure 15-3 shows the result of a search for *flashlight.*

Figure 15-2: The Apps drop-down menu.

Display drop-down menu   See All link

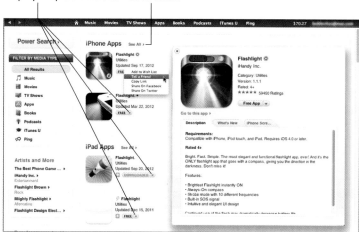

Figure 15-3: I want to use my iPhone as a flashlight, so I searched for the word *flashlight*.

The bad news is that you have to search the entire iTunes Store, which includes music, television shows, movies, and other stuff in addition to iPhone apps.

Ah, but we have more good news: Your search results are segregated into categories — one of which is iPhone Apps (refer to Figure 15-3). And here's even more good news: If you click the See All link to the right of the words *iPhone Apps,* all iPhone apps that match your search word or phrase appear.

Click the little downward-pointing triangle to the right of each item's price to display a drop-down menu, as shown for the first Flashlight app in Figure 15-3. This menu lets you add the product to your wish list, send an e-mail with a link to this product, copy the link to this product to the Clipboard so you can paste it elsewhere, or share it on Facebook or Twitter.

Finally, if you hover the cursor over an app's icon, a tiny *i* in a circle will appear in its lower-right corner. Click the *i* and a small information window pops up.

Getting more information about an app

Now that you know how to find apps in the App Store, this section delves a little deeper and shows you how to get additional info about an app that interests you.

Checking out the detail screen from your computer

To find out more about an app icon, a featured app, or a text link on any of the iTunes App Store screens, just click it. A detail screen like the one shown in Figure 15-4 appears.

This screen should tell you most of what you need to know about the app, such as basic product information and a narrative description, what's new in this version, the language it's presented in, and the system requirements to run the app. Click the blue More link to the right of the Description and What's New sections to expand them and see additional details.

Bear in mind that the app description on this screen was written by the app's developer and may be somewhat biased. Never fear, gentle reader: In the next section, we show you how to find reviews of the app written by people who have used it.

Notice that this app is rated 9+, as labeled in Figure 15-4. And just below the rating is the reason for that rating: Frequent/Intense Cartoon or Fantasy Violence.

Free App button   Link to developer   Link to support   More links

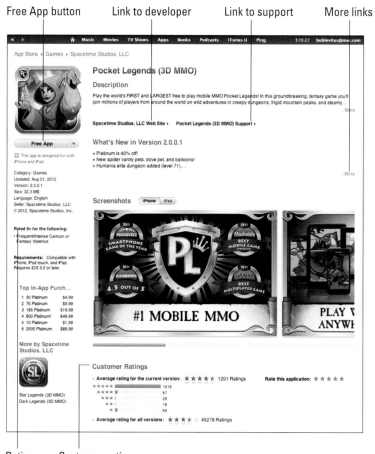

Rating   Customer ratings

Figure 15-4: The detail screen for the Pocket Legends app.

Following is a list of the ratings as of this writing:

- **4+:** Contains no objectionable material.

- **9+:** May contain mild or infrequent occurrences of cartoon, fantasy, or realistic violence; or infrequent or mild mature, suggestive, or horror-themed content that may not be suitable for children under the age of 9.

- **12+:** May contain infrequent mild language; frequent or intense cartoon, fantasy, or realistic violence; mild or infrequent mature or suggestive themes; or simulated gambling that may not be suitable for children under the age of 12.

✔ **17+:** May contain frequent and intense offensive language; frequent and intense cartoon, fantasy, or realistic violence; mature, frequent, and intense mature, suggestive, or horror-themed content; sexual content; nudity; depictions of alcohol, tobacco, or drugs that may not be suitable for children under the age of 17. You must be at least 17 years old to purchase apps with this rating.

One other feature of the detail pages that's worth mentioning is that most apps include one or more useful links, right below the app description. In Figure 15-4, one link goes to the website of the developer (Spacetime Studios, LLC), and the other goes to the Pocket Legends Support web page. We urge you to explore such links at your leisure.

Reading reviews from your computer

If you scroll down the detail screen, below the customer ratings, you find a series of reviews by the folks who own the app (not shown 15-4). Each review includes a star rating, from zero to five; if an app is rated four or higher, it's probably well liked by people who own it.

Downloading an app

Downloading an app is simple. When you find an app you want to try, just click its Get App or Buy App button. At that point, you have to log in to your iTunes Store account, even if the app is free.

After you log in, the app begins downloading. When the app has finished downloading, it appears in the Apps section of your iTunes library, as shown in Figure 15-5.

We are using the Grid view for the apps in Figure 15-5, but you can view your apps in three other ways, namely List view, Album list view, and Cover Flow view. To change views, click one of the four icons just to the left of the search field (labeled in Figure 15-5). Also note the two tabs below the icons, which say Apps and Genres (selected in Figure 15-5). These tabs, which are exclusive to Grid view, provide two additional ways to look at your collection of apps; we suggest you try both options for Grid view and experiment with the three other views.

Downloading an app to your iTunes library on your computer is only the first half of getting it onto your iPhone. After you download an app, you have to sync your iPhone before the app will be available on it, unless you've enabled Automatic Downloads as described earlier in this chapter.

List view   Album list view

View all apps   View all genres   Grid view   Cover Flow view

Figure 15-5: Apps you downloaded appear in the Apps section of your iTunes library.

Updating an app

Every so often, the developer of an iPhone app releases an update. Sometimes these updates add new features to the app, or squash bugs, or both. In any event, updates are usually a good thing for you and your iPhone, so it makes sense to check for them every so often. To do this on your computer using iTunes, select Apps in the Library list on the left, and then click the Check for Updates link, which appears near the lower-right corner of the iTunes window when Apps is selected in the Library (as shown in Figure 15-5).

If you click the Get More Apps link at the bottom of the screen, you find yourself back at the main screen of the iTunes App Store (refer to Figure 15-1).

Downloading other content on your iPhone

You may have noticed that the App Store app on your iPhone offers nothing but apps. iTunes on your computer, on the other hand, includes sections for Music, Movies, TV Shows, Books, Podcasts, and iTunes U in addition to Apps.

On your iPhone, you obtain music, movies, and TV shows with the iTunes app, and books and magazines with the free iBooks app, which you'll have to download if you don't already have it. To download podcasts or iTunes U content, however, you'll need the Podcasts or iTunes U apps, which (curiously) are not included with your iPhone out of the box.

The good news is that both apps are free in the App Store, so if you want to shop for podcasts

or iTunes U content on your iPhone, you should probably go download one or both apps now.

Our tech editor Dennis Cohen explained it to his teenage granddaughter thusly:

> Think of iTunes as a shopping mall with a bunch of stores (that is, the Music, Movies, TV Shows, Books, Podcasts, and iTunes U links) in a single location. Your iPhone doesn't have a mall, so you shop for different kinds of content in the appropriate store (that is, the App Store, iTunes, iBooks, Newsstand, Podcasts, and iTunes U apps).

The good news is that because these "store" apps all work pretty much the same, and you know how to use the App Store app, you also know how to use all of the store apps.

Using Your iPhone to Find Apps

Finding apps with your iPhone is almost as easy as finding them by using iTunes. The only requirement is that you have an Internet connection of some sort — Wi-Fi or wireless data network — to browse, search, download, and install apps.

To get started, tap the App Store icon on your iPhone's Home screen. After you launch the App Store, you see five icons at the bottom of the screen, representing five ways to interact with the store, as shown in Figure 15-6.

Looking for apps from your iPhone

The first four icons at the bottom of the screen — Featured, Charts, Genius, and Search — offer four ways to explore the virtual shelves of the App Store.

Tap the Featured icon and you'll see a miniature version of the iTunes App Store (shown in Figure 15-1), with the same departments, namely Amazing Apps on iPhone 5 and Great Games on iPhone 5.

At the bottom of the screen are icons for Charts, Genius, Search, and Updates. Genius is perhaps the most interesting — it suggests apps you might enjoy based on the apps currently installed on your iPhone. The Charts section works much the same as the Featured section. Its three departments — Top Paid, Top Free, and Top Grossing — represent the most popular apps that either cost money (paid and top grossing) or don't (free).

Each page displays dozens upon dozens of apps, but you see only a handful at a time on the screen. Remember to flick up and down and left and right to see all the others.

Know exactly what you're looking for? Instead of simply browsing, you can tap the Search icon and type a word or phrase.

Or use the Categories button, which appears at the top of the Featured and Charts sections, which works a little differently because it has no apps. Instead, it offers a list of categories such as Games, Newsstand, Entertainment, Utilities, and Social Networking, to name a few, as shown in Figure 15-7.

Figure 15-6: The icons across the bottom represent the five sections of the App Store.

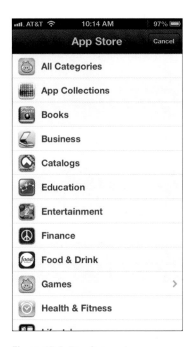

Figure 15-7: The Categories section lets you browse for apps in categories such as these.

Tap a category to see either a page full of apps of that type or a list of sub-categories for that type. For example, the Games category offers subcategories such as Action, Arcade, Kids, Music, and Puzzle. Other categories have no subcategories — you'll go directly to the page full of apps when you tap them. To make your browsing easier, each category or subcategory page has four sections — New, What's Hot, Paid, and Free.

If you're wondering about Updates, the fifth icon at the bottom of the screen, we discuss it a little later in this chapter in the imaginatively named "Updating an App" section.

Finding more information about an app

Now that you know how to find apps in the App Store, the following sections show you how to find additional information about a particular app.

Checking out the detail screen from your iPhone

To find out more about any app on any page, tap the app. You see a detail screen like the one shown in Figure 15-8.

Remember that the app description on this screen was written by the developer and may be somewhat biased.

Reading reviews from your iPhone

Tap the Reviews button (between Details and Related in Figure 15-8) to see the star ratings and reviews for that app. At the bottom of that page is another button: More Reviews. Tap it to see (what else?) more reviews.

Game Center means social gaming

We'd be remiss if we didn't at least say a few words about Game Center, the free social-gaming app that comes with every iPhone. Thousands of games in the App store support Game Center. All you have to do to get involved is tap the Game Center app and log in with your Apple ID.

When you do, you'll find a list of the games on your iPhone with Game Center support, some recommendations for other games you might enjoy, a list of your achievements in games

you own, and a button that lets you invite your friends to play.

If you're the type who enjoys social networking (and you know who you are, Facebook and Twitter fans), you should definitely open and log in to Game Center. That way, even if you don't use it much, your friends will be able to find you and challenge you to a game — you'll see an alert and a numeric badge on the Game Center icon by default when a friend request or game challenge arrives.

Downloading an app

To download an app to your iPhone, tap the price button near the top of its detail screen. In Figure 15-8, the price button is the gray rectangle that says Free. You may or may not be asked to type your iTunes Store account password before the App Store disappears and the Home screen, where the new app's icon will reside, appears in its place. The new icon is slightly dimmed, and appears with a blue progress indicator and the word *Loading* or *Installing,* as shown in Figure 15-9.

Progress bar

Figure 15-8: Remote, the free app from Apple, lets you control iTunes or AppleTV from your iPhone.

Figure 15-9: The blue progress bar indicates that the app is more than halfway through downloading.

By the way, if the app is rated 17+, you see a warning screen after you type your password. You have to tap the OK button to confirm that you're 17 or older before the app will download.

The app is now on your iPhone, but it isn't copied to your iTunes library on your Mac or PC until your next sync — unless, of course, you've turned on Automatic Downloads as described earlier in the chapter. If your iPhone suddenly loses its memory (unlikely) or you delete the app from your iPhone before you sync (as described later in this chapter), that app is gone forever. That's the bad news.

The good news is that after you've paid for an app, you can download it again if you need to — from iTunes on your computer or the App Store app on your iPhone — and you don't have to pay for it again.

After you download an app to your iPhone, the app is transferred to your iTunes Apps library the next time you sync your phone.

Or, if you've turned on Automatic Downloads in iTunes (which is in iTunes Preferences on its Store pane), the app will appear automatically in your iTunes library almost immediately after you purchase the app on your iPhone.

Updating an app

As mentioned earlier in this chapter, every so often (or, for some apps, far too often), the developer of an iPhone app releases an update. If one (or more) of these is waiting for you, a little number in a circle appears on the App Store icon on your Home screen as well as on the Updates icon at the bottom of the screen. Tap the Updates icon if any of your apps need updating.

If you tap the Updates button and see (in the middle of the screen) the message *All Apps Are Up-to-Date,* none of the apps on your iPhone requires an update at this time. If an app needs updating, an Update button appears next to the app. Tap the button to update the app. If more than one app needs updating, you can update them all at once by tapping the Update All button in the upper-right corner of the screen.

If you try to update an app purchased from any iTunes Store account except your own, you're prompted for that account's ID and password. If you can't provide them, you can't download the update.

Deleting and Organizing Your Apps

That's almost everything you need to know about installing apps on your iPhone. However, you might find it helpful to know how to delete and organize apps.

Deleting an app

You can delete an app in two ways: in iTunes on your computer or directly from your iPhone.

To delete an app in iTunes, click Apps in the source list and then do one of the following:

- Click the app's icon to select it and then choose Edit⇨Delete.
- Right-click (or Control+click on a Mac) the app's icon and choose Delete.

Either way, you see a dialog asking whether you're sure you want to remove the selected app. If you click the Remove button, the app is removed from your iTunes library, as well as from any iOS device that syncs with your iTunes library.

You can't delete any Apple apps that came with your iPhone, but here's how to delete any third-party app on your iPhone:

1. **Press and hold down any icon until all the icons begin to jiggle.**

2. **Tap the little x in the upper-left corner of the app you want to delete, as shown in Figure 15-10.**

   A dialog appears, informing you that deleting this app also deletes all its data, as shown in Figure 15-11.

3. **Tap the Delete button.**

Deleting an app from your iPhone this way doesn't get rid of it permanently. The app remains in your iTunes library until you delete it from iTunes, as described earlier in this chapter. Put another way: Even though you deleted the app from your iPhone, it's still in your iTunes library. If you want to get rid of an app for good and for always after you delete it on your iPhone, you must delete it also from your iTunes library. Even then it's not *really* gone forever because you can download purchased apps again for free.

If you see a warning that deleting the app also deletes any associated data, you may want to save the data before deleting the app. Different apps have different schemes for importing and exporting data; the important thing is that if you create documents with an app (notes, images, videos, and such), deleting the app will delete any files you've created with that app. Forewarned is forearmed.

Little x's

Figure 15-10: Tap an app's little x to mark the app for deletion.

Figure 15-11: Tap Delete to remove the app from your iPhone.

 If you delete an app and later change your mind and want it back on your iPhone, you can tap the Updates button and then tap Purchased, where you'll find all the apps you've ever purchased in your life, or at least all the apps you bought with the Apple ID you're currently using. Tap the Not on This iPhone tab at the top of the screen to limit the display to only apps that aren't currently installed on your iPhone. Then tap the little cloud icon (shown in the margin) to reinstall the app on your iPhone.

Organizing your apps

You can have up to 11 Home screens (or pages) of apps. And if you're like many iPhone users, you'll soon have a substantial collection of apps in your iTunes library and on your iPhone. So let's look at a few ways to organize those apps for easy access.

On your computer (in iTunes)

First things first: On your computer, make sure you've selected your iPhone in the Devices section below the iTunes Store on the left side of the iTunes window. Then click the Apps tab near the top of the window (shown in Figure 15-12).

Scrolling list of Home screens with screen 6 selected

Sync Apps section   iPhone section displaying Home screen 6

Figure 15-12: Eight screens of apps with screen 6 selected.

You can organize your apps in the following ways:

- ✔ In the iPhone section, you can click and drag an app icon to a new location on the same screen.

- ✔ You can drag an app from the Sync Apps section on the left to any of the 11 screens in the Home screen list on the right, as long as the screen has no empty screens before it. In other words, you can drag an app to screen 7 as long as at least one app is on each of the screens numbers 1 through 6.

- ✔ You can change the order of screens in the Home screen list by clicking and dragging a screen upward or downward in the list and dropping it in its new location. After you have a few pages' worth of apps, give it a try — it's easy and kind of fun.

You can change the order of Home screens only in iTunes. No mechanism exists for reordering Home screens on your iPhone.

On your iPhone

To rearrange apps on your iPhone, first press and hold down on any app until all the apps begin to jiggle and dance, and the little black "delete me" x's appear. Figure 15-13 shows the screen before (left) and after (right) moving an app. The app you press and hold down doesn't have to be the one you want to move — any app will do.

Figure 15-13: The way things were (left), and what happens when we drag the Dr. Bob icon from the next-to-bottom row to the top row.

To move an app after the jiggling starts, press it, drag it to its new location (other apps on the screen will politely move out of its way to make space for it), and release it, as shown on the right of Figure 15-13.

To move an app to a different Home screen after the jiggling starts, press the app and drag it all the way to the left or right edge of the screen. The preceding or next Home screen, respectively, will appear. Keep dragging the app to the left or right edge of each successive Home screen until you reach the screen you want. Then drop the app in its new location on that screen. If the screen already holds 16 apps (20 if you have an iPhone 5), the last icon on the page will be pushed to the next Home screen. Be persistent — sometimes it takes a few tries to make the screens switch.

All these techniques for iTunes and iPhones work with apps in the dock: by default, Phone, Safari, Mail, and Music.

You can add apps beyond the 11th Home screen. To do so, just keep selecting check boxes for apps in the Sync Apps section after all 11 screens are filled. You won't be able to see the icons for these apps on any Home screen, so you'll have to access them via Spotlight search.

You use the same technique — drag one app on top of another app — to create folders in both iTunes and on your iPhone. And to place an app into an existing folder, you drag that app on top of the folder. If you've forgotten how to create folders, refer to the section on organizing icons into folders in Chapter 2.

A few more facts about Home screens. We mention this elsewhere, but in case you missed it: The little dots above the four apps in the dock indicate how many Home screens you have. The white dot denotes the Home screen you're currently looking at. So, for example, the dots in Figure 15-12 tell us we're looking at screen 9 of 10 Home screens.

And last but not least, we'd be remiss if we didn't at least provide the following reminders. You can create folders that hold up to 12 apps each (16 on the iPhone 5), put Spotlight to work to quickly find and launch apps no matter which Home screen they're on, and take advantage of multitasking (by double-tapping the Home button) to quickly switch between recently used apps. If you're hazy on any of these three concepts, we suggest that you flip back to Chapter 2, where they are expounded upon in full and loving detail.

There you have it — you now know everything you need to know to find, install, delete, and organize iPhone apps!

Books, Newspapers, and Magazines

Before we leave the subject of apps and the App Store, we want to tell you how to find, buy, and read books and magazines on your iPhone.

We've run into plenty of skeptics who beg the question, "What's so wrong with paper books, which folks have been reading for centuries, that we now have to go digital?" The short answer is that nothing is wrong with physical books — except maybe that, over the long term, paper is fragile, and books tend to be bulky, a potential impediment for travelers.

On the other hand, when asked why he prefers paper books, Bob likes to drop one from shoulder height and ask, "Can your iPad (or Kindle) do that?"

Having read that, consider the electronic advantages:

- ✓ **Forget weight constraints:** You can cart a whole bunch of e-books around when you travel, without breaking your back. To the avid bookworm, this could change the way you read. Because you can carry so many books wherever you go, you can read whatever type of book strikes your fancy at the moment, kind of like listening to a song that fits your current mood. And you'll always have your reference library in your pocket or purse when you need it.

- ✓ **Switch genres at will:** Go for it. Rather immerse yourself in classic literature? Go for that. You might read a textbook, cookbook, or biography. Or gaze in wonder at an illustrated beauty. What's more, you can switch among the various titles and styles of books at will, before finishing any single title.

- ✓ **Change fonts and type sizes:** With e-books, or what Apple prefers to call *iBooks,* you can change the text size and fonts on the fly, quite useful for those with less than 20/20 vision.

- ✓ **Get the meaning of a word on the spot:** No more searching for a physical dictionary. You can look up an unfamiliar word on the spot.

- ✓ **Search with ease:** Looking to do research on a particular subject? Enter a search term to find each and every mention of the subject in the book you're reading.

- ✓ **See all the artwork in color:** Indeed, you're making no real visual sacrifices anymore. For example, the latest iBooks software from Apple lets you experience (within certain limits) the kind of stunning art book once reserved for a coffee table. Or you can display a colorful children's picture book. Although artwork is even more stunning on an iPad, it's still impressive on the iPhone's smaller screen.

- ✓ **Read in the dark:** The iPhone has a high-resolution backlit display so that you can read without a lamp nearby, which is useful in bed when your partner is trying to sleep.

Truth is, this backlit story has two sides. The grayscale electronic ink displays on Amazon's Kindle and several other e-readers may be easier on the eyes and reduce fatigue, especially if you read for hours on end. And although you may indeed have to supply your own lighting source to read in low-light situations, those screens are somewhat easier to see than the iPhone screen when you're out and about in bright sunshine.

iBooks for your iPhone

To start reading electronic books on your iPhone, the simplest option is to fetch the iBooks app in the App Store. You should know how to do that (if not, the instructions for finding and downloading apps are in this very chapter, just a few pages back from here).

The app is free and comes with access to Apple's iBookstore, which looks and feels almost exactly like the App Store, which is to say it's an inviting place to browse and shop for books 24 hours a day.

iBooks and the iBookstore aren't the only game in town. Check out other e-book options such as the Kindle, Nook, Bluefire, or Stanza apps, which many users prefer over the iBooks experience. Your mileage may vary.

You can buy iBooks on your computer in the App Store's Books section or on your iPhone by tapping the Store button at the top of the iBooks app's main screen.

You can only *read* iBooks on an iPhone, iPad, or iPod touch. You can *buy* an iBook using iTunes on your Mac or PC but you can't *read* that iBook using iTunes (or any other app we know of) on your Mac or PC. We hope this anomaly will be corrected, but as we write this you can read iBooks only on i-devices.

Newspapers and magazines

Those in the newspaper business know that it's been tough sledding in recent years. The Internet has proved to be a disruptive force in media, as it has in so many areas.

It remains to be seen what role Apple generally, and the iPhone specifically, will play in the future of electronic periodicals or in helping to turn around sagging media enterprises. It's also uncertain which pricing models will make the most sense from a business perspective.

What we can tell you is that reading newspapers and magazines on the iPhone is not like reading newspapers and magazines in any other electronic form. The experience can be slick, but only you can decide whether it's worth paying the tab (in the cases where you do have to pay).

Don't look for newspapers and magazines in the iBooks app's iBookstore. Periodicals are not considered books and are handled differently.

Newspaper and magazine apps

You can follow two paths to subscribe to or read a single issue of a newspaper or magazine. The first includes several fine publishing apps worth checking out, including USA TODAY (where Ed works), The Wall Street Journal, The New York Times, Thomson Reuters News Pro, BBC News, and Popular Mechanics. We also recommend fetching the free Zinio app, which offers publications including *Rolling Stone, The Economist, Macworld, PC Magazine, Car and Driver, National Geographic, Spin, Business Week,* and *Sporting News.* You can buy single issues of a magazine or subscribe, and sample and share some articles without a subscription.

You have to pay handsomely or subscribe to some of these newspapers and magazines, and most (if not all) of them contain ads (somebody has to pay the freight).

Newsstand

The second path to periodicals is iOS 6's Newsstand. This handy icon on your Home screen is a special folder that gathers newspaper and magazine apps from participating publishers in a single convenient location.

To shop for periodicals on your computer, launch iTunes and then click the iTunes Store in the list on the left. Next, press and hold down the Apps link near the top of the screen, and then select Newsstand from the drop-down menu.

On your iPhone, you can peruse periodicals in the Newsstand section of the App Store. Tap App Store, tap the Categories icon at the bottom of the screen, and then tap Newsstand. In addition, you can tap the Store button in the Newsstand icon on your Home screen to go to the App Store's Newsstand section.

It's too soon to tell how many publications will adopt the Newsstand paradigm, how many will choose custom apps or Zinio, and how many will do both. Stay tuned.

As the late Steve Jobs was so fond of saying in his keynotes, "There is one last thing": If you're into apps, we are happy to inform you that Chapters 17 and 18, in the famous Part of Tens, are about our ten favorite free iPhone apps and our ten favorites with a price on their virtual heads.

When Good iPhones Go Bad

In This Chapter

▶ Fixing iPhone issues

▶ Dealing with network and calling problems

▶ Eliminating that sinking feeling when you can't sync

▶ Perusing the Apple website and discussion forums

▶ Sending your iPhone to an Apple Store

*I*n our experience, iPhones are usually reliable devices. And most users we talk to report trouble-free operation. Notice our use of the word *most*. That's because every so often, a good iPhone goes bad. It's not a common occurrence, but it does happen. So in this chapter, we look at the types of bad things that can happen, along with suggestions for fixing them.

What kind of bad things are we talking about? Well, we're referring to problems involving

▸ The phone itself

▸ Making or receiving calls

▸ Wireless networks

▸ Sync, computers (both Mac and PC), or iTunes

After all the troubleshooting, we tell you how to get even more help if nothing we suggest does the trick. Finally, if your iPhone is so badly hosed that it needs to go back to the mothership for repairs, we offer ways to survive the experience with a minimum of stress or fuss.

iPhone Issues

Our first category of troubleshooting techniques applies to an iPhone that's frozen or otherwise acting up. The recommended procedure when this happens is to perform the seven *Rs* in sequence:

- ✓ Recharge your iPhone
- ✓ Restart your iPhone
- ✓ Reset your iPhone
- ✓ Remove content from your iPhone
- ✓ Reset your iPhone's settings and content
- ✓ Restore your iPhone
- ✓ Renew your iPhone in Recovery mode

If your iPhone acts up on you — if it freezes, doesn't wake up from sleep, doesn't do something it used to do, or in any other way acts improperly — don't panic. This section describes the things you should try, in the order that we (and Apple) recommend.

If the first technique doesn't do the trick, go on to the second. If the second one doesn't work, try the third. And so on.

But first . . .

But before you even start those procedures, Apple recommends you take these steps:

1. **Verify that you have the current version of iTunes installed on your Mac or PC.**

   You can always download the latest and greatest version here at www.apple.com/itunes/download.

2. **Verify that you're connecting your iPhone to your computer using a USB 2.0 or 3.0 port.**

   If you encounter difficulties at this point, we implore you to read the paragraph in the next section that begins with this:

   "*Don't* plug the iPhone's Lightning connector cable (iPhone 5) or dock connector–to–USB cable (earlier models) into a USB port on your keyboard, monitor, or an unpowered USB hub."

3. **Make sure that your iPhone software is up-to-date.**

   To check your iPhone software by using iTunes on your Mac or PC:

   a. **Connect your iPhone to your computer, launch iTunes (if necessary), and then click your iPhone in the iTunes sidebar.**

   b. **Click the Summary tab, and then click the Check for Update button.**

   To check your iPhone software by using your iPhone:

   a. **Tap Settings on your Home screen.**

   b. **Tap General in the Settings list.**

   c. **Tap Software Update.**

If your iPhone requires an update, you receive instructions for doing so. Otherwise, please continue.

If those three easy steps didn't get you back up and running and your iPhone is still acting up — it freezes, doesn't wake up from sleep, doesn't do something it used to do, or in any other way acts improperly — don't panic. The following sections describe the things you should try, in the order that we (and Apple) recommend.

Recharge your iPhone

If your iPhone acts up in any way, shape, or form, the first thing you should try is to give its battery a full recharge.

Don't plug the iPhone's Lightning connector cable (iPhone 5) or dock connector–to–USB cable (earlier models) into a USB port on your keyboard, monitor, or an unpowered USB hub. You need to plug the cable into one of the USB ports on your computer itself or a powered hub (one that requires an AC power source) because the USB ports on your computer supply more power than the other ports.

Most powered USB hubs, the kind you plug into an AC outlet, will charge your iPhone just fine. But passive, or unpowered, hubs — ones that don't plug into the wall for power — won't cut it when it comes to charging your phone.

Note that you can use the included USB power adapter to recharge your iPhone from an AC outlet rather than from a computer. So if your iPhone isn't charging when you connect it to your computer, try charging it from a wall outlet instead. In addition, some power strips by Belkin and other vendors include one or more powered USB ports that will work.

If you're in a hurry, charge your iPhone for a minimum of 20 minutes. We think a full charge is a better idea, but a 20-minute charge is better than no charge at all. And for faster charging in any circumstances, turn your iPhone off while it charges.

Restart your iPhone

If you recharge your iPhone and it still misbehaves, the next thing to try is restarting it. Just as restarting a computer often fixes problems, restarting your iPhone sometimes works wonders.

Here's how to restart:

1. **Press and hold the sleep/wake button.**

2. **Slide the red slider to turn off the iPhone, and then wait a few seconds.**

3. **Press and hold the sleep/wake button again until the Apple logo appears on the screen.**

If your phone is still frozen, misbehaves, or doesn't start up, it's time to try the third *R,* resetting your iPhone.

Reset your iPhone

To reset your iPhone, merely press and hold the sleep/wake button while pressing and holding the Home button on the front. When you see the Apple logo, you can release both buttons.

Resetting your iPhone is like forcing your computer to restart after a crash. Your data shouldn't be affected by a reset. So don't be shy about giving this technique a try. In many cases, your iPhone goes back to normal after you reset it this way.

Remember to press *and hold* both the sleep/wake button and the Home button. If you press both and then release them, you create a *screen shot* — a picture of whatever is on your screen at the time — rather than reset your iPhone. (This type of screen picture, by the way, is stored in the Photos app's camera roll. Find out more about this feature at the end of Chapter 19.)

Unfortunately, sometimes resetting *doesn't* do the trick. When that's the case, you have to take stronger measures.

At this point, it's a good idea to back up your iPhone's contents by right- or Control-clicking the phone's name in the list on the left side of the iTunes window (on your Mac or PC) and choosing Back Up. Or you can initiate a backup to iCloud from your iPhone by tapping Settings↪iCloud↪Storage & Backup↪Back Up Now.

Feel free to look in the Backup section of the Summary pane in iTunes, which will show you when the last backup occurred or that your iPhone has never been backed up. However, we highly recommend that you back up again, just in case.

Remove your content

Nothing you've done so far should have taken more than a minute or so (or 20 if you tried the 20-minute recharge). We hate to tell you, but that's about to change because the next thing you should try is removing some or all of your data, to see whether it's the cause of your troubles.

To do so, you need to sync your iPhone and reconfigure it so that some or all of your files are removed from the phone. The problem could be contacts, calendar data, songs, photos, videos, or podcasts. If you suspect a particular data type — for example, you suspect your photos because whenever you tap the Photos icon on the Home screen, your iPhone freezes — try removing that type of data first.

Or, if you have no suspicions, deselect every item on every tab in iTunes (Info, Apps, Music, Movies, Photos, and so on) on your Mac or PC and then sync. When you're finished, your iPhone should have almost no data on it. We say *almost* because data created by apps on the iPhone — for example, documents created on your iPhone with apps such as Pages, Numbers, or Keynote — may remain on your iPhone. If you really want to be thorough, click every app in the File Sharing section of the Apps pane in iTunes and delete any documents you see in the Documents area.

If that method fixed the problem, try restoring your data, one type at a time. If the problem returns, keep experimenting to determine which particular data type or file is causing the problem.

If you're still having problems, the next step is to reset your iPhone's settings.

Reset your settings and content

Resetting involves two steps: The first one, resetting your iPhone settings, resets every iPhone *setting* to its default — the way it was when you took it out of the box. Resetting the iPhone's settings doesn't erase any of your data or media. The only downside is that you may have to go back and change some settings afterward, so you can try this step without (much) trepidation. Tap the Settings icon on your Home screen, and then tap General⟳Reset⟳Reset All Settings.

Be careful *not* to tap Erase All Content and Settings, at least not yet. Erasing all content takes more time to recover from (because your next sync takes a long time), so try Reset All Settings first.

At this point, you could try resetting some of the other options available on the Reset screen, such as Reset Network Settings. If you're desperate, it won't hurt to try Reset Keyboard Dictionary, Reset Home Screen Layout, and Reset Location Warnings; they're not likely to help but might be worth a try before you resort to erasing all content and settings, as we're about to describe.

Now, if resetting all settings didn't cure your iPhone, you have to try Erase All Content and Settings. (Read the next Warning first.) You find that option in the same place as Reset All Settings (tap Settings⮞General⮞Reset).

This strategy deletes everything from your iPhone — all your data, media, and settings. Because all these items are stored on your computer and are backed up when you sync — at least in theory — you should be able to put things back the way they were during your next sync. But you will lose any photos you've taken since your last sync, as well as contacts, calendar events, and playlists you've created or modified since your last sync.

After using Erase All Content and Settings, check to see whether your iPhone works properly. If it doesn't cure what ails your iPhone, the next *R,* restoring your iPhone using iTunes, might help.

Restore your iPhone

Restoring your iPhone is a fairly drastic step, but it often succeeds after recharging, restarting, resetting, removing content, and resetting settings and content have failed.

To restore your phone, connect it to your computer as though you were about to sync. But when the iPhone appears in the iTunes source list, click the Restore button on the Summary tab. This action erases all your data and media and resets all your settings.

If your computer isn't available, you can trigger this step from your iPhone by tapping Settings⮞General⮞Reset⮞Erase All Content and Settings.

All your data and media should still exist on your computer or in iCloud, with the possible exception of photos you've taken since your last sync if you aren't using Photo Stream and any contacts, calendar events, notes, and playlists you've created or modified since your last sync. You may also lose any iTunes or App Store content you've purchased or downloaded on the iPhone since its last sync, but you can always download them again at no cost if they disappear. In other words, you probably won't lose anything by restoring. Your next sync will take longer than usual, and you may have to reset any settings you've changed since you got your iPhone. But other than those inconveniences, restoring shouldn't cause you any trouble.

If restoring your iPhone didn't fix things, we have one more thing you can try before you give up the ghost on your poor, sick iPhone.

Renew your iPhone with Recovery mode

If you've gone through all the previous suggestions or you couldn't attempt some or all of them because your iPhone is so messed up, you can try one last thing: Recovery mode. Here's how it works:

1. **Disconnect the USB cable from your iPhone, but leave the other end of the cable connected to the USB port on your computer.**

2. **Turn off the iPhone by pressing and holding the sleep/wake button for a few seconds until the red slider appears on-screen, and then slide the slider.**

   Wait for the iPhone to turn off.

3. **Press and hold the Home button while you reconnect the USB cable to your iPhone.**

   When you reconnect the USB cable, your iPhone should power on.

   If you see a battery icon with a thin red band and an icon displaying a wall plug, an arrow, and a lightning bolt, you need to let your iPhone charge for at least 10 to 15 minutes. When the battery picture goes away or turns green instead of red, go back to Step 2 and try again.

4. **Continue holding the Home button until you see the Connect to iTunes screen, and then release the Home button.**

   If you don't see the Connect to iTunes screen on your iPhone, try again from Step 1.

5. **If iTunes didn't open automatically already, launch it now.**

   You should see a Recovery Mode alert on your computer screen telling you that your iPhone is in recovery mode and that you must restore it before it can be used with iTunes.

6. **Use iTunes to restore the device, as we describe in the preceding section.**

Okay. So that's the gamut of things you can do when your iPhone acts up. If you tried all this and none of it worked, skim through the rest of this chapter to see whether anything else we recommend looks like it might help. If not, your iPhone probably needs to go into the shop for repairs.

Never fear, gentle reader. Be sure to read the section near the end of the chapter, "If Nothing We Suggest Helps." Your iPhone may be quite sick, but we help ease the pain by sharing some tips on how to minimize the discomfort.

Problems with Calling or Networks

If you're having problems making or receiving calls, problems sending or receiving SMS text messages, or problems with Wi-Fi or your wireless carrier's data network, this section may help. The techniques here are short and sweet — except for the last one, restore. The inconvenient, time-consuming restore technique, which we describe in the preceding section, entails erasing all your data and media and then restoring it.

First, here are some simple steps that may help. Once again, we (and Apple) suggest that you try them in this order:

1. **Check the cell signal icon in the upper-left corner of the screen.**

   If you don't have at least one or two bars, you may not be able to use the phone or messaging function.

2. **Make sure you haven't left your iPhone in airplane mode, as described in Chapter 14.**

   In airplane mode, all network-dependent features are disabled, so you can't make or receive phone calls, send or receive messages, or use any apps that require a Wi-Fi or data network connection (that is, Mail, Safari, Stocks, Maps, and Weather).

3. **Try moving around.**

   Changing your location by as little as a few feet can sometimes mean the difference between four bars and zero bars or being able to use a Wi-Fi or wireless data network or not. If you're inside, try going outside. If you're outside, try moving 10 or 20 paces in any direction. Keep an eye on the cell signal or Wi-Fi icon as you move around, and stop when you see more bars than you saw before.

4. **Try changing your grip on the phone (or if it's an iPhone 4, try using a case).**

   Apple says, "Gripping any mobile phone will result in some attenuation of its antenna performance, with certain places being worse than others depending on the placement of the antennas. This is a fact of life for every wireless phone. If you ever experience this on your iPhone 4, avoid gripping it in the lower-left corner in a way that covers both sides of the black strip in the metal band, or simply use one of many available cases."

5. **Turn on airplane mode by tapping Settings on the Home screen, and then tapping the airplane mode On/Off switch to turn it on. Wait 15 or 20 seconds, and then turn it off again.**

Toggling airplane mode on and off like this resets both the Wi-Fi and wireless data-network connections. If your network connection was the problem, toggling airplane mode on and off may correct it.

6. **Restart your iPhone.**

If you've forgotten how, refer to the "Restart your iPhone" section, a few pages back. Restarting your iPhone is often all it takes to fix whatever was wrong.

7. **Make sure your SIM card is firmly seated.**

A *SIM* (Subscriber Identity Module) card is a removable smart card used to identify mobile phones. You can change phones by moving the SIM card from one phone to another.

To remove the SIM card, straighten one end of a fine-gauge paper clip and stick the straight end *gently* into the hole on the SIM tray, as shown in Figure 16-1 for the iPhone 4 and 4S and in Figure 16-2 for the nano-SIM used in the iPhone 5.

Figure 16-1: Removing the micro-SIM tray on an iPhone 4 or 4S.

Figure 16-2: Removing the nano-SIM tray on an iPhone 5.

When the SIM tray slides out, carefully lift out the SIM card and then reinsert it, making sure it's firmly situated in the tray before you *gently* push the tray back in until it locks.

If none of the preceding suggestions fixes your network issues, try restoring your iPhone as described previously, in the "Restore your iPhone" section.

Performing a restore deletes everything on your iPhone — all your data, media, and settings. You should be able to put things back the way they were with your next sync. If that doesn't happen, for whatever reason, you can't say we didn't warn you.

Sync, Computer, or iTunes Issues

The last category of troubleshooting techniques in this chapter applies to issues that involve synchronization and computer–iPhone relations. If you're having problems syncing or your computer doesn't recognize your iPhone when you connect it (or your phone issue is not resolved by any of our previous suggestions), we have some more things you can try.

Once again, we suggest that you try these procedures in the order they're presented here:

1. **Recharge your iPhone.**

   If you didn't try it previously, try it now. Go back to the "iPhone Issues" section, at the beginning of this chapter, and read what we say about recharging your iPhone. Every word there applies here.

2. **Try a different USB port or a different cable if you have one available.**

   It doesn't happen often, but occasionally USB ports and cables go bad. When they do, they invariably cause sync and connection problems. Make sure that a bad USB port or cable isn't to blame. And check all plugs, connectors, cables, and adapters to ensure that they're properly inserted and seated correctly.

   If you don't remember what we said about using USB ports on your computer rather than the ones on your keyboard, monitor, or hub, we suggest that you reread the "Recharge your iPhone" section, earlier in this chapter.

   Apple has used the same USB cable for iPods and iPhones for many years and also uses that same cable for iPads, so if you happen to have one of those cables handy, give it a try. Unless . . .

Unless, that is, you've purchased your iDevice after September or October 2012, when the iPhone 5 and the 2012 models of the iPod touch and iPod Nano were introduced. These devices all sport the new Lightning connector instead of the same USB–to–dock–connector cable we've known and loved all these years. To use an old cable with these new devices requires a Lightning–to–30–pin adapter, which Apple sells for $29 or $39.

3. Restart your iPhone and try to sync again.

We describe restarting your iPhone in full and loving detail in the "Restart your iPhone" section, earlier in this chapter.

4. Restart your computer.

We have found that restarting your computer often fixes issues with syncing your iPhone.

Restarting your computer can fix non-iPhone issues as well. It's a good idea to reboot your computer before you do any kind of troubleshooting, be it with your iPhone or your computer.

5. Reinstall iTunes.

Even if you have an iTunes installer handy, you probably should visit the Apple website and download the latest-and-greatest version, just in case. You'll always find the latest version of iTunes at `www.apple.com/itunes/download`.

More Help on the Apple Website

If you try everything we suggest earlier in this chapter and still have problems, don't give up just yet. This section describes a few places you may find helpful. We recommend that you check out some or all of them before you throw in the towel and smash your iPhone into tiny little pieces (or ship it back to Apple for repairs, as described in the next section).

First, Apple offers an excellent set of support resources on its website at `www.apple.com/support/iphone`. You can browse support issues by category, search for a problem by keyword, or even get personalized help by phone, as shown in Figure 16-3.

While you're visiting the Apple support pages, another section could be helpful: the discussion communities. You find them at `http://discussions.apple.com`, and they're chock-full of questions and answers from other iPhone users. Our experience has been that if you can't find an answer to a support question elsewhere, you can often find something helpful in these forums. You can browse by community — Using iPhone, iPhone Hardware, iPhone in the Enterprise, or iPhone Accessories, as shown in Figure 16-4 — or search by keyword.

Browse by category

Search by keyword

Participate in discussion communities

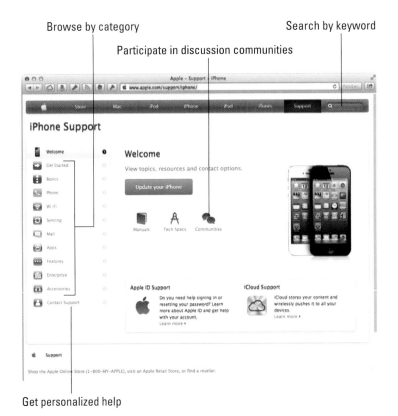

Get personalized help

Figure 16-3: The Apple iPhone support pages offer several kinds of helpful information.

Either way, you'll find thousands of iPhone discussions (for example, 335,457 on using the iPhone when Figure 16-4 was captured) about almost every aspect of using your iPhone. Better still, frequently you can find the answer to your question or a helpful suggestion.

Now for the best part: If you can't find a solution by browsing or searching, you can post your question in the appropriate Apple community. Check back in a few days (or even in a few hours), and some helpful iPhone user may well have replied with the answer. If you've never tried this fabulous tool, you're missing out on one of the greatest support resources available anywhere.

Last, but certainly not least, before you give up the ghost, you might want to try a carefully worded Google (or Yahoo! or Bing) search. It couldn't hurt, and you might just find the solution.

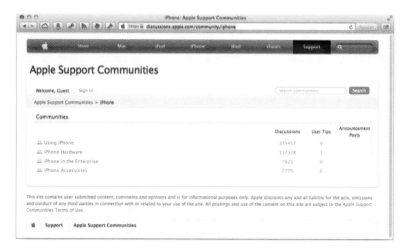

Figure 16-4: Four iPhone communities have thousands of discussions about all things iPhone.

If Nothing We Suggest Helps

If you tried every trick in the book (this one) and still have a malfunctioning iPhone, it's time to consider shipping it off to the iPhone hospital (better known as Apple, Inc.). The repair is free if your iPhone is still under its one-year limited warranty.

You can extend your warranty as long as two years from the original purchase date. To do so, you need to buy the AppleCare+ Protection Plan for your iPhone. You don't have to do it when you buy the phone, but you must buy it before your one-year limited warranty expires. The cost is $99.

Here are a few things you should do before you take your phone in to be repaired:

- *Your iPhone is erased during its repair,* so you should sync your iPhone with iTunes before you take it in, if you can. If you can't and you entered data on the phone since your last sync, such as a contact or an appointment, the data won't be there when you restore your iPhone upon its return.

- Remove any third-party accessories, such as a case or screen protector.

✔ Remove the SIM card from your iPhone (as described in the earlier section "Problems with Calling or Networks") and keep it in a safe place.

Do not, under any circumstances, forget to remove your SIM card. Apple doesn't guarantee that your SIM card will be returned to you after a repair. If you forget this step, Apple suggests that you contact your local AT&T, Verizon, or Sprint store and obtain a new SIM card with the proper account information. Ouch.

Although you may be able to get your iPhone serviced by your provider or by mail, we recommend that you take it to your nearest Apple Store, for three reasons:

✔ **No one knows your iPhone like Apple.** One of the geniuses at the Apple Store may be able to fix whatever is wrong without sending your iPhone away for repairs.

✔ **The Apple Store will, in some cases, swap out your wonky iPhone for a brand-new one on the spot.** You can't win if you don't play, which is why we always visit our local Apple Store when something goes wrong (with our iPhones, iPads, iPods, and even our laptops and iMacs).

✔ **Only the Apple Store offers an Express Replacement Service (ERS) for iPhones needing repairs.** The AppleCare Express Replacement Service costs $29 when your iPhone is under warranty or covered by an AppleCare Protection Plan. This service provides you with a new iPhone when you have to send in your old one for service.

If your iPhone *isn't* under warranty or AppleCare, you can still take advantage of the Express Replacement Service — it costs you a lot more, though. See Figure 16-5 for the costs at press time or visit `http://support.apple.com/kb/index?page=servicefaq&geo=United_States&product=iphone` for current pricing and more information on the ERS service.

If visiting an Apple, AT&T, Verizon, or Sprint store isn't possible, call Apple at 1-800-MY-IPHONE (1-800-694-7466) in the United States or visit `www.apple.com/contact` to find the number to call in other countries.

If you choose the AppleCare Express Replacement Service, you don't have to activate the new phone and it has the same phone number as the phone it replaces. All you need to do is pop your old SIM card into the new phone, sync it with iTunes or iCloud to fill it with the data and media files that were on your sick iPhone, and you're good to go.

If you've done everything we've suggested, we're relatively certain that you're now holding an iPhone that works flawlessly. Again.

iPhone 5	ERS Fee	Late Fee	Replacement Value
16GB		$210	$649
32GB	$29	$260	$749
64GB		$310	$849
iPhone 4S			
16GB		$175	$549
32GB	$29	$225	$649
64GB		$275	$749
iPhone 4			
8GB		$150.50	$450
16GB	$29	$225	$599
32GB		$250	$649
iPhone 3GS			
8GB		$113	$375
16GB	$29	$225	$599
32GB		$275	$699
iPhone 3G			
8GB	$29	$175	$499
16GB		$175	$499
Original iPhone			
4GB & 8GB	$29	$125	$399
16GB		$175	$499

Figure 16-5: Prices for Express Replacement Service at press time.

If at this point you aren't holding an iPhone that works flawlessly and has most (if not all) of your stuff on it, it's time to break out the big guns and make an appointment with a Genius at your local Apple Store. Call the support hotline (800-275-2273) or visit the support web page at www.apple.com/support/iphone.

That said, some or all of your stuff may not be on it. If that's the case, the following section offers a two-trick solution that usually works.

Dude, Where's My Stuff?

If you performed a restore or had your iPhone replaced or repaired, you have one more task to accomplish. Your iPhone may work flawlessly at this point, but some or all of your stuff — your music, movies, contacts, iMessages, or whatever — is missing. You're not sunk, at least not yet. You still have a couple of tricks up your sleeve.

- **Trick 1: Sync your iPhone with iTunes and then sync it again.** That's right — sync and sync again. Why? Because sometimes stuff doesn't get synced properly on the first try. Just do it.

- **Trick 2: Restore from backup.** Right-click your iPhone in the iTunes sidebar and choose Restore from Backup. The Restore from Backup dialog appears and offers you a choice of backups. Select the one you want, click the Restore button, and let the iPhone work some magic.

If you have more than one backup for a device, try the most recent (undated) one first. If it doesn't work or you're still missing files, try restoring from any other backups before you throw in the towel.

These backups include photos in the camera roll or in Saved Photos, text messages, notes, contact favorites, sound settings, and more, but not media such as music, videos, or photos. If media is what's missing, try performing Trick 1 again.

Part VI
The Part of Tens

*1*t's written in stone somewhere at John Wiley & Sons, Inc., world headquarters that we *For Dummies* authors must include a Part of Tens in every single *For Dummies* book we write. It's a duty we take quite seriously. So in this part, you find not just one but two lists of our favorite apps plucked from the iPhone App Store — ten apps that are free and ten that are not. These include programs to turn your iPhone into a goofy photo booth, a baseball reference, and a capable Internet radio. Plus you find a couple of addictive games, and even an app to let you control your Mac or PC remotely from your iPhone.

We close the show with one of our favorite topics: hints, tips, and shortcuts that make life with your iPhone even better. Among the ten, you find out how to share web pages and pick up another trick or two on using iPhone's virtual keyboard.

17

Ten Appetizing Apps

*K*iller app is familiar jargon to anyone who has spent any time around computers. The term refers to an app so sweet or so useful that just about everybody wants or must have it.

You could make the argument that the most compelling killer app on the iPhone is the very App Store we expound on in Chapter 15. This online emporium has an abundance of splendid programs — dare we say killer apps in their own right? — many of which are free. These apps cover everything from social networking tools to entertainment. Okay, so some rotten apples are in the bunch too. But we're here to accentuate the positive.

son Mayhem   Empire B

With that in mind, in this chapter we offer ten of our favorite free iPhone apps. In Chapter 18, you see ten iPhone apps that aren't free but that we believe are worth every penny.

We're showing you ours and we encourage you to show us yours. If you discover your own killer iPhone apps, by all means, let us know so we can check them out.

Shazam

Ever heard a song on the radio or television, in a store, or at a club, and wondered what it was called or who was singing it? With the Shazam app, you may never wonder again. Just launch Shazam and point your iPhone's microphone at the source of the music. In a few seconds, the song title and artist's name magically appear on your iPhone screen, as shown in Figure 17-1.

Figure 17-1: Point your phone at the music and Shazam tells you the artist, title, and more.

In Shazam parlance, that song has been *tagged.* Now, if tagging were all Shazam could do, that would surely be enough. But wait, there's more. After Shazam tags a song you can

- Buy the song at the iTunes Store
- Watch related videos on YouTube
- Tweet the song on Twitter

✓ Read a biography, a discography, or lyrics

✓ Take a photo and attach it to the tagged item in Shazam

✓ E-mail a tag to a friend

Shazam isn't great at identifying classical music, jazz, big bands, show tunes, or opera, nor is it adept at identifying obscure indie bands. But if you use it primarily to identify popular music, it rocks (pun intended).

The free version of Shazam offers unlimited tagging but also displays lots of ads. If that works for you, you're all set. But if you're like us, you may prefer Shazam Encore, which eliminates the ads and has several exclusive features, including premium recommendations.

We've tried other apps that claim to do what Shazam does, but we've yet to find one as good as Shazam (free) or Shazam Encore ($4.99 for a 1-year subscription or $5.99 for a lifetime subscription, for which we gladly coughed up the money). It has worked for us in noisy airport terminals, crowded shopping malls, and even once at a wedding ceremony.

Wolfgang's Concert Vault

Wolfgang's Concert Vault is an app that provides you with free access to the largest collection of concert recordings in the world. Some of our favorites include The Who, Led Zeppelin, King Crimson, Neil Young, Pink Floyd, Creedence Clearwater Revival, Elvis Costello, and David Bowie. And if those particular artists don't appeal to you, check out concert recordings by hundreds upon hundreds of other artists.

What's cool is that these offerings are exclusive recordings you probably haven't heard before and probably won't hear elsewhere. You can find master recordings from the archives of Bill Graham Presents, the King Biscuit Flower Hour, and many others.

Wolfgang's Concert Vault is a superb iPhone app with its roots in a superb website (www.wolfgangsvault.com), as shown in Figure 17-2.

The Wolfgang's Concert Vault iPhone app offers a clean, uncluttered interface (see Figure 17-3) and provides many of the website's best features, including playlists (see Figure 17-4). After you create a free account, you can access your playlists and favorite songs on either the website or the iPhone app.

Figure 17-2: The Wolfgang's Vault website is more graphical than the iPhone app, but the latter delivers most of the same free goodies.

Both app and website let you tag a concert as a favorite, search for songs or artists, and listen to complete concert recordings at no charge. On the website, you can also create playlists by culling songs from different concert recordings. We wish the app allowed you to create playlists on your iPhone, but it does let you *listen* to the playlists you've created.

If you love music and want to hear unique live performances of songs you know and love, Wolfgang's Concert Vault is the app for you.

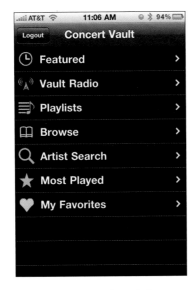

Figure 17-3: The Wolfgang's Concert Vault iPhone app has a simple, clean interface.

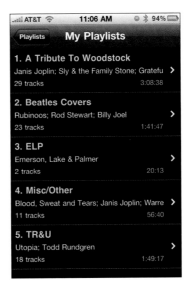

Figure 17-4: Some of Bob's playlists. (Can you tell the kind of music he likes?)

Comics

We really love the Comics app. Not only do we find many of the latest comics and graphic novels in its built-in comic store the same day as print versions hit the stores, but the selections also include both *DC* and *Marvel Comics,* which publish Bob's all-time favorite: Spider-Man! Many of the titles are classics, including issue #1 of *The Amazing Spider-Man.* Released in 1963 for 12¢, a copy in excellent condition goes for at least $25,000 today! Thanks to the Comics app, we can enjoy this out-of-print classic in pristine condition on our iPhones for a mere $1.99. That's just too cool. Other comics are priced from 99¢ per issue.

One of the coolest features is called Guided View (motion comics), which looks great on an iPhone screen. It's difficult to describe in words and still images, but we're going to try anyway. First, take a look at a full page as it would appear in the printed version of the comic, as shown in Figure 17-5.

Figure 17-5: The first page of the first issue of *The Amazing Spider-Man* as displayed on the iPhone screen.

With Guided View, the first thing you'd see is Figure 17-6, left. When you tap in the right one-third of the screen, to indicate you're ready to read the next panel, the first panel slides off the left edge of the screen as the next panel (shown in Figure 17-6, right) slides onto the screen from the right.

Figure 17-6: The first panel of the same page as it appears in Guided View (left). The first panel slides off the screen as this next panel slides on (right).

We don't know of any other app that makes reading a comic so enjoyable on the small screen. And we're delighted that the Comics app's built-in store offers classic Marvel and DC titles including *Superman, Batman, Wonder Woman,* and the *Justice League,* as well as new classics such as *The Walking Dead* and *Scott Pilgrim.*

If you like comics or graphic novels, you're sure to enjoy the free Comics app.

Bill Atkinson PhotoCard

Who is Bill Atkinson? He had a hand (or both hands) in the first Macintosh computer as well as the MacPaint and HyperCard Mac applications. Today, he's a world-renowned nature photographer, which brings us to his app.

Bill Atkinson PhotoCard is a free app that lets you create gorgeous high-resolution postcards and send them by e-mail or by the U.S. Postal Service. E-mail is always free. And though sending by USPS costs between $1.50 and $2.00 per card, depending on how many print-and-mail credits you purchase, the 8½-x-5½-inch postcards are stunning. Printed on heavy, glossy stock on a state-of-the-art HP Indigo Digital Press and laminated for protection against damage in the mail, they're as beautiful as any postcard you've ever seen.

You can create a postcard using one of the 200 included nature photos by Bill Atkinson, as shown in Figure 17-7, or any picture in your Photos library.

Figure 17-7: Send a postcard with a gorgeous nature photo by Bill Atkinson.

You can also add any of 400 decorative stickers and 200 decorative stamps, as shown in Figure 17-8. You can even add voice notes if you e-mail the card!

Figure 17-8: You can compose text, and add stickers and stamps like these to your cards.

If you take pictures and have friends, you're going to love Bill Atkinson PhotoCard.

IMDb

We like movies, so we both use the IMDb (Internet Movie Database) app a lot. In a nutshell, it knows everything there is to know about almost every movie ever made and many TV shows as well. For example, let's say you want to know something (anything) about the 1997 classic *The Fifth Element.* Just type *Fifth Element,* tap the Search button, and everything (and we mean everything) about the movie appears — release date, original theatrical trailer, a plot summary, synopsis, the entire cast, the entire crew, critic's reviews, user reviews, trivia, goofs, and more (some of which are shown in Figure 17-9).

But that's not all. IMDb also includes all movies playing in theaters nearby (or near any zip code), showtimes for movies playing nearby, shows on TV tonight, lists such as STARmeter (most-viewed stars on IMDb this week), star birthdays, DVD and Blu-ray discs released recently or to be released soon, and U.S. box office results, all accessible from a well-organized and customizable Home screen, shown in Figure 17-10.

We appreciate that we can read reviews, play movie trailers, and e-mail movie listings to others with a single tap. We also enjoy perusing information and movie trailers for soon-to-be-released films and DVDs.

You won't find a more comprehensive guide to films and you can't beat the price!

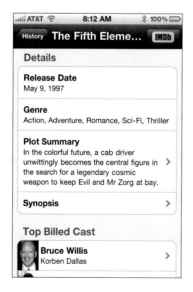

Figure 17-9: Details like these are available for almost every movie.

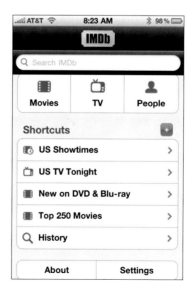

Figure 17-10: The IMDb Home screen can be customized to your liking.

Pandora Radio

We've long been fans of Pandora on the computer. So we're practically delirious that this custom Internet radio service is available *gratis* on the iPhone.

And Pandora is better than ever, at least on the multitasking iPhone, because you can listen to music in the background while doing other stuff. But we're getting ahead of ourselves.

Pandora works on the iPhone in much the same way it does on a PC or a Mac. You type the name of a favorite musician or song title and Pandora creates an instant personalized radio station with selections that exemplify the style you chose. Figure 17-11 shows some of the eclectic stations we created. Tapping QuickMix plays musical selections across all your stations. Tapping the New Station button, at the bottom of the screen, displays a search field. Tap that field and the iPhone keyboard appears so that you can add a new station built around an artist, a song title, or a composer. You can also select from stations Pandora has packaged together around a particular genre.

In Figure 17-12, we typed *Beatles* and Pandora created a Beatles station that includes performances from John, Paul, George, and Ringo, as well as tunes from other artists whose songs are similar to songs by The Beatles both collectively and individually.

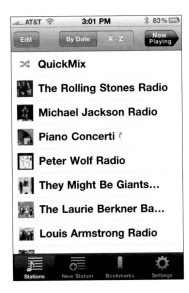

Figure 17-11: Eclectic online radio stations from Pandora.

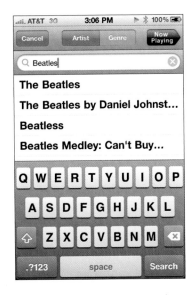

Figure 17-12: Creating a new station couldn't be easier.

And say you type in a song title, such as *Have I Told You Lately.* Pandora constructs a station with similar music after you tell it whether to base tunes on the Van Morrison, Rod Stewart, or other rendition.

Pandora comes out of the Music Genome Project, an organization of musicians and technologists who analyze music according to hundreds of attributes (such as melody, harmony, and vocal performances).

You can help fine-tune the music Pandora plays by tapping the thumbs-up or thumbs-down icon below the album cover of the song being played, as shown in Figure 17-13.

Return to station list

Explanation of why song is playing and artist info

Figure 17-13: Have we told you lately how much we like Pandora?

If you tap the triangular icon, you can bookmark the song or artist being played, e-mail to a friend the station that the song is playing on, or head to iTunes to purchase the song directly on the iPhone (if available).

Apple iBooks

"Did people once read books on paper?"

Don't be surprised if you have to answer this query from a curious kid someday. Although we figure that time is still a ways off, the idea behind the question no longer seems so far off or far-fetched. For proof, check out Apple's own iBooks.

The beauty of electronic books, or e-books (or iBooks according to the Apple lexicon), is that you can schlep a boatload of reading material with you when you travel without breaking your back. And e-books can enhance your reading experience with a bevy of nifty tricks: You can look up the meaning of a word on the spot, change fonts and type sizes, and easily add highlights or bookmarks. Moreover, you can search for every mention of a particular term or subject in a book. Heck, with the iPhone, you can even read in the dark.

Apple introduced its iBooks app and companion iBookstore online bookseller with the iPad tablet. Apple eventually brought both app and bookseller to the iPhone (though you still have to go to the App Store to download the iBooks app). As a result, electronic reading will never be the same.

The covers for the books you buy in iBookstore — more than 700,000 titles were available in the U.S. as our own book went to press, with hundreds of thousands outside America — land on the handsome virtual wooden bookshelf shown in Figure 17-14. More than 180 million books have been downloaded. Some are gorgeous illustrated children's books, photo books, and cookbooks. Apple has also made a push into textbooks. You can stash Adobe PDF-formatted documents on the bookshelf too. And iBooks supports an e-book industry standard format known as ePub as well.

Tap a book cover to start reading the book. When you tap a page or drag its corner edge, the page changes, curling like a real book. We think that bit of razzle-dazzle is very cool. Check out Figure 17-15 to sample the controls that make virtual reading a veritable pleasure.

Figure 17-14: Your virtual bookshelf.

Figure 17-15: Handy reading tools.

Shopping in iBookstore — to enter, tap the Store button from the bookshelf, or library, view — is an equal pleasure, with numerous ways to browse or search books you want to read, including from the *New York Times* bestseller lists.

Figure 17-16 shows one of the storefront views in the joint. Explore the various buttons for other views and to uncover books of interest.

Tap any of the books that intrigue you to read reviews, get a free sample, and make a purchase. Pricing for iBooks varies, but the $11.99 sum for Jeff Lindsay's *Double Dexter,* the title shown in Figure 17-17, is not atypical for a new work. (Many are in the $9.99 to $12.99 range.) And the good news is that prices are almost always less expensive than their hardcover counterparts — check out the section for free books (refer to Figure 17-16).

And, assuming you sync your iPhone and other devices with your computer regularly, your bookmarks, highlights, notes, and last location in a book will remain in sync with copies of the same book on an iPad or an iPod touch that uses the same Apple ID in your Store account.

Figure 17-16: Exploring the virtual aisles of iBookstore.

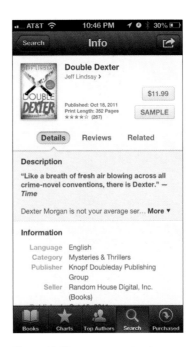

Figure 17-17: Buying an e-book is almost always cheaper than a hardcover work.

WebMD

As the old saying goes, you have nothing if you don't have your health. Carrying the free WebMD app on your iPhone provides a rich repository of health and medical information in your pocket, as the app's Home screen displayed in Figure 17-18 shows.

Let's explore a few of these areas:

✔ **Symptom Checker:** First let WebMD know your age and sex, and then you see an illustrated male or female body so that you can tap on the area of concern. Tap the Flip icon, shown on the bottom-left corner of Figure 17-19, to go from a front view to a back view and vice versa. Pinch and zoom to zero in on a specific body part.

Tap the appropriate body part (or tap the List button instead), and WebMD serves up a list of potential symptoms. Tap a symptom to detect possible conditions and find articles (on the WebMD website) that may help you out.

Figure 17-18: WebMD can help you grasp what's going on health-wise.

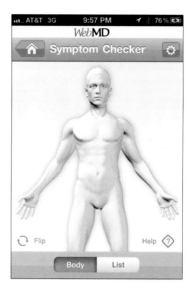

Figure 17-19: Find a symptom by tapping on a body part.

✔ **Drugs and Treatments:** Among the tools you'll find here is one that helps you identify drugs just by their shape, color, or the letters or numbers imprinted on the pill, tablet, or capsule.

✔ **First Aid:** You can search for remedies, or consult a scrollable A to Z list to find treatments for everything from food poisoning to snakebites.

✔ **Local Health Listings:** By using your current location (or entering another location), WebMD can help you find a physician by name or specialty, a pharmacy, or a hospital. You can even tap a phone number in any listing you find to add to your contacts.

If you sign up for a free WebMD account, you can save lists of drugs, conditions, first-aid topics, and articles.

WhitePages Mobile

Yea, yea, we know: Plenty of phone directories are on the Internet. But WhitePages Mobile is an incredibly handy resource for finding home and business numbers on the fly or doing a reverse phone lookup (you have the number but have no clue whose number it is). Figure 17-20 shows the different types of searches you can make.

When new listings pop up, you can add them to your contacts or update existing contacts. You can also get maps and directions to where folks live or work. In some cases, WhitePages Mobile provides other information, including the age range of the person and some of the other people living in the person's household. And WhitePages Mobile uses GPS to detect your current whereabouts.

RedLaser

You're out and about shopping and wondering whether you're getting a decent deal. Pull out RedLaser and scan the barcode imprinted on the package. Doing so searches online and local prices for hundreds of retailers. If the barcode isn't readily available, you can type a product search with the iPhone's keyboard.

If RedLaser properly identifies a product, as it did with a bottle of McCormick garlic powder, as shown in Figure 17-21, it can serve up pricing results from a number of sources, including Google, Buy.com, TheFind, SDC.com, Milo.com, Half.com, Target, and of course eBay, which owns this handy app. It can find prices in U.S. dollars, pounds sterling, and euros.

When you scan a food item, RedLaser can help you uncover nutrition facts. It'll also show you top deals of the day.

RedLaser can recognize a variety of barcode types, as well as QR codes, which give you access to web addresses, contact information, calendar events, and more. Inside the app you can even create your own QR code.

The app keeps the results of previous scans in a History list.

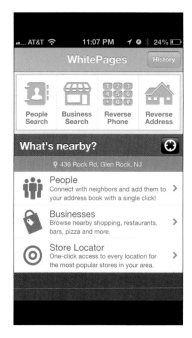

Figure 17-20: Finding a number through WhitePages Mobile.

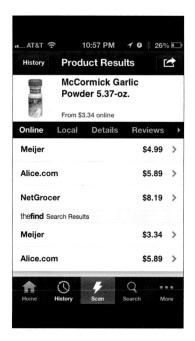

Figure 17-21: RedLaser turns your iPhone camera into a spicy barcode scanner.

18

Ten Apps Worth Paying For

In This Chapter

▶ Instapaper

▶ OldBooth

▶ GottaGo

▶ WordsWorth

▶ iTeleport

▶ Baseball Statistics 2012 Edition

▶ Glee

▶ Air Video

▶ My Secret Folder

▶ TurboScan

*I*f you read Chapter 17, you know that lots of great free apps are available for your iPhone. But as the cliché goes, some things are worth paying for. In some cases, the apps in this chapter are free up front, but you have to part with some loot to fully take advantage of them. Still, none of the ten for-pay apps we've chosen as some of our favorites are likely to break the bank. As you're about to discover, some of the apps on this list are practical and others are downright silly. The common theme? We think you'll like carrying these apps around on your iPhone.

Instapaper ($3.99)

Do you ever come across a web page you'd like to read later, when you have the time? Sure, you can bookmark those pages or use Safari's Reading list, but neither is much help if you prefer a browser other than Safari. Wouldn't it be nice if you could somehow save web pages to your iPhone and read them at your convenience, regardless of whether or not you're a Safari user, and with or without an Internet connection (such as when you're on an airplane)?

We're happy to inform you that you can if you just download the Instapaper iPhone app from Marco Arment. Then, when you're surfing the web on your Mac, PC, iPhone, iPad, or iPod touch and see a page you want to read later, select the special Instapaper Read Later *bookmarklet* (a special bookmark that uses JavaScript). From then on, you can read the page whenever you choose with the Instapaper iPhone app.

Figure 18-1 shows the Instapaper app displaying some of the web pages we've saved with the Read Later bookmarklet. And Figure 18-2 shows what one of the articles looks like when you read it with the Instapaper app.

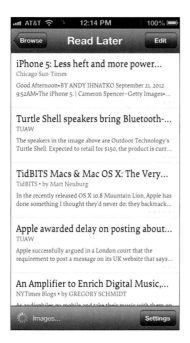

Figure 18-1: Instapaper displaying some web pages we saved for our future reading pleasure.

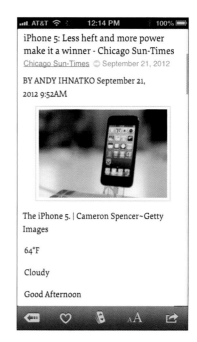

Figure 18-2: Using Instapaper to read Andy Ihnatko's iPhone 5 review from the *Chicago Sun Times*.

Instapaper is particularly good for long airplane trips. The week before Bob travels, he makes a point of grabbing lots of web pages with his Read Later bookmarklet to ensure that he doesn't run out of good stuff to peruse during his flight. One last thing: Bob says the tilt-scrolling feature is so good it ought to be included in any app that displays text.

If tilt-scrolling feels unnatural, try reversing its direction by tapping the Settings button on Instapaper's main screen.

OldBooth ($1.99)

OldBooth is just plain fun. It lets you take any full-face photo and apply wonderfully goofy transformations to it. A picture is worth a thousand words, so we'll start this description with Figure 18-3, which clearly demonstrates just what it is that OldBooth does.

Figure 18-3: The original photos of Bob and his wife Lisa are on the left; the OldBooth images of each appear to the right.

You get the picture, don't you? (Pun completely intended.)

Using OldBooth is as easy as 1-2-3:

1. **Select a gender and then select one of the 20 mask styles available for each gender.**

2. **Select a picture.**

   You can either take a new photo with your iPhone's camera or select a picture from your iPhone's Photo library.

3. **Resize the picture by pinching or unpinching, rotate the picture by pressing and dragging, and adjust the brightness of the picture, the mask, or both.**

When you're happy with the image, save it to your iPhone's camera roll, where you can use it as wallpaper, e-mail it to a friend, assign it to a contact, or just save it to the Photos app's camera roll, where it will be exported to your Mac or PC the next time you sync and added to your Photo Stream automatically.

OldBooth is easy and lots of fun for less than two bucks.

If two bucks sounds like too much to pay, you can get a free version called OldBooth Lite, which has a limited number of masks. We predict that once you've tried the free version, you'll gladly shell out $1.99 for the real deal.

GottaGo ($1.99)

If you've ever wanted a perfect excuse to leave a meeting (or anywhere else, for that matter), you'll love GottaGo. This clever little app lets you create a bogus phone call or text message and have it appear on your iPhone at any time you choose. At the appropriate moment, your iPhone rings or chimes and you receive what looks and sounds just like a real phone call or text message.

The GottaGo Unlock screen is animated just like the real thing. You can attach an image to your GottaGo call so it truly looks like you're receiving a real phone call. You can record custom audio that you hear when you answer the fake call. And you can select your own wallpaper and ringtone to make the effect even more realistic. The call settings screen is shown in Figure 18-4, and the resulting fake call appears in Figure 18-5.

When you gotta go, nothing gets you out of there faster than the GottaGo iPhone app. Isn't two bucks a tiny price to pay for your freedom?

WordsWorth ($1.99)

Being writers ourselves, we love a good word game, and one of our favorites so far is WordsWorth. You form words by tapping letters on the screen. Longer words using rarer letters (such as *J, Z,* and *Qu,* for example) score more points than shorter words with more common letters.

To make things interesting, the app includes certain special tiles, such as blue wild cards, green bonuses, and red timers, all shown in Figure 18-6. A gold tile (see Figure 18-7) helps you grow your score. The timer tiles are the most insidious; if their time runs out before you've used the letter, the game is over.

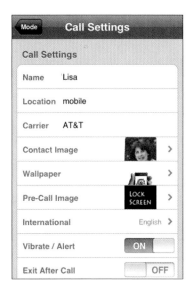

Figure 18-4: GottaGo makes your fake call (or text message) look like the real thing.

Figure 18-5: Even you might be fooled by GottaGo.

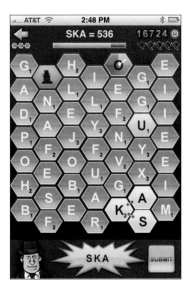

Figure 18-6: Special tiles make WordsWorth a challenge.

Figure 18-7: Going for the gold in WordsWorth.

WordsWorth doesn't have a fixed time limit per game. Instead, it's level-based — each time you achieve the prescribed number of points, you advance to the next level. And, of course, the levels grow increasingly harder with more and rarer timed tiles, fewer vowels, and rarer consonants.

If you can't find any more words on the screen, you can shuffle the tiles by shaking your iPhone. But be careful: A limited number of shuffles are available for each level.

Although WordsWorth is simple, it's also engaging and addictive. And you can even compete against other players over Bluetooth or Wi-Fi, or challenge your friends on the Facebook social network.

Lots of terrific word-based games are available for the iPhone. Another favorite worth checking out is a Boggle-like game called Wurdle from Semi Secret Software, which will also set you back only $1.99.

iTeleport ($24.99)

We admit that iTeleport isn't cheap and is more than a little geeky, but it's so cool and potentially useful that we would have been remiss had we not included it.

iTeleport is technically a VNC (Virtual Network Computing, also known as remote screen control) client. Put another way, it's an iPhone app for controlling your Mac, Windows, or Linux computer "from a few feet away or from halfway around the world."

Yes, you can actually see your computer screen and control its keyboard and mouse from anywhere in the world (as long as your iPhone can connect to the Internet through Wi-Fi, 3G, EDGE, or whatever).

Figure 18-8 shows an iPhone running iTeleport, which is controlling a Mac in another room (though the Mac could just as easily be in a different city, state, or country).

iTeleport is an iPhone app, so you pinch and unpinch to zoom in and out. In Figure 18-8, we zoomed in on the upper-left corner of the Mac screen, where a chapter is being edited in Microsoft Word.

There's little you can do on your Mac, PC, or Linux computer that you can't control remotely with iTeleport — though of course you're dealing with a smaller screen on the iPhone. We use iTeleport to check mail accounts other than the ones on our iPhones, to grab files from our hard drive and e-mail them to ourselves (at our iPhone e-mail addresses) or others, and to make sure backups are running when scheduled.

Disconnect   Settings   Modifier   Shortcuts   Keyboard

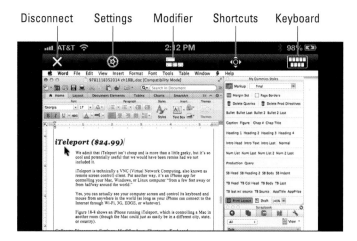

Figure 18-8: I'm editing this chapter with Microsoft Word while controlling my Mac remotely with iTeleport.

Another cool use for the app is as a spy cam. This feature requires that you have a computer with a built-in camera, such as an iMac or any of the MacBook models. Open an app that uses the built-in camera (for example, Photo Booth on the Mac or a webcam program under Windows), and you'll be able to watch what's happening in front of that computer on your iPhone no matter where in the world you happen to be.

Several free or less expensive VNC apps are available in the iTunes Store, but iTeleport is the only one we've found that is robust and reliable enough to recommend.

Baseball Statistics 2012 Edition ($2.99 for Latest Stats)

Consider Baseball Statistics 2012 Edition a dream app for a passionate baseball fan. One of the things that makes baseball such a great game is the statistics that have defined the sport since, well, the 19th century. (We won't add a steroids comment — oops, just did.) Baseball Statistics from Bulbous Ventures puts all those stats at your fingertips, so you can settle barroom bets or just relive memories of favorite ballplayers from when you were a kid.

The app has easily accessible yearly stats for every Major League player and team since 1871 — nope, we weren't around — from batting, fielding, and pitching statistics to team wins, losses, and attendance. As of this writing, the stats go through the 2011 season — heck, none of the 2012 pennant winners have been declared yet.

If a player has a Wikipedia entry, you can tap a button to see it. A baseball card feature displays a player's career stats, as if it were the back of a baseball card, when you rotate the iPhone to its side. We only wish we also could get a front baseball-card view with a picture of a uniform-clad player, but we're quibbling.

Poking around is fun. We found stats for outfielder Cherokee Fisher of the 1872 Baltimore Canaries. (Check out Figure 18-9 for evidence that the Canaries existed.) And to help decide one of those classic "who-was-better" debates, we compared Mickey Mantle's career stats to Willie Mays's.

Ed, a passionate New York Mets junkie, would gladly spring for the $2.99 tab, required for the latest (2011 at press time) season's statistics. Heck, that sum would have bought an awfully good seat at the ballpark when Tom Seaver was pitching brilliantly for the 1969 Miracle Mets. His stats from that season are shown in Figure 18-10.

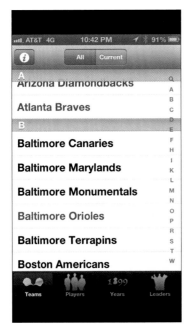

Figure 18-9: And you thought the Orioles were the only Major League team in Baltimore.

Figure 18-10: An amazing year for Tom Terrific and the Miracle Mets of 1969.

Glee (Free but $1.99 to $2.99 for Songs)

Do you love to sing in the shower or car, especially when no one is listening. Or can you actually belt out a tune?

Either way, let us highly recommend Glee, an app based on the popular Fox TV musical series *Glee.* It's yet another addictive app from Smule, a company that initially burst onto the scene by turning an iPhone into an ancient flutelike instrument called an ocarina.

The instrument you use in Glee is your own voice, of course, and you get to compete globally for starbursts, which you earn every time you pretend to be, say, Sinatra, Streisand, or Freddie Mercury. You earn extra points for keeping to the melody.

If you share your songs via Twitter or Facebook, or e-mail them, you might gain a following of gleeks, as fans of the TV series are called.

You start by practicing along to *Twinkle, Twinkle, Little Star* before graduating to more challenging material such as *We Are the Champions,* butchered by Ed in Figure 18-11 (take our word for it). As with any karaoke machine, you are backed up by a soundtrack and can follow the words on the screen. You can sing with a harmonious choir or turn on a pitch correct feature, if needed. Songs are recorded, but based on our own efforts, you save them at your own risk.

You can choose to sing a cappella, or sing along to tracks in your iTunes library, which unlike other material here, cannot be shared because of licensing restrictions.

If you tap World from the main Glee screen, the globe shown in Figure 18-12 appears. Drag the globe around with your finger to find talent from around the world. If you're so inspired by what you hear, you can join in, leave a comment, or become a gleek.

Although the app is free, you'll probably find yourself quickly spending more loot on extra songs, some for an additional 99¢ each, some for $1.99 a pop, some a buck more.

Figure 18-11: Freddie Mercury might be rolling over in his grave.

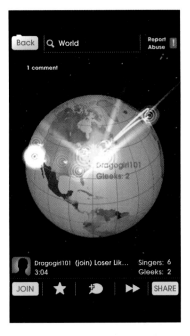

Figure 18-12: Sing along with new friends from around the globe.

Air Video ($2.99)

We both have more than 100GB of movies and TV shows in our iTunes library, so an iPhone with 32GB or even 64GB of storage just doesn't cut it. Having to decide which movies and TV shows to sync to our iPhones makes us crazy — we want all our movies and TV shows available on our iPhones all the time.

Well, with Air Video, we can. Air Video lets you stream video from your Mac or PC to your iPhone. It works over a cellular or Wi-Fi connection. You can use it with almost all common video formats, and you can convert most formats on-the-fly, so you can usually start watching your video immediately after you select it.

If you're thinking this sounds a bit like Apple's AirPlay or Home Sharing, you're right. The big deal is that AirPlay and Home Sharing work only with devices on the same Wi-Fi network. Air Video works over any Wi-Fi or cellular data connection, so you can watch movies stored on your computer regardless of where in the world you happen to be.

If you don't have an unlimited wireless data plan, be careful about watching movies because streaming video consumes data at an alarming rate. If you're iPhone is using a 3G or 4G network, watching a movie could cost you more than you expect. We recommend connecting via Wi-Fi before you stream a movie in this or any other app so you won't have to worry about exceeding your wireless data plan's cap.

After you've purchased the Air Video iPhone app, the first step is to download the free Air Video server and launch it on your Mac or PC. The second step is to tell the server which folder or folders contain the video you want to access remotely. That's all there is to it!

What Bob loves most about Air Video is that he can carry around an entire season of his son's high school football games without them using up a single megabyte of precious storage on his 32GB iPhone. Figure 18-13 shows the Air Video movie selection screen; remember that these huge movie files are stored on a computer in a remote location, not on his iPhone.

The only thing that makes Air Video less than perfect is that it doesn't work with video protected with DRM (digital rights management). So it won't work with video content you purchase from the iTunes Store, though it works fine with free video podcasts and iTunes U courseware that you download from the iTunes Store.

Even so, for a mere $2.99, we can access any and all of our personal video collection without using a single bit (or byte) of space on our iPhones. (You can even try a free version with a limited number of movies.) And that, friends, is a wonderful thing.

My Secret Folder (99¢)

Psst, we probably shouldn't spill the beans on My Secret Folder, but here goes.

We figure most of you most of the time are more than willing to share the pictures you take with or store on your iPhone. But what about those naughty or embarrassing images, that, dare we suggest, might get you in trouble. Sure you could delete them, but you kind of like having them somewhere.

That somewhere is My Secret Folder. As the app's name suggests, it gives you a secret place to stash photos you want to keep at bay from nosy family members, your boss, and anyone else who might get at your phone and peep. It's not just images either. You can create albums for secret contacts, secret notes, and even bookmarks you can visit from a secret web browser. You can take pictures from within the app, or import them from elsewhere on your phone. (You just have to manually delete them from your otherwise public albums.)

To start, you choose a passcode that is the key to your folder. But you can also set up a decoy password to make others think they've penetrated your secret stash — put real files in the decoy folder to really throw them off. From within the app, you can purchase additional Lock screens.

Moreover, as Figure 18-14 shows, you can also have the phone snap a picture of anyone who gets hold of your phone and tries, unsuccessfully, to log in with an incorrect passcode. After you load the app on your phone, it goes by the name My Folder, so as not to call too much attention to itself.

Figure 18-13: We can watch any of these movies on our iPhone.

Figure 18-14: Who is that sneaky guy trying to get at my secret folders?

TurboScan ($1.99)

If you travel for work, your pockets are probably littered with business cards, expense receipts, notes, pictures, and documents. If only you could carry a scanner in your pocket to get all that paper into some semblance of order.

Stop dreaming. TurboScan turns your iPhone into one.

Pixoft's app lets you scan and spit out high-quality PDFs. TurboScan is fast — processing a page in less than four seconds — and can detect paper edges to help improve accuracy. And by tapping the SureScan 3x button, shown in Figure 18-15, you can take three pictures of the same document, and the app processes them into a single superior image. You can process scans in color or black-and-white.

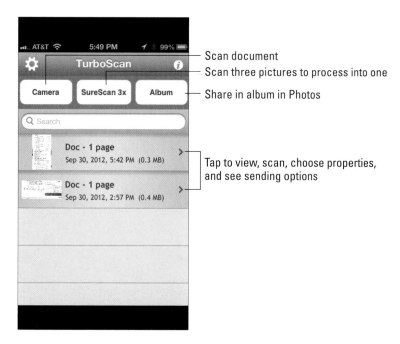

Figure 18-15: TurboScan turns your iPhone into a pocket scanner.

After you've scanned a document, you can choose a name, choose an appropriate size (such as U.S. letter, receipt, or business card), and add a datestamp. Then you can e-mail it to yourself as a PDF or a JPEG, print it, or save it to your camera roll or another Photos album. You can also open it as a PDF to view in other apps on your iPhone that can read documents in the PDF format (such as CloudReaders, Evernote, or iBooks).

19

Ten Helpful Hints, Tips, and Shortcuts

In This Chapter

▷ Typing faster with the slide
▷ Typing faster with autocorrection
▷ Altering the speed of scrubbing in iTunes
▷ Exploiting links
▷ Sharing web pages and links
▷ Choosing a Safari home page
▷ Storing stuff
▷ Creating free ringtones with GarageBand
▷ Dumping apps from the multitasking tray
▷ Capturing a screen grab

*A*fter spending a lot of quality time with our iPhones, it's only natural that we've discovered more than a few helpful hints, tips, and shortcuts. In this chapter, we share some of our faves.

Do the Slide for Accuracy and Punctuation

Our first tip can help you type faster in two ways: by helping you type more accurately and by enabling you to type punctuation and numerals faster than ever before.

While reading this book, you find out how to tap, double-tap, and even double-tap with two fingers. Now we want to introduce you to a new gesture we like to call the *slide*.

To do the slide, you start by performing the first half of a tap. That is, you touch your finger to the keyboard screen but don't lift your finger up. Now, without lifting your finger, slide it onto the key you want to type. You'll know you're on the right key because it pop ups and enlarges.

First, try the slide during normal typing. Stab at a key. If you miss, rather than lifting your finger, backspacing, and trying again, do the slide onto the proper key. After you get the hang of the slide, you'll see that it saves a lot of time and improves your accuracy as well. Get in the habit of not lifting your finger until you're certain it's on the correct key.

Now here's the best part: You can use the slide to save time with punctuation and numerals, too. The next time you need to type a punctuation mark or number, try this technique:

1. **Start a slide action with your finger on the 123 key.**

   The 123 key is to the left of the space key when the alphabetical keyboard is active. This is a slide, not a tap, so don't lift your finger just yet.

2. **When the punctuation and numeric keyboard appears on-screen, slide your finger onto the punctuation mark or number you want to type.**

3. **Lift your finger.**

The cool thing is that the punctuation and numeric keyboard disappears and the alphabetical keyboard reappears — all without tapping the 123 key to display the punctuation and numeric keyboard and without tapping the ABC key (the key to the left of the space key when the punctuation and numeric keyboard is active).

If you slide onto certain characters and your finger lingers for a couple of seconds without lifting, your slide will be spoiled. A set of alternate characters will appear, as shown in Figure 19-1, preventing you from continuing the slide action. The keys that react this way are all vowels and some consonants, including N, Z, and L.

Figure 19-1: Press certain keys for too long and your slide will end in a flurry of alternate character options.

Practice the slide for typing letters, punctuation, and numerals. If you remember not to pause when your finger is pressing a character with pop-up alternatives, we guarantee that you'll be typing faster and more accurately in a few days.

Autocorrect Is Your Friend

In this section, we describe two related tips about autocorrection that can also help you type faster and more accurately.

Auto apostrophes are good for you

First, before moving on from the subject of punctuation, you should know that you can type *dont* to get to *don't.* We told you to put some faith in the iPhone's autocorrection software. And that applies to contractions. In other words, save time by letting the iPhone's intelligent keyboard insert the apostrophes on your behalf for these and other common words.

We're aware of a few exceptions. The iPhone cannot distinguish between *it's,* the contraction of *it is,* and *its,* the possessive adjective and possessive pronoun. It has the same issue with other contractions such as won't (wont).

Make rejection work for you

If the autocorrect suggestion isn't the word you want, reject it instead of ignoring it. Finish typing the word and then tap the x to reject the suggestion before you type another word. Doing so makes your iPhone more likely to accept your word the next time you type it (or less likely to make the same incorrect suggestion the next time you type the word).

Here you thought you were buying a tech book, and you get grammar and typing lessons thrown in at no extra charge. Just think of us as full-service authors.

The Way-Cool Semi-Hidden Audio Scrub Speed Tip

Here's the situation: You're listening to a podcast or an audiobook and trying to find the beginning of a specific segment by moving the scrubber (that little round dot on the scrubber bar) left and right. The only problem is that the scrubber isn't very precise and your fat finger keeps moving it too far one way or the other.

Never fear — your iPhone has a wonderful (albeit somewhat hidden) fix. Just press your finger on the scrubber, but instead of sliding your finger to the left or right, slide it downward toward the bottom of the screen (see Figure 19-2). As you slide, the scrubbing speed changes like magic and the amount of change is displayed above the scrubber bar. The default (normal) speed is called high-speed scrubbing; when you slide your finger downward, the speed changes to half-speed scrubbing, then to quarter-speed scrubbing, and finally to fine scrubbing. This scrub trick is easier to do than to explain, so give it a try.

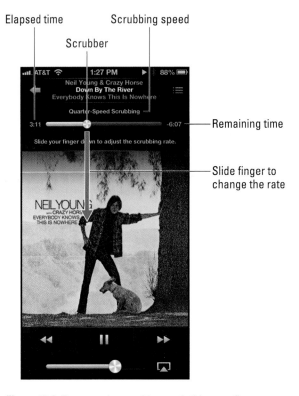

Elapsed time   Scrubbing speed

Scrubber

Remaining time

Slide finger to
change the rate

Figure 19-2: Press on the scrubber and slide your finger
downward to change the scrubbing rate.

While you're sliding, keep an eye on the elapsed time and remaining time indicators because they provide useful feedback on the current scrubbing speed.

Assault on batteries

Because this is a chapter of tips and hints, we'd be remiss if we didn't include some ways that you can extend your battery life. First and foremost: If you use a carrying case, charging the iPhone while it's in that case may generate more heat than is healthy. Overheating is bad for both battery capacity and battery life. So take the iPhone out of the case before you charge it.

If you're not using a 3G, 4G, or Wi-Fi network or a Bluetooth device (such as a headset or car kit), consider turning off the features you don't need in Settings. Doing so could mean the difference between running out of juice and being able to make that important call later in the day.

Activate Auto-Brightness to enable your iPhone to adjust its screen brightness based on current lighting conditions, which can be easier on your battery. From the Home screen, tap Settings⇨Brightness, and then tap the On/Off switch, if necessary, to turn it on.

Turning off Location Services (tap Settings⇨Location Services, and then tap the On/Off switch) and turning off Push (tap Settings⇨Mail, Contacts, Calendars⇨Fetch New Data, and then tap the On/Off switch) can also help to conserve battery life.

Finally, turning on EQ (see Chapter 8) when you listen to music can make it sound better but also uses more processing power. If you've added EQ to tracks in iTunes using the Track Info window, and you want to retain the EQ from iTunes, set the EQ on your iPhone to flat. Because you're not turning off EQ, your battery life will be slightly worse but your songs will sound just the way you expect them to sound. Either way, to alter your EQ settings from the Home screen, tap Settings⇨iPod⇨EQ.

Apple says a properly maintained iPhone battery will retain up to 80 percent of its original capacity after 400 full charge and discharge cycles. You can replace the battery at any time if it no longer holds sufficient charge. Your one-year limited warranty includes the replacement of a defective battery. Coverage jumps to two years with the AppleCare and AppleCare+ Protection Plans. Apple will replace the battery if it drops below 50 percent of its original capacity.

If your iPhone is out of warranty, Apple will replace the battery for $79 plus $6.95 shipping and local tax, and will also dispose of your old battery in an environmentally friendly manner.

Tricks with Links and Phone Numbers

The iPhone does something special when it encounters a phone number or URL in e-mail and SMS text messages. The iPhone interprets as a phone number any sequence of numbers that looks like a phone number: 1-123-555-4567, 555-4567, 1.123.555.4567, and so on. The same goes for sequences of characters that look like a web address (URL), such as http://www. *WebsiteName*.com or www.*WebsiteName*.com. When the iPhone sees what it assumes to be a URL, it appears as a blue link on your screen.

If you tap a phone number or URL sequence like the ones just shown, the iPhone does the right thing. It launches the Phone app and dials the number for a phone number, or it launches Safari and takes you to the appropriate web page for a URL. That's useful but somewhat expected. What's more useful and not so expected is the way Safari handles phone numbers and URLs.

Let's start with phone numbers. When you encounter a phone number on a web page, give it a tap. A little dialog appears on the screen displaying that phone number and offering you a choice of two buttons: Call or Cancel. Tap Call to switch to the Phone app and dial the number; tap Cancel to return to the web page.

Here's another cool Safari trick, this time with links. If you press and hold down on a link rather than tapping it, a little floating text bubble appears and shows you the underlying URL.

You also see the underlying URL if you press and hold down on a URL in Mail or Messages. Having this information in Mail or Messages is even more useful because it enables you to spot bogus links and phishing attempts without switching to Safari or actually visiting the URL.

Finally, here's one last Safari trick. If you press and hold down on most graphic images, Save Image and Copy Image buttons appear. Tap Save Image and the picture is saved to the camera roll in the Photos app. Tap Copy Image and the picture is copied to the Clipboard so you can paste it into any app that accepts pasted images, including but not limited to Messages and Mail.

Share the Love . . . and the Links

Ever stumble on a web page you just have to share with a buddy? The iPhone makes it dead simple. From the site in question, tap the action icon at the bottom of the browser (shown in the margin). Then tap the appropriate button to share via Mail, iMessage (or SMS), Twitter, or Facebook.

What happens next depends on which button you tap. For example, if you tap Mail, a new mail message appears with the Subject line prepopulated with the name of the website you're visiting and the body of the message prepopulated with the URL. Just type something in the message body, supply your pal's e-mail address, and then tap the Send button.

Choosing a Home Page for Safari

You may have noticed that the iPhone version of Safari does not have an option to specify a home page, though the popular option exists on Mac and PC versions of the Safari (and for that matter, every other web browser in common use today). Instead, when you tap the Safari icon, you return to the last site you visited.

The trick to having Safari open to the page of your choosing rather than to the last page you visited is to create an icon for the page you want to use as your home page. This technique is called creating a *web clip* of a web page. Here's how to do it:

1. **Open the web page you want to use as your home page and tap the action button (shown in the margin).**

2. **Tap the Add to Home Screen button.**

   The Add to Home screen appears.

3. **(Optional) Change the name of the icon if you like.**

4. **Tap Add.**

   An icon that will open this page appears on your Home screen (or one of your Home screens if you have more than one).

5. **Tap this new web clip icon instead of the Safari icon, and Safari opens to your home page instead of the last page you visited.**

You can even rearrange the icons so that your home page icon, instead of or in addition to the Safari icon, appears in the dock, as shown in Figure 19-3.

See the tip in Chapter 1 for rearranging icons if you've forgotten how. And consider moving the Safari icon from the dock onto one of your Home screens so that you never tap it by accident. If you like, place both Safari and your new web clip icon in the dock so that you can tap either one depending upon your needs.

Safari icon

My Home page icon

Dock

Figure 19-3: The B.L. Dot Com icon now replaces the Safari icon in the dock (between Mail and Music on the dock).

Storing Files

A tiny Massachusetts software company — Ecamm Network — sells an inexpensive piece of OS X software called PhoneView ($29.95), which lets you copy files from your Mac to your iPhone and copy files from the iPhone to a Mac. (No Windows version is available.) Better still, you can try the program for a week before deciding whether you want to buy it. Go to www.ecamm.com to fetch the free demo.

The big deal here is that while automatic backups protect most of the files on your iPhone, you can't manipulate them. They're backed up and restored, but heaven help you if you want to extract one or more individual iMessages, SMS, and MMS messages, specific songs, videos, notes, or other types of data from your iPhone. The bottom line is that there's no easier way to manage files on your iPhone than by using PhoneView.

In a nutshell, here's how PhoneView works. After downloading the software to your Mac, double-click the program's icon to start it. Then do one of the following:

- **To transfer files and folders to the iPhone** (assuming that you have room on the device), click the Copy to iPhone button on the toolbar and then select the files you want to copy. The files are copied into the appropriate folder on the iPhone. Alternatively, you can drag files and folders from the Mac Desktop or a folder into the PhoneView browser.

- **To go the other way and copy files from your iPhone to your computer,** highlight the files or folders you want to be copied and then click the Copy from iPhone button on the toolbar. Select the destination on your Mac where you want to store the files and then click Save. You can also drag files and folders from the PhoneView file browser to the Mac desktop or folder. Or you can double-click a file in the PhoneView browser to download it to your Mac's Documents folder.

If you need access to the files on your iPhone or if you want to use your iPhone as a pseudo–hard drive, PhoneView is a bargain.

Bob says: I use Printopia, also from Ecamm ($19.95), to print from my iPhone to several of my non-AirPrint printers. It works great and costs a lot less than a new AirPrint-enabled printer.

Create Ringtones for Free in GarageBand

The capability to create free iPhone ringtones with Apple's GarageBand application (which is bundled with every Mac) was beyond the purview of the ringtone discussions in previous chapters. Creating those ringtones, however, is relatively easy. Start by launching GarageBand on your Mac and creating a new iPhone ringtone project. Then:

1. **Click the Media Browser button to reveal the media browser pane.**

2. **Click the disclosure triangle to reveal the contents of your iTunes library.**

3. **Click your iTunes music library to reveal its contents.**

4. **Select the song you want to turn into a ringtone and drag it onto the timeline (*Hello Muddah, Hello Faddah!* in Figure 19-4).**

    You can't use songs purchased from the iTunes Store for ringtones if they're protected by Apple's digital rights management copy protection. GarageBand won't let you drag a protected song onto its timeline.

Disclosure triangle for iTunes   Media Browser pane

Timeline   iTunes music libary

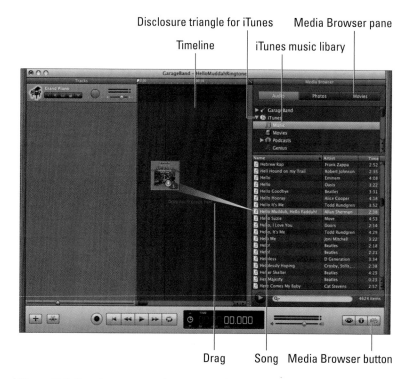

Drag   Song   Media Browser button

Figure 19-4: Creating a custom ringtone, part I.

Apple stopped using copy protection for music files in April 2009. If you purchased the song after that, you're good to go. If you purchased the song before then, you can pay a small upgrade fee (30¢ at press time) to convert the song to iTunes Plus, Apple's new higher-quality, non-copy-protected format.

The bottom line is that you can make ringtones only from songs you've ripped yourself from CD or downloaded without rights management or other copy protection (such as MP3s from Amazon.com or files in Apple's iTunes Plus format).

5. **Click the cycle region button to enable the cycle region.**

6. **Click in the middle of the cycle region and drag it to the portion of the song you want to use as your ringtone.**

7. **Fine-tune the start and end points by clicking and dragging the cycle region's left and right edges, as shown in Figure 19-5.**

   For best results, keep your ringtones under 30 seconds.

8. **Click the play button to hear your work. When you're satisfied with it, choose Share⇨Send Ringtone to iTunes.**

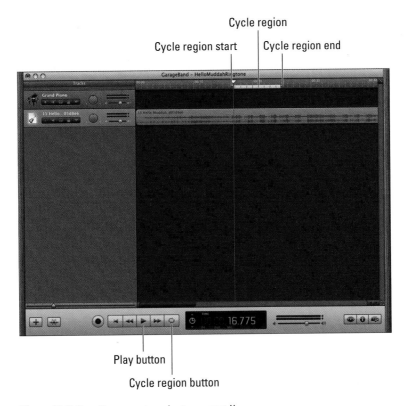

Figure 19-5: Creating a custom ringtone, part II.

If you have a microphone, you can record ringtones featuring voice recordings such as the following. "Yo! It's your bro!" "This is your mother. Pick up the phone right this moment." "Ed Baig calling." "Incoming! Incoming!" "This is your iPhone and I'm ringing." And so on. You get the picture.

The next time you sync, your new ringtone becomes available on your iPhone. To use it as your ringtone, tap Settings⇨Sounds⇨Ringtone, and then tap the ringtone in the list of available sounds. To associate the ringtone with a specific contact or contacts, find the contact in either the Contacts app or the Phone app's Contacts tab, tap Ringtone, and then tap the specific ringtone in the list of available ringtones.

iOS 5 and above let you use ringtones as text tones, so you can associate custom ringtones with text messages from a specific contact. The procedure is as just described, but you tap Text Tone instead of Ringtone.

Getting Apps Out of the Multitasking Tray

iOS 6's multitasking is great, but sometimes you don't want to see an app's icon in the multitasking tray. Don't worry — it's easy to remove any app that's cluttering up your tray.

To get rid of an app icon in the multitasking tray, here's what you do:

1. **Double-press the Home button.**

   The multitasking tray appears. Don't forget that you can swipe the tray from right to left (or left to right) to see additional icons representing other multitasking apps.

2. **Press any icon in the tray until all the icons begin to wiggle and display a little red – symbol, as shown in Figure 19-6.**

3. **Tap the little red – symbol for the app (or apps) you want to remove from the tray.**

   The app disappears from the multitasking tray. (We tapped the Apple Store app in Figure 19-6.) To fill the gap in the tray, apps slide to the left, as shown in Figure 19-7. Icons from the group of apps you'd see if you swiped from right to left on the tray slide onto the screen as needed.

4. **Press the Home button to end the wiggling and hide the red – symbols.**

5. **Press the Home button again to dismiss the multitasking tray.**

   You can also tap anywhere above the multitasking tray to end the wiggling, hide the red – symbols, and dismiss the multitasking tray — all in one fell swoop.

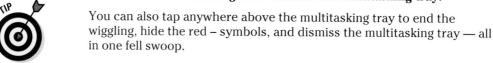

You can use this trick to stop an app that's running in the background, too. For example, if Pandora Radio is playing in the background and you decide you've had enough Pandora for now, just follow the preceding steps and Pandora will shut the heck up. Without this trick, you'd have to open Pandora, tap the Pause button, then press the Home button to close Pandora (but the Pandora icon remains in the multitasking tray).

The bottom line is that using this tip is an easier, faster way to quit an app that's running in the background, as well as the only way (short of restarting your iPhone) to remove an icon from your multitasking tray.

Figure 19-6: Press an icon in the multitasking tray until the icons wiggle and grow red – symbols.

Figure 19-7: After removing the Apple Store icon, the iTunes and Video icons slide to the left to fill the gap.

Taking a Snapshot of the Screen

True confession: We threw in this final tip because, well, it helps people like *us*.

Permit us to explain. We hope you've admired the pictures of the iPhone screens that are sprinkled throughout this book. We also secretly hope that you're thinking what marvelous photographers we must be.

Well, the fact is, we couldn't take a blurry picture of the iPhone using its built-in screen-grab feature if we wanted to.

Press the sleep/wake button at the same time you press the Home button, but just for an instant. The iPhone grabs a snapshot of whatever is on the screen. The picture lands in the iPhone's camera roll; from there, you can synchronize it with your PC or Mac, along with all your other pictures. And from there, the possibilities are endless. Why, your picture could wind up just about anywhere, including in a *For Dummies* book.

Index

• C •

• S •

Apple & Mac

iPad 2 For Dummies,
3rd Edition
978-1-118-17679-5

iPhone 4S For Dummies,
5th Edition
978-1-118-03671-6

iPod touch For Dummies,
3rd Edition
978-1-118-12960-9

Mac OS X Lion
For Dummies
978-1-118-02205-4

Blogging & Social Media

CityVille For Dummies
978-1-118-08337-6

Facebook For Dummies,
4th Edition
978-1-118-09562-1

Mom Blogging
For Dummies
978-1-118-03843-7

Twitter For Dummies,
2nd Edition
978-0-470-76879-2

WordPress For Dummies,
4th Edition
978-1-118-07342-1

Business

Cash Flow For Dummies
978-1-118-01850-7

Investing For Dummies,
6th Edition
978-0-470-90545-6

Job Searching with Social
Media For Dummies
978-0-470-93072-4

QuickBooks 2012
For Dummies
978-1-118-09120-3

Resumes For Dummies,
6th Edition
978-0-470-87361-8

Starting an Etsy Business
For Dummies
978-0-470-93067-0

Cooking & Entertaining

Cooking Basics
For Dummies, 4th Edition
978-0-470-91388-8

Wine For Dummies,
4th Edition
978-0-470-04579-4

Diet & Nutrition

Kettlebells For Dummies
978-0-470-59929-7

Nutrition For Dummies,
5th Edition
978-0-470-93231-5

Restaurant Calorie Counter
For Dummies,
2nd Edition
978-0-470-64405-8

Digital Photography

Digital SLR Cameras &
Photography For Dummies,
4th Edition
978-1-118-14489-3

Digital SLR Settings
& Shortcuts
For Dummies
978-0-470-91763-3

Photoshop Elements 10
For Dummies
978-1-118-10742-3

Gardening

Gardening Basics
For Dummies
978-0-470-03749-2

Vegetable Gardening
For Dummies,
2nd Edition
978-0-470-49870-5

Green/Sustainable

Raising Chickens
For Dummies
978-0-470-46544-8

Green Cleaning
For Dummies
978-0-470-39106-8

Health

Diabetes For Dummies,
3rd Edition
978-0-470-27086-8

Food Allergies
For Dummies
978-0-470-09584-3

Living Gluten-Free
For Dummies,
2nd Edition
978-0-470-58589-4

Hobbies

Beekeeping
For Dummies,
2nd Edition
978-0-470-43065-1

Chess For Dummies,
3rd Edition
978-1-118-01695-4

Drawing For Dummies,
2nd Edition
978-0-470-61842-4

eBay For Dummies,
7th Edition
978-1-118-09806-6

Knitting For Dummies,
2nd Edition
978-0-470-28747-7

Language &
Foreign Language

English Grammar
For Dummies,
2nd Edition
978-0-470-54664-2

French For Dummies,
2nd Edition
978-1-118-00464-7

German For Dummies,
2nd Edition
978-0-470-90101-4

Spanish Essentials
For Dummies
978-0-470-63751-7

Spanish For Dummies,
2nd Edition
978-0-470-87855-2

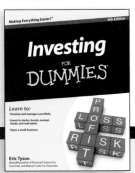

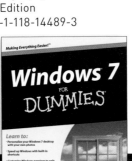

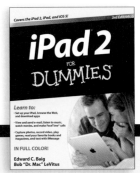

Available wherever books are sold. For more information or to order direct: U.S. customers visit www.dummies.com or call 1-877-762-2974.
U.K. customers visit www.wileyeurope.com or call (0) 1243 843291. Canadian customers visit www.wiley.ca or call 1-800-567-4797.

Connect with us online at www.facebook.com/fordummies or @fordummies

Math & Science

Algebra I For Dummies, 2nd Edition
978-0-470-55964-2

Biology For Dummies, 2nd Edition
978-0-470-59875-7

Chemistry For Dummies, 2nd Edition
978-1-1180-0730-3

Geometry For Dummies, 2nd Edition
978-0-470-08946-0

Pre-Algebra Essentials For Dummies
978-0-470-61838-7

Microsoft Office

Excel 2010 For Dummies
978-0-470-48953-6

Office 2010 All-in-One For Dummies
978-0-470-49748-7

Office 2011 for Mac For Dummies
978-0-470-87869-9

Word 2010 For Dummies
978-0-470-48772-3

Music

Guitar For Dummies, 2nd Edition
978-0-7645-9904-0

Clarinet For Dummies
978-0-470-58477-4

iPod & iTunes For Dummies, 9th Edition
978-1-118-13060-5

Pets

Cats For Dummies, 2nd Edition
978-0-7645-5275-5

Dogs All-in One For Dummies
978-0470-52978-2

Saltwater Aquariums For Dummies
978-0-470-06805-2

Religion & Inspiration

The Bible For Dummies
978-0-7645-5296-0

Catholicism For Dummies, 2nd Edition
978-1-118-07778-8

Spirituality For Dummies, 2nd Edition
978-0-470-19142-2

Self-Help & Relationships

Happiness For Dummies
978-0-470-28171-0

Overcoming Anxiety For Dummies, 2nd Edition
978-0-470-57441-6

Seniors

Crosswords For Seniors For Dummies
978-0-470-49157-7

iPad 2 For Seniors For Dummies, 3rd Edition
978-1-118-17678-8

Laptops & Tablets For Seniors For Dummies, 2nd Edition
978-1-118-09596-6

Smartphones & Tablets

BlackBerry For Dummies, 5th Edition
978-1-118-10035-6

Droid X2 For Dummies
978-1-118-14864-8

HTC ThunderBolt For Dummies
978-1-118-07601-9

MOTOROLA XOOM For Dummies
978-1-118-08835-7

Sports

Basketball For Dummies, 3rd Edition
978-1-118-07374-2

Football For Dummies, 2nd Edition
978-1-118-01261-1

Golf For Dummies, 4th Edition
978-0-470-88279-5

Test Prep

ACT For Dummies, 5th Edition
978-1-118-01259-8

ASVAB For Dummies, 3rd Edition
978-0-470-63760-9

The GRE Test For Dummies, 7th Edition
978-0-470-00919-2

Police Officer Exam For Dummies
978-0-470-88724-0

Series 7 Exam For Dummies
978-0-470-09932-2

Web Development

HTML, CSS, & XHTML For Dummies, 7th Edition
978-0-470-91659-9

Drupal For Dummies, 2nd Edition
978-1-118-08348-2

Windows 7

Windows 7 For Dummies
978-0-470-49743-2

Windows 7 For Dummies, Book + DVD Bundle
978-0-470-52398-8

Windows 7 All-in-One For Dummies
978-0-470-48763-1

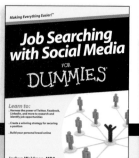

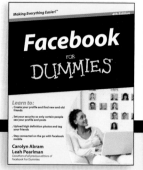

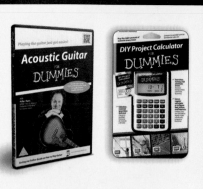